LEGENDARY LOCALS

OF

HAMILTON

OHIO

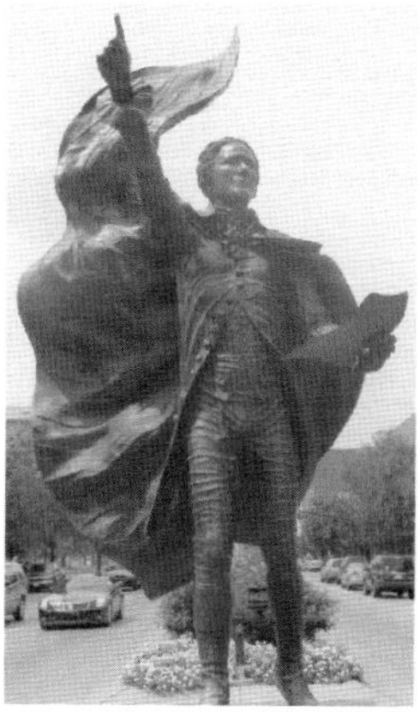

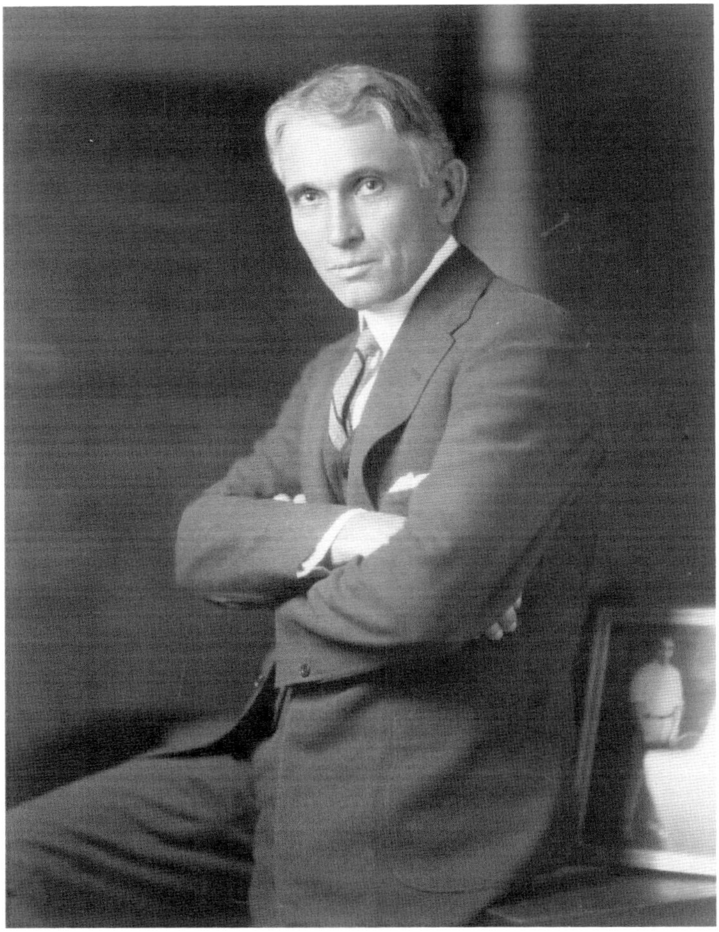

Homer Gard

For more than 60 years, Homer Gard (1866–1952) was an outstanding community leader, public benefactor, and major contributor to the welfare of Hamilton's residents, especially its youth. In 1887, he began an exemplary career as a newspaper editor, publisher, and owner of the *Hamilton Journal News*. He was one of the 18 charter members of the Associated Press and a member of the National Press Club. Gard was a clerk for the city council and served as Hamilton's postmaster for eight years. He helped organize the Hamilton Chamber of Commerce in 1910, assisted in its reorganization in 1924, and was a director of the Chamber of Commerce of the United States. He was a founder of the local Rotary Club; a trustee of Mercy Hospital, the Ohio Association for Care of Mentally Sick, and Miami University; and was active in the Boy Scouts, Hamilton Welfare Federation, Red Cross, and local chapters of the Veterans of Foreign Wars and American Legion. Gard gave extensive support to the city's Young Men's Christian Association, serving as the group's president and on its board of trustees from 1923 to 1952. He was truly a dynamic force that made Hamilton a better place to live. (Courtesy of Butler County Historical Society.)

Page 1: The American Cape

Sculptor Kristen Visbal of Lewes, Delaware, created *The American Cape*, the 13-foot-tall bronze statue of Alexander Hamilton that stands in the High Street median in Journal Square. The $230,000 sculpture of the city's namesake, dedicated in 2004, was jointly commissioned by Historic Hamilton and Hamilton, Ohio, City of Sculpture, Incorporated. (Courtesy of the author.)

LEGENDARY LOCALS

OF

HAMILTON

OHIO

RICHARD N. PILAND

LEGENDARY LOCALS

ISBN 978-1-4671-0069-4

Legendary Locals is an imprint of Arcadia Publishing
Charleston, South Carolina

Printed in the United States of America

Library of Congress Control Number: 2012952402

For all general information, please contact Arcadia Publishing:
Telephone 843-853-2070
Fax 843-853-0044
E-mail sales@arcadiapublishing.com
For customer service and orders:
Toll-Free 1-888-313-2665

Visit us on the Internet at www.arcadiapublishing.com

Dedication

To the Butler County Historical Society and the Hamilton Lane Library, for their efforts to collect, archive, and preserve the area's history. Their work has made this book possible.

On the Cover: From left to right:
(TOP ROW) James McBride, early settler (Courtesy of Lane Library, page 13); Nathaniel Sherman, civic activist (Courtesy of the Butler County Historical Society, page 36); Mike Fox, politician (Courtesy of the Butler County Historical Society, page 39); Ella Mae Cope, educator (Courtesy of Hamilton City School District, page 47); George Rentschler, industrialist (Courtesy of Lane Library, page 62).
(MIDDLE ROW) Nancy Wiley, community volunteer (Courtesy of the Butler County Historical Society, page 125); Clark Lane, philanthropist (Courtesy of the Butler County Historical Society, page 20); Joe Nuxhall, baseball player (Courtesy of the Butler County Historical Society, page 99); Will H. Lebo, educator (Courtesy of Hamilton City School District, page 45); Alta Harvey Heiser, author (Courtesy of the Butler County Historical Society, page 84).
(BOTTOM ROW) Harry T. Wilks, philanthropist (Courtesy of the Butler County Historical Society, page 120); Eva D. Lande, civic activist (Courtesy of the Butler County Historical Society, page 115); Terry Malone, coach (Courtesy of the Butler County Historical Society, page 106); Janet Baker, educator (Courtesy of the Butler County Historical Society, page 58); Thomas Beckett, industrialist (Courtesy of the Butler County Historical Society, page 66).

CONTENTS

ACKNOWLEDGMENTS

The creation of this book required the cooperation and generosity of many people. I first must thank Kathy Creighton, executive director of the Butler County Historical Society, and her board of directors, for giving me unlimited access to the society's large photograph collection and archival resources. Volunteers Richard Scheid and, especially, Marlene Carmack, were enormously helpful. A large majority of the photographs in the society's collection were donated by the *Hamilton Journal News*. I would like to salute the work of the newspaper's photojournalists, including Cheryl Bauer, Dick Burns, Jim Denny, Michael Heinz, John Janco, Bob McMaken, David Schwegmann, and July Tomasi.

Special thanks go to Audrey Morrison, of the Hamilton Lane Library, for helping me with the library's local history and Cummins collection of photographs. I greatly appreciate Susan Myers for giving me access to the collection. I would also like to express my deep gratitude to Joni Copas, director of communications for the Hamilton City School District, for allowing me to have full access to the district's archival resources.

Unless otherwise noted, all images used in this book appear courtesy of the Butler County Historical Society. Additional contributions to the project were made by several people. I would like to thank the following for the photographs they provided for the book: Diane Kuhlmann Beaty, Sherrie Bluester, Michael P. Dingeldein, Jackie Freyberg, Timothy L. Gillespie, Scott Grant, Rick H. Jones, Tully Milders, Nancy Schon, Charles J. Stinger, Jon Theim, Rob Wile, and Craig Wilks.

I especially want to indicate my indebtedness to Diane Kuhlmann Beaty for all of the background research she provided. The support and inspiration given by Tiffany Frary, my publisher at Arcadia, is greatly appreciated. I know I caused her headaches.

Finally, I want to acknowledge the unquestioned support of my wife, Marcy. She has been a source of constant encouragement. She makes my life better and has done so for the last 40 years.

INTRODUCTION

When soldiers under the command of Gen. Arthur St. Clair arrived to build Fort Hamilton in 1791, the land along the Great Miami River was wilderness. After the area was made safe for immigrants, enterprising men cleared the forest and began to build their homes and community. Many of the early settlers had been soldiers, and most came from Pennsylvania, Virginia, and Kentucky. They were industrious and moral people who valued hard work, ability, dedication, purpose, service, and craftsmanship.

Hamilton, nearly always an important center of activity, has evolved from an agricultural center and seat of justice for Butler County to the "greatest manufacturing city of its size in the world," to the "City of Sculpture." The city has endured rough times, ranging from devastating floods to economic depressions to the loss of jobs attributable, in part, to the end of local ownership of businesses. The people of Hamilton have worked to adapt and solve their community's problems and build a good place in which to live.

For convenience, the book is divided into chapters covering key aspects of life in Hamilton rather than structured chronologically. It should be noted, however, that many legendary citizens made contributions in several areas of community life. For example, Dave Belew was chief executive of a large manufacturing company, a leading philanthropist, and a contributor to the community's artistic activities. The men and women included here are among the people who made lasting and significant contributions to the growth of Hamilton. They are not, however, the only people who made a substantial impact on the community.

Among Hamilton's founding fathers were pioneers James McBride and John Woods, involved in much of the town's early development; John Cleves Symmes, developer of the "Hollow Earth Theory"; industrialist William Beckett, who built one of the first paper mills in Hamilton; and philanthropist Clark Lane, the donor of the public library. Some of the prominent public servants were the popular Dr. Mark Millikin; Rear Adm. Donald Wulzen, who ordered the first combat Marines ashore at the start of the Vietnam War; John Holcomb, who brought mass murderer James Ruppert to justice; and Mike Fox, who helped secure funds for the Government Services Center and the connector to I-75 before pleading guilty to federal charges and being sentenced to prison. William P. Cope and his daughter Ella Mae served a combined 70 years in Hamilton's public schools; Superintendent D.R. Baker kept the schools open during the Great Depression; Dr. Bernie Phelps got the Miami University campus under way; and Janet Baker led the school district into the 21st century. Local business legends include William Murstein, George Rentschler, Frederick Brant Rentschler, and Joel Schmidt. In the fields of arts and entertainment, Hamilton has been home to such luminaries as Lou Jenks Beauchamp, Stella Weiler Taylor, Robert McCloskey, and Ray Combs. Great athletes include Joe Nuxhall, Bill Wilks, Mary Bowermaster, and Frank Clair. Hamilton has benefited from the philanthropy of many people, such as publisher Homer Gard, banker Richard Fitton, attorney Harry Wilks, and Donna and Pat Carruthers. Other business leaders, educators, political figures, city officials, and fascinating citizens have contributed to the common good. They have made this book possible.

Many writers have contributed helpful accounts of Hamilton's history; some in the context of telling the story of Butler County and others in recounting the development of the community, an industry, or a company. For this book, the most helpful of the former were Western Biographical Publishing Company's *History and Biographical Cyclopaedia of Butler County, Ohio with Illustrations and Sketches of its Representative Men and Pioneers* (1882); Lewis Historical Publishing Company's *History of Southwestern Ohio, The Miami Valleys* (1964); and *Centennial History of Butler County, Ohio* (1905), edited by Bert S. Bartlow, W.H. Todhunter, Stephen D. Cone, Joseph J. Pater, and Frederick Schneider. Among Hamilton-oriented books, the most valuable were D.W. McClung's *Centennial Anniversary of the City of Hamilton, September*

17–19, 1891 (1892); Stephen D. Cone's *A Concise History of Hamilton, Ohio* (1901); *Memoirs of the Miami Valley* (1919), edited by John C. Hover, Willard J. Wright, Joseph D. Barnes, Clayton A. Leiter, Walter D. Jones, John Ewing, Charlotte Reeve Conover, and W.C. Culkins; Stella Weiler Taylor's wonderful stories of life in Hamilton published in the two-volume *Rosemary, That's for Remembrance—A Series of Lavender Scented Memories of Other Days in Hamilton* (1940); and *Hamilton in the Making* by Alta Harvey Heiser (1941). Special notice should be given to the several books published by local historian Jim Blount. Several of his titles, as well as his many columns written for the *Hamilton Journal News* and, more recently, the Lane Library, have been especially useful for this book.

CHAPTER ONE

Founding Fathers

One of the primary goals of the Land Ordinance of 1785, passed by the Continental Congress, was to raise money through the sale of land in the territory west of the original 13 states. John Cleves Symmes purchased the large tract of land between the Great Miami and Little Miami Rivers in 1787. Gen. Arthur St. Clair and his soldiers built Fort Hamilton four years later as the first in a chain of posts to aid in removing the threat posed by Indians. St. Clair's soldiers, including Gen. Richard Butler, were defeated, and it remained for Gen. Anthony Wayne and his army to secure the territory for settlers at the Battle of Fallen Timbers in 1794. Fort Hamilton was abandoned by the military in 1796, and a steady stream of settlers began to come to the Miami Valley.

Many of Hamilton's founding fathers were industrious and versatile men who cleared the wilderness, created homes, developed a government, and established commerce. Perhaps the most important of these early community builders were John Reily, James McBride, Dr. Daniel Millikin, and John Woods. There were others, to be sure, but these men laid the foundation on which Hamilton was built.

Brewer John Sohn, Dr. Cyrus Falconer, and Superintendent David McClung gave considerable attention to starting a public school system, which was organized in 1851 and started with two buildings. Lawyer Thomas Millikin drafted the merger agreement that unified the communities of Rossville and Hamilton. By 1857, when the population reached 5,000 people, the town achieved status as a city. William Beckett began one of the earliest paper manufacturers in the city.

Attorney John Millikin left his law firm partnership with William Bebb to raise pigs and work to develop the lovely Greenwood Cemetery. Bebb, who worked with Lewis D. Campbell and others to create the Hamilton hydraulic system, went on to become Ohio's 19th governor. Industrialist Clark Lane, probably the city's first philanthropist, donated the building and books that started the public library. Dr. Dan Millikin, son of lawyer John Millikin and one of the first three graduates of Hamilton High in 1862, was a popular and admired man in the community for more than 30 years.

Much is owed to these men. They, and others like them, provided the foundation for the growth of Hamilton as a truly special city.

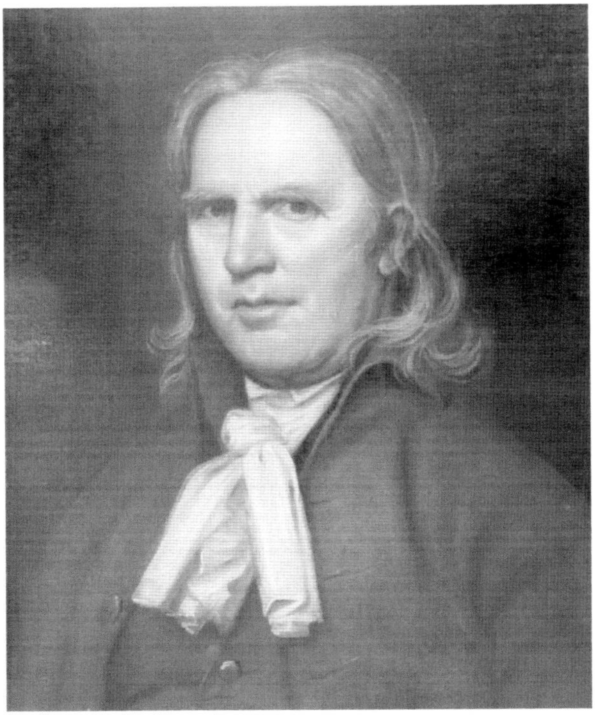

John Cleves Symmes

In 1788, John Cleves Symmes (1742–1814) moved to Ohio after serving as a justice of the New Jersey Supreme Court and a delegate to the Continental Congress. Symmes is most noted for buying 311,682 acres of land between the Great Miami and Little Miami Rivers in the "Miami Purchase" for $225,000. Following the purchase, he served as judge of the territorial court from 1788 to 1803, often conflicting with the governor of the territory, Gen. Arthur St. Clair.

Gen. Arthur St. Clair

In 1791, soldiers under General St. Clair built Fort Hamilton, the first in a chain of posts meant to remove the threat posed by Indians. St. Clair (1737–1818), a Revolutionary War officer and close friend of George Washington, marched his men into battle against the Indians. His army was routed, and hostile tribes remained a problem in the territory. St. Clair was exonerated of any blame for the defeat, and he served as governor of the Northwest Territory from 1788 to 1802.

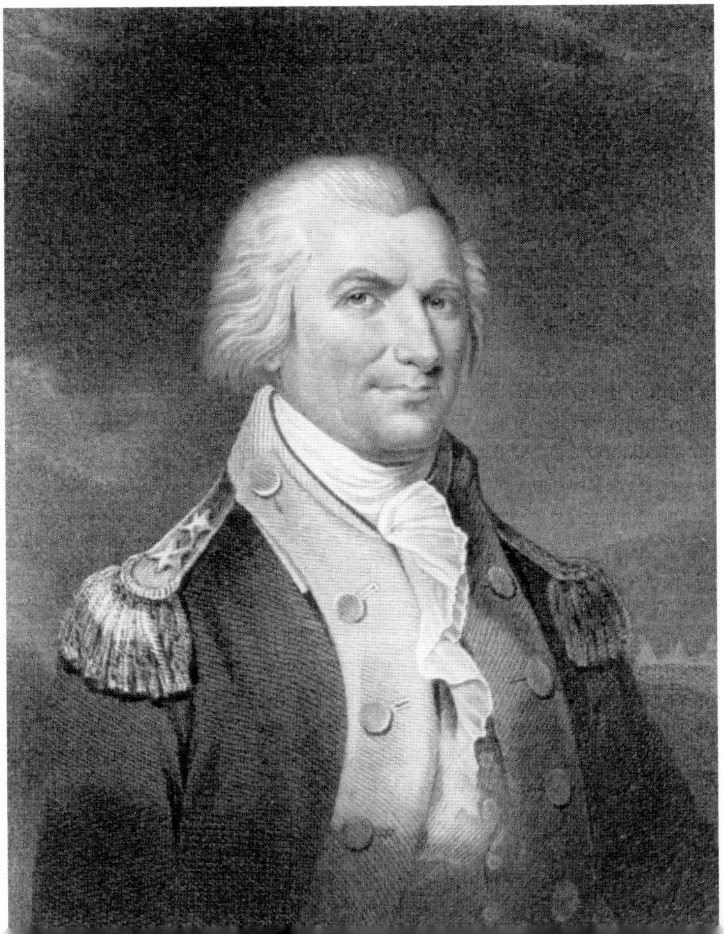

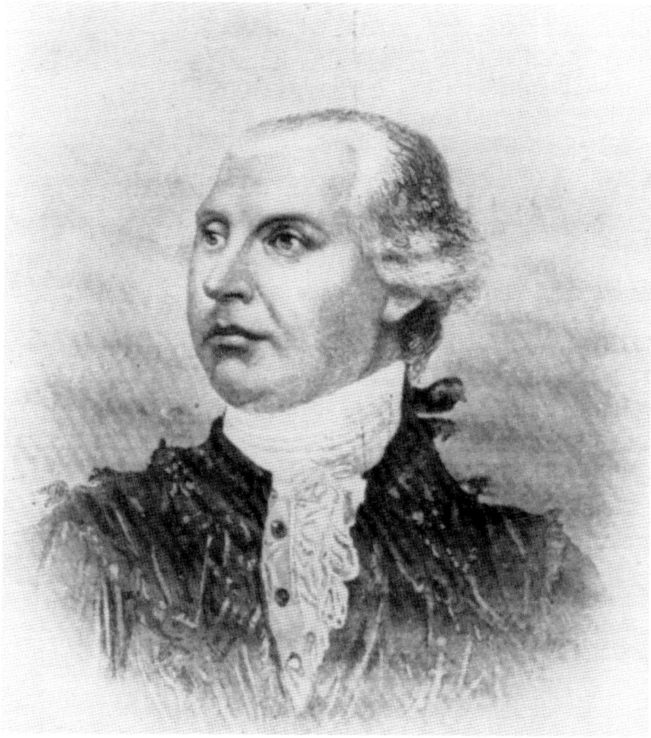

Gen. Richard Butler
Richard Butler (1743–1791), a Revolutionary War veteran and successful negotiator of treaties with several Indian tribes, was second in command of St. Clair's army at Fort Hamilton. He was mortally wounded during St. Clair's defeat. Butler was carried behind the lines to have his wounds dressed by a surgeon, only to be tomahawked and scalped by a lone Indian who had penetrated the ranks of the regiment. Butler County was named in his honor.

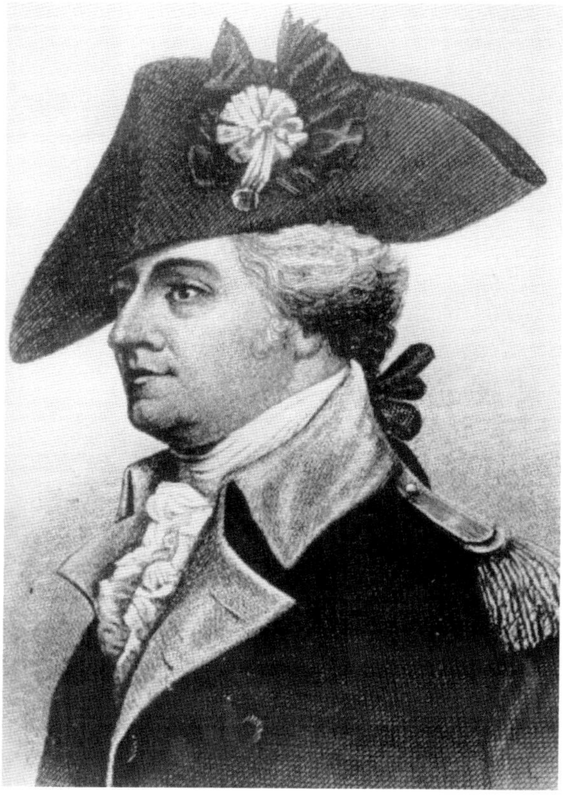

Gen. Anthony Wayne
Anthony Wayne's exploits during the Revolutionary War earned him the rank of general and the nickname "Mad Anthony." President Washington chose Wayne to reverse the loss suffered by General St. Clair. Wayne (1745–1796) took his army north of Hamilton to build Fort Defiance in 1794 and defeated the combined Indian forces at Fallen Timbers. His victory effectively ended the Indian wars. The Treaty of Greenville, which he negotiated, was signed in 1795. This brought peace and made the territory safe for settlers.

John Reily

John Reily (1763–1850) served as clerk of the territorial general assembly and helped write Ohio's constitution in 1802. Starting in 1803, Reily served as Butler County's recorder for eight years, auditor for 16 years, clerk of the common pleas court for 37 years, and clerk of the Supreme Court for 39 years. He surveyed and laid out Rossville in 1804 and was Hamilton's first postmaster, serving from 1804 to 1832. He was an original trustee of Miami University, a position he held from 1809 to 1840.

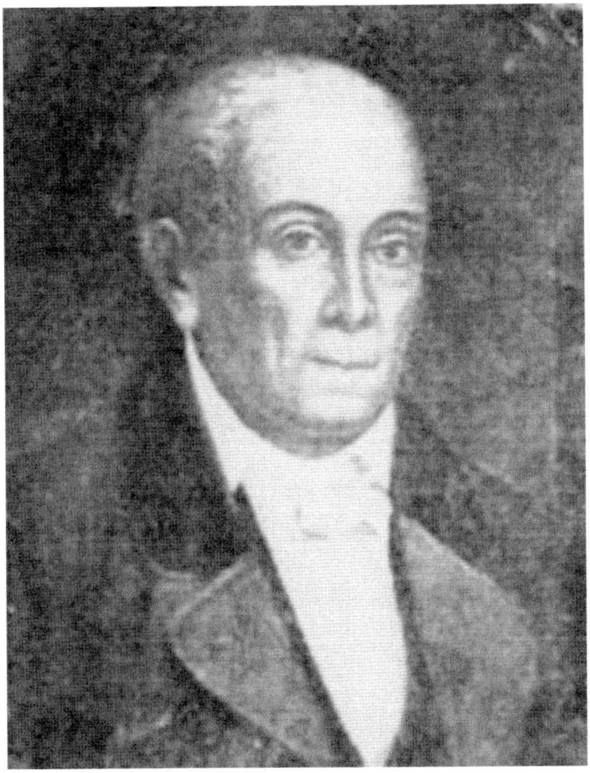

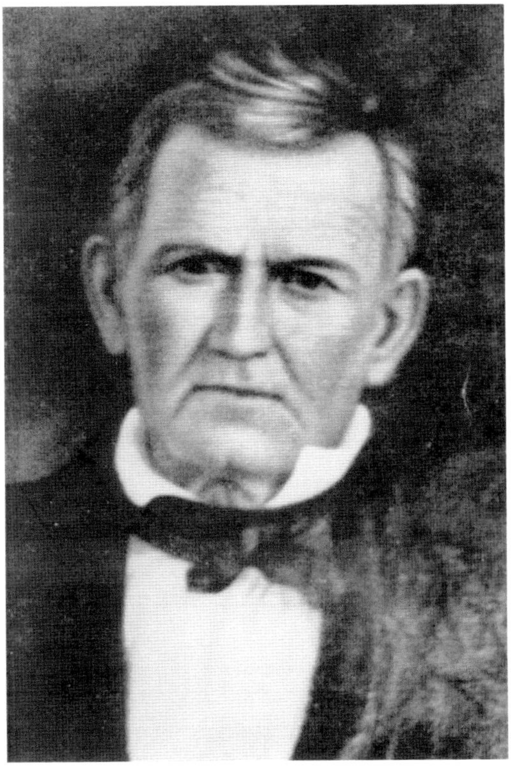

Dr. Daniel Millikin

Dr. Millikin (1779–1849) was the first physician to permanently reside in Hamilton. He provided health care to county residents and those in adjoining counties. Millikin also served eight years as a court of common pleas judge, two years as state representative, and 11 years as a Miami University trustee. His life as a pioneer doctor was full of hardship, extensive travel on horseback over bad roads in all types of weather, and exposure to infectious diseases. The poor health Millikin suffered late in his life was attributed to his career in medicine. (Courtesy of Lane Library.)

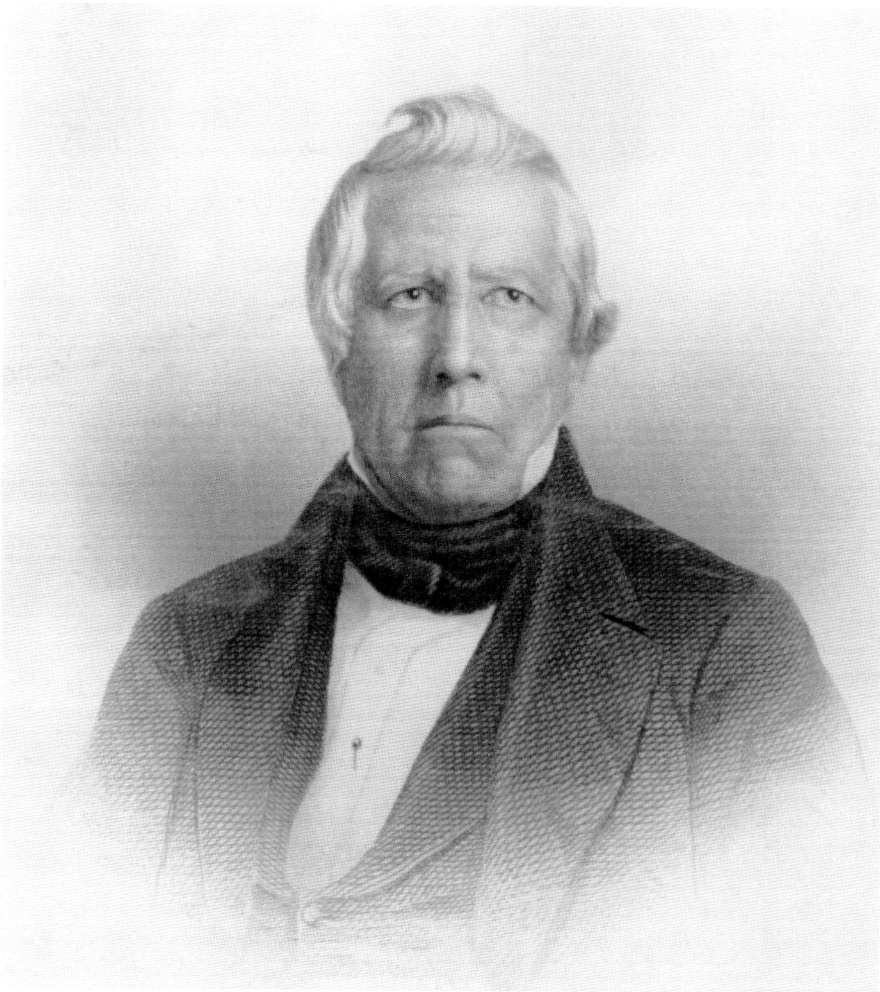

James McBride

Very few early settlers match the contributions to the development of Hamilton made by James McBride (1788–1859). He came to Hamilton in 1806 and, by 1811, had become involved in town and county government, frequently clerking for John Reily. He served as Butler County sheriff from 1813 to 1817; state legislator from Hamilton during 1822 and 1823; and the town's first mayor in 1833, serving four years, during which he helped codify town ordinances and law enforcement. As county surveyor in 1836, McBride drew the first detailed map of the county. He returned to Columbus in 1845 to help John Woods in the state auditor's office and influenced the development of the Miami-Erie Canal. From 1846 to 1852, he served as Butler County clerk of courts. McBride, who had no formal education, played a major role in the development of Miami University in Oxford. In 1809, he became the first secretary of the university's board of trustees, serving until 1820. He was appointed trustee in 1821 and served in that post until his death in 1859. McBride brought the first printing press to Hamilton in 1814 for the town's first newspaper, the *Miami Intelligencer*; built the first hotel in town sometime before 1820; and in 1818, he designed the first bridge across the Great Miami River to connect Hamilton and Rossville. He was involved in the creation of turnpike roads and the financing and development of the Cincinnati, Hamilton & Dayton Railroad. McBride also wrote a two-volume work of biographical sketches of Butler County pioneers, a history of Hamilton, and a history of Oxford. His personal library comprised about 5,000 books. (Courtesy of Lane Library.)

John Woods

John Woods (1794–1855) established his law practice in Hamilton in 1819 and served as county prosecuting attorney from 1820 to 1825. As representative of Butler and Warren Counties in the US Congress from 1825 to 1829, he worked to pass a bill that enabled Ohio to acquire land to extend the Miami Canal from Dayton to Lake Erie. Attorney Woods became the publisher and editor of the Hamilton *Intelligencer* newspaper from 1829 to 1832. In 1845, he was elected state auditor, a position he held until 1851. His other activities included working to establish the Hamilton and Rossville Female Academy, being president of two railroad lines, leading the effort to merge Rossville and Hamilton, securing funding for the Hamilton and Rossville Hydraulic, and working to get a road built between Hamilton and Cincinnati. Many of Woods's correspondence, legal briefs, and similar documents are archived at the Butler County Historical Society. (Courtesy of Lane Library.)

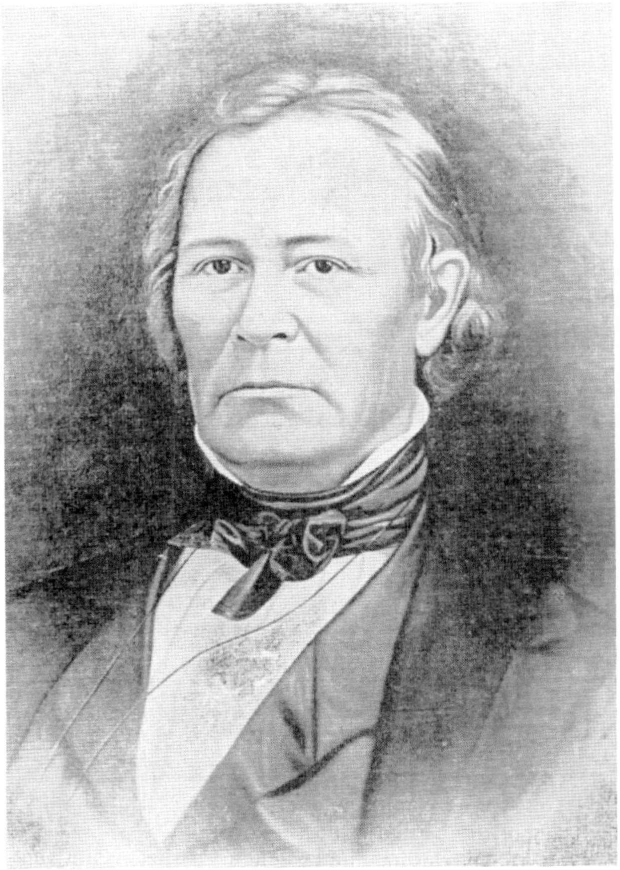

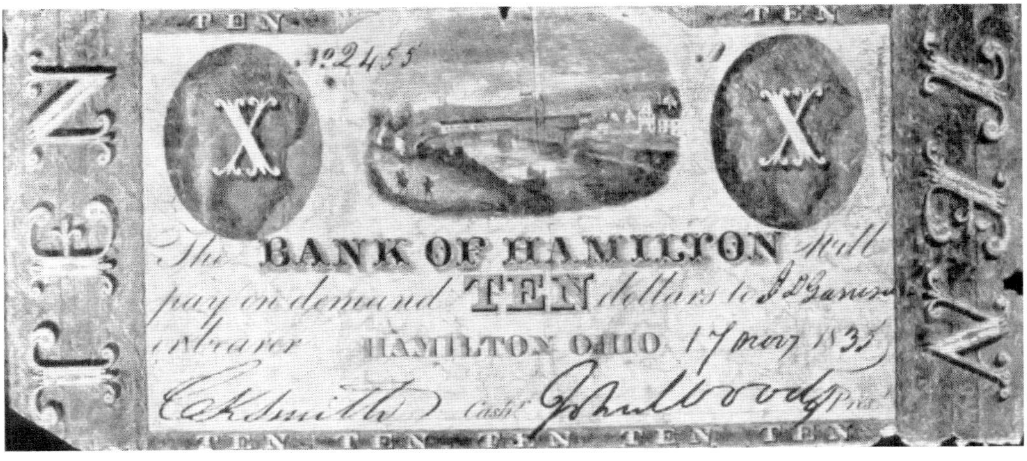

Bank of Hamilton $10 Bill

The Bank of Hamilton, incorporated in 1817, was Butler County's first bank. This 1835 $10 bill, signed by bank president John Woods, shows the first bridge over the Great Miami River between Hamilton and Rossville. The covered bridge was designed by James McBride, one of the bank's trustees. The bridge, which collapsed during an 1866 flood, outlived the bank, which survived only until 1843.

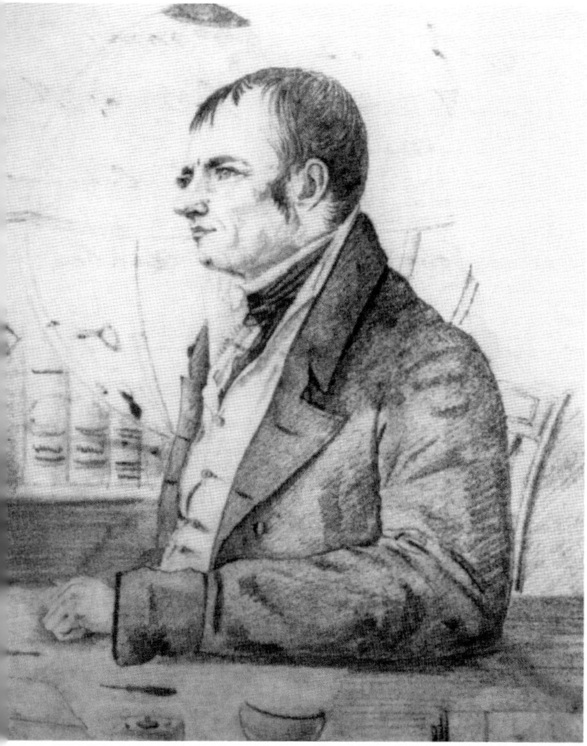

John Cleves Symmes Jr.
In an 1818 circular, John Cleves Symmes Jr. (1780–1829) declared that the Earth was hollow and habitable within, had concentric spheres, and was open at the poles. Symmes, seen above in an 1820 pencil-on-paper drawing by John J. Audubon, devoted his time to publicizing his theory and his reasons for believing it, despite the wide ridicule it received. Known as Captain Symmes to distinguish himself from his uncle, John Cleves Symmes, he traveled the country, giving lectures and trying to get funding for explorations to the poles. Even though he won the support of many people, including James McBride, Symmes did not live to see his theories disproved. His health declined during his travels, and he returned to his Hamilton farm less than three months before his death in 1829, deeply in debt. Captain Symmes's remains were buried with full military honors at the burying ground in Ludlow Park. His son Americus Vespucius Symmes arranged for a four-sided stone monument topped with a hollow globe, shown to the right, to be placed on the grave. Inscriptions on the stone memorialize Symmes as a soldier, philosopher, and originator of the theory of a hollow, habitable Earth. Over the years, the hollow globe was occasionally stolen, returned, or replaced.

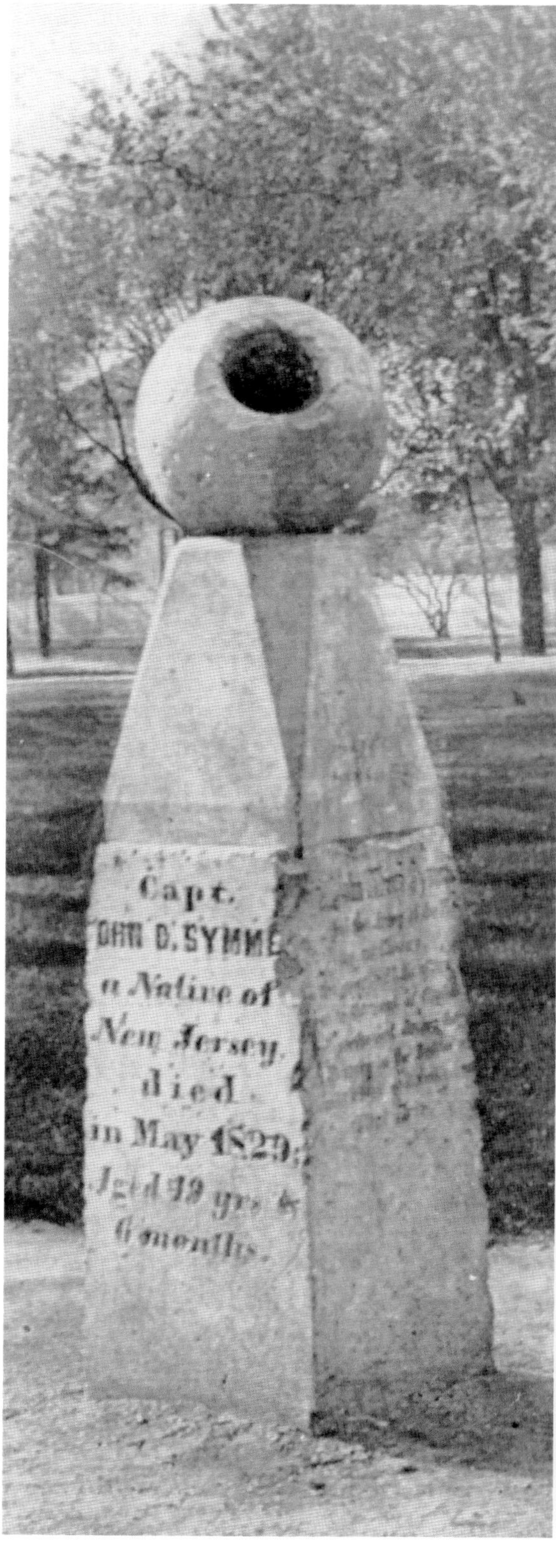

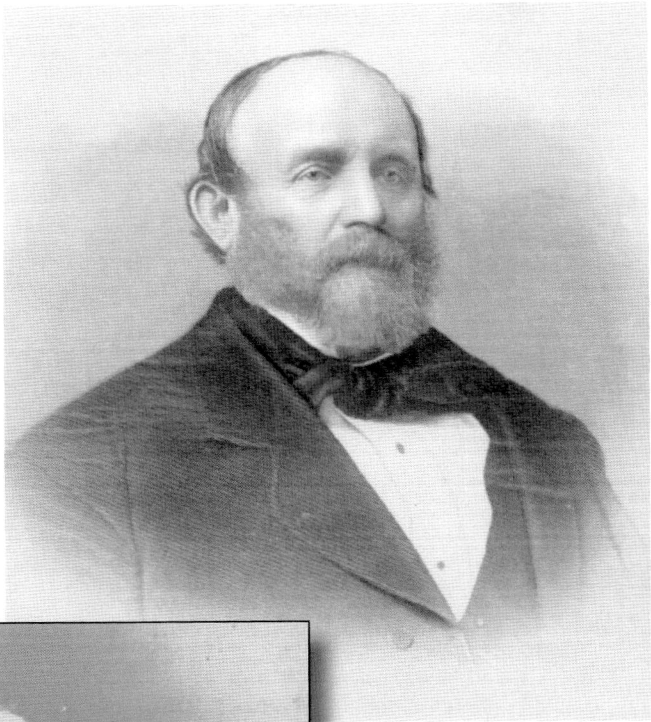

John W. Sohn

German-born John W. Sohn began the first of the German lager breweries in Hamilton in 1839 and operated his breweries until 1865. He also owned a malt house, a large pork-packing plant, two tanneries, and a vineyard, and held interests in woodworking machinery made by his son-in-law, William C. Margedant. Sohn (1815–1889) was a city councilman, county commissioner, and a member of the very first board of education of Hamilton's school district, formed in 1851. (Courtesy of Lane Library.)

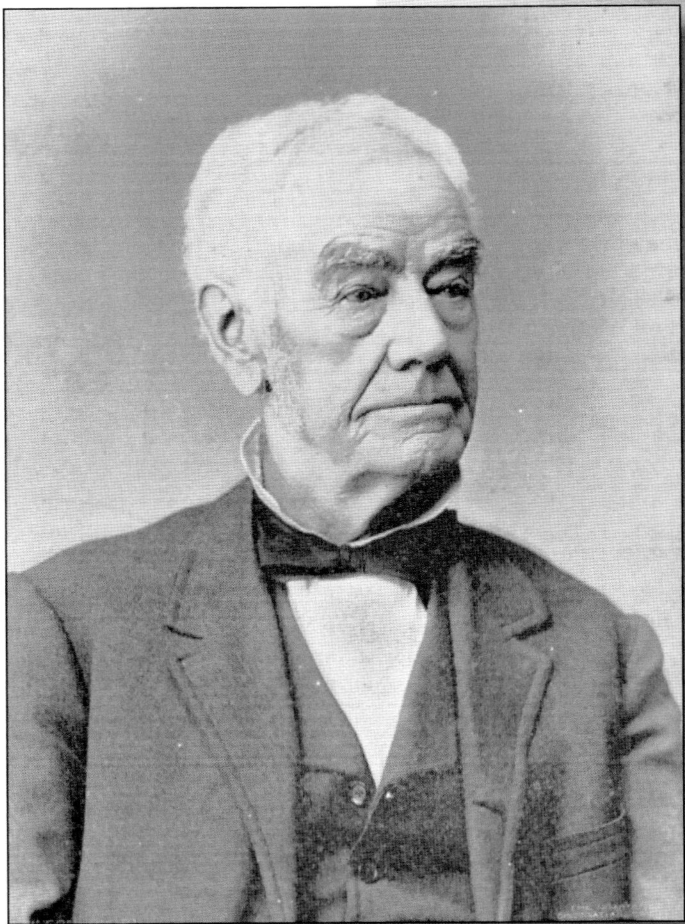

Dr. Cyrus Falconer

For 63 years, Cyrus Falconer (1810–1895) practiced medicine in Hamilton. In 1837, he was a founder of the county medical society and helped it reorganize as the Hamilton Medical Society in 1848. He contributed articles to scholarly medical journals as early as 1834, five years before he married Mary Woods, daughter of pioneer John Woods. When Hamilton's school district was created in 1851, Falconer was elected one of the first three school examiners. An abolitionist, he helped slaves travel the Underground Railroad and was an ardent advocate of temperance. (Courtesy of Lane Library.)

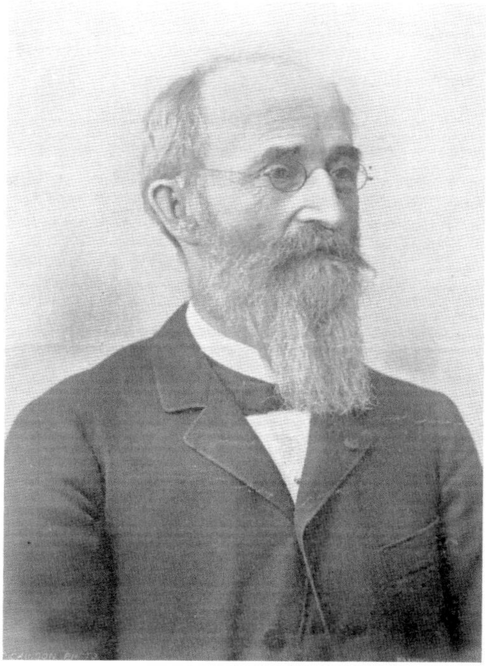

David W. McClung
McClung began his years in Hamilton as a high school teacher and became the district's first superintendent in 1854. He published the *Hamilton Intelligencer* newspaper and was a county probate court judge between 1857 and 1860. After the Civil War, McClung (1831–1916) was president of the Second National Bank for two years and manager of a paper company from 1868 to 1879. He served two terms as a Miami University trustee (1866–1875 and 1887–1896). In 1879, he and his wife, Anna Carter Harrison, a granddaughter of Pres. William Henry Harrison, moved to Cincinnati, where McClung was a surveyor, postmaster, and collector of internal revenue for the federal government. He edited the history book *The Centennial Anniversary of the City of Hamilton, Ohio, September 17–19, 1891*. (Courtesy of Lane Library.)

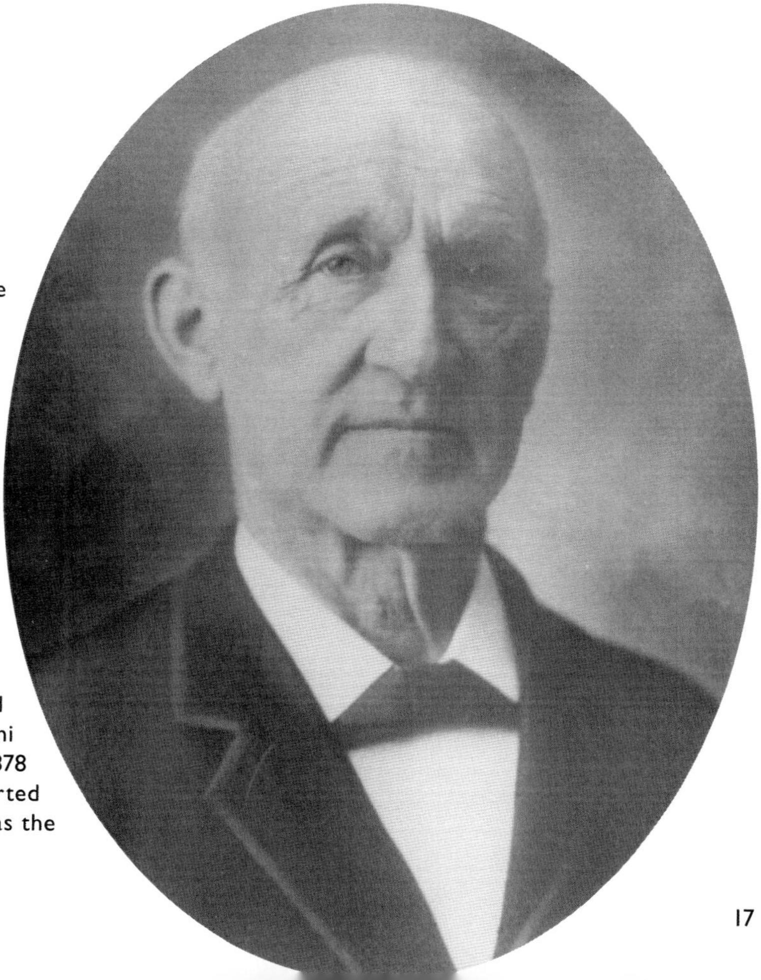

Thomas Millikin
Millikin was considered one of the best lawyers in Ohio. In 1838, he graduated from Miami University and studied law with Elijah Vance, the county's prosecuting attorney. He opened his firm in 1840 and practiced law for nearly 60 years. Millikin (1819–1899) was a member of the committee that drafted the terms of the 1854 merger of Hamilton and Rossville. He was a Miami University trustee from 1878 to 1887. The firm he started in 1840 is known today as the Millikin & Fitton Law Firm.

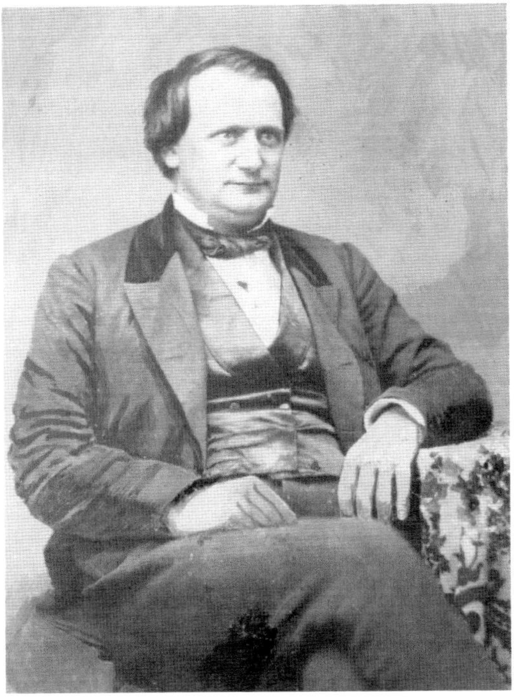

William Beckett

William Beckett (1821–1895) graduated from Miami University in 1844, studied law with his father-in-law, John Woods, and was admitted to the bar in 1846. He and F.D. Rigdon formed the Miami Paper Mill in 1848, an operation that evolved into the Beckett Paper Company. Beckett promoted building the Cincinnati, Hamilton, & Dayton Railroad and became its director in 1855. He was appointed a trustee of Miami University in 1857 and served the school until his death in 1895.

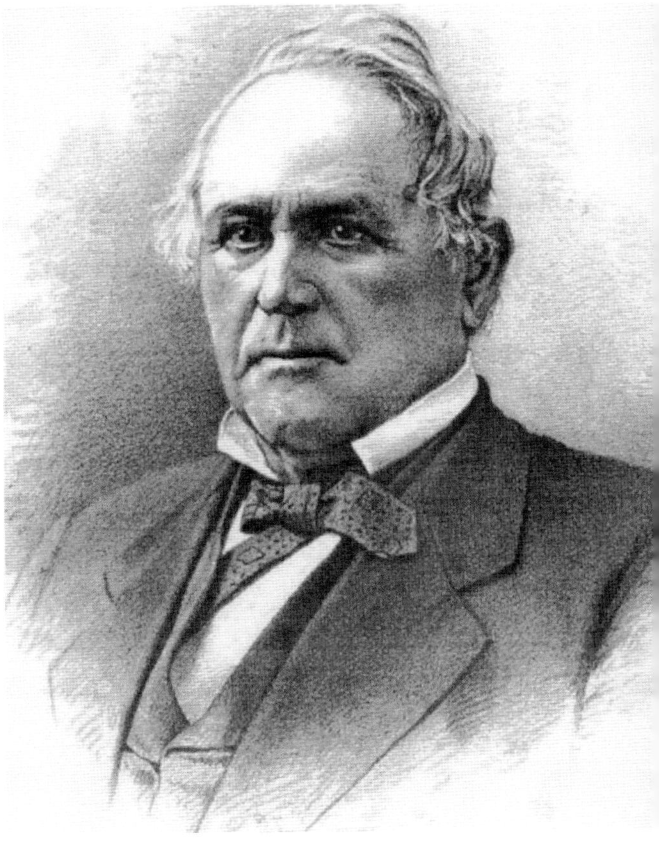

John M. Millikin

Millikin (1804–1884) came to Hamilton with his father, pioneer doctor Daniel Millikin, in 1807. He started his law practice in 1827 before forming a 13-year law partnership with William Bebb in 1834. In 1846, he stopped practicing law and moved to his farm, where he raised Poland China pigs. Millikin was Ohio treasurer from 1875 to 1878 and a Miami University trustee from 1860 until his death in 1884. He was a major influence on the development of Greenwood Cemetery, serving as trustee from 1848 to 1884.

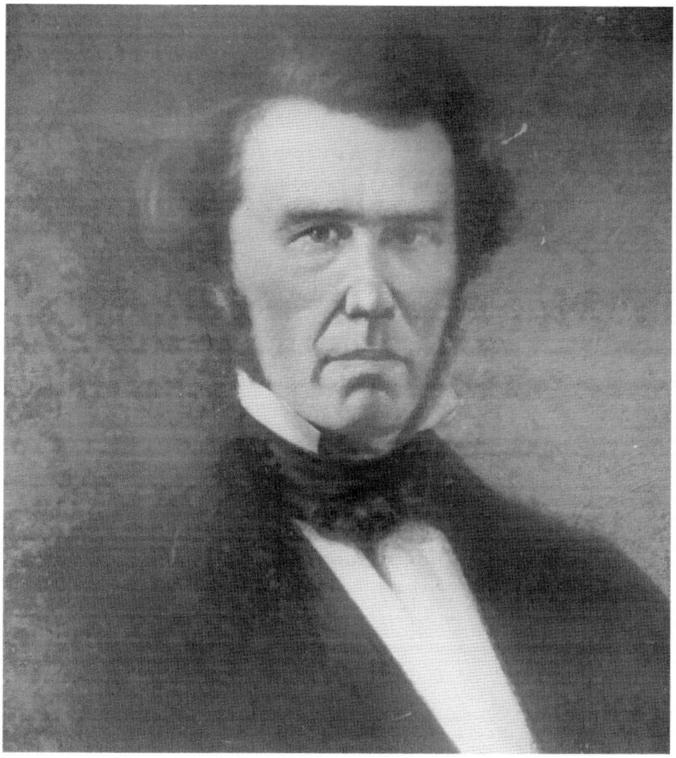

William Bebb
From 1827 until 1832, William Bebb operated a boarding school for boys in Morgan Township. He joined a law firm partnership with John M. Millikin and practiced law until 1846. He was president and board member of the Hamilton & Rossville Hydraulic Company during the 1840s. Bebb (1802–1873) was elected Ohio's 19th governor, serving from 1846 to 1849. During the Civil War, he served in Lincoln's administration as an examiner in the pension department.

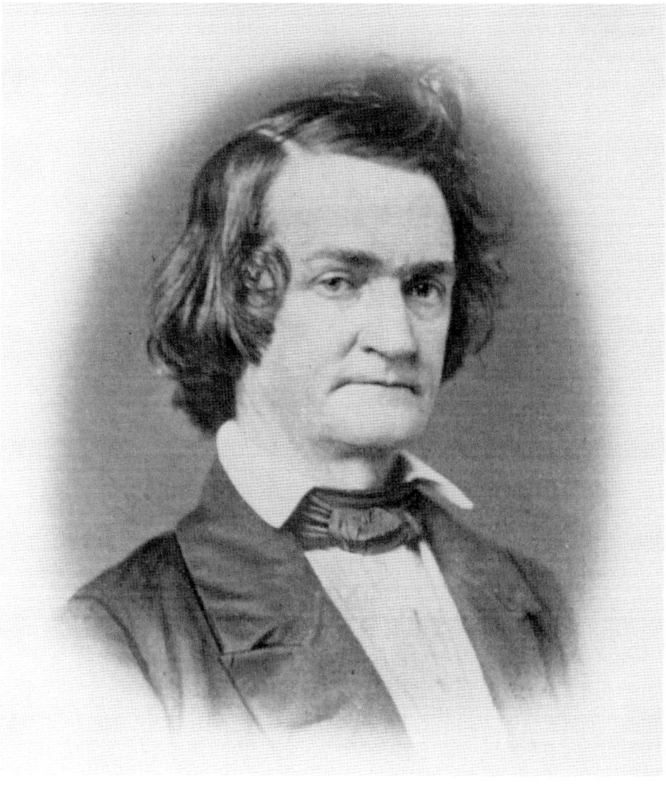

Lewis D. Campbell
Campbell (1811–1882) was editor of the Hamilton *Intelligencer* from 1832 until 1838 and a lawyer who practiced from 1835 to 1850. He was a director of the Hamilton & Rossville Hydraulic Company and a founder of the Cincinnati, Hamilton, & Dayton Railroad Company. Campbell represented Butler County in the US House of Representative for six terms, from 1849 to 1858 and from 1871 to 1873. After the Civil War, he was appointed US Minister to Mexico. His wife was Jane Reily, daughter of pioneer John Reily. (Courtesy of Library of Congress, Prints and Photographs Division.)

Clark Lane

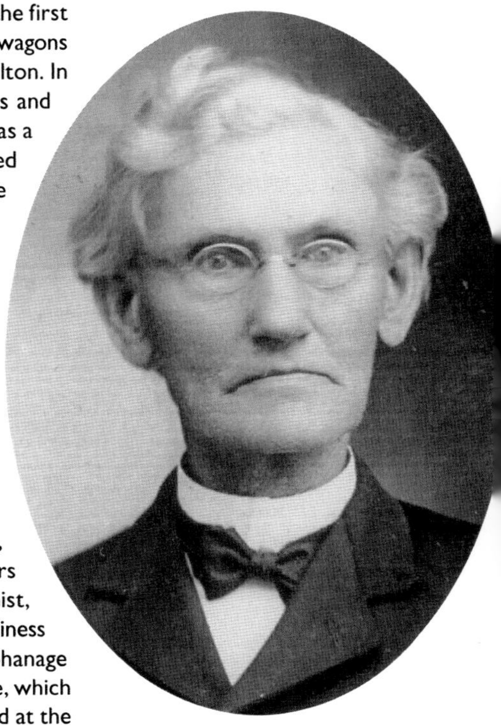

Hamilton's first philanthropist was very likely Clark Lane (1823–1907). As a youth, he helped his father and brothers build the first reaping machines in the territory and make a variety of farm wagons at their home near Mount Healthy, 10 miles south of Hamilton. In 1844, Lane came to Hamilton to do ironwork for wagons and several paper mills. He developed an excellent reputation as a blacksmith and formed Clark Lane & Company in 1854, helped by a $1,000 loan from industrialist William Beckett. The company evolved first into the firm of Owens, Lane & Dyer, a large foundry that did work for sawmills, gristmills and paper mills, and, after Lane sold his interest in the business in 1875, it became the Hooven, Owens, & Rentschler Company in 1882. During the 1850s and 1860s, Lane's company was successful and quite profitable. In 1863, Lane began construction of his family's home in Hamilton, an octagonal structure that many locals called "Lane's Folly." Then, three years later, he had a second octagonal structure built across the street from his home. It was this building that Lane furnished, stocked with more than 2,000 books, and opened as a public library on October 20, 1866. He offered the library as a gift to the city, and voters in a special election accepted the offer. Lane, an abolitionist, bought the Elbridge Dyer farm and home from his former business partner and donated it to Butler County for use as an orphanage and children's home. One of the first residents of the home, which opened in 1875, was Lane's invalid son, Harry, who resided at the facility until his death in 1886 at age 29. Lane's octagonal home is today the headquarters of the Hamilton Community Foundation.

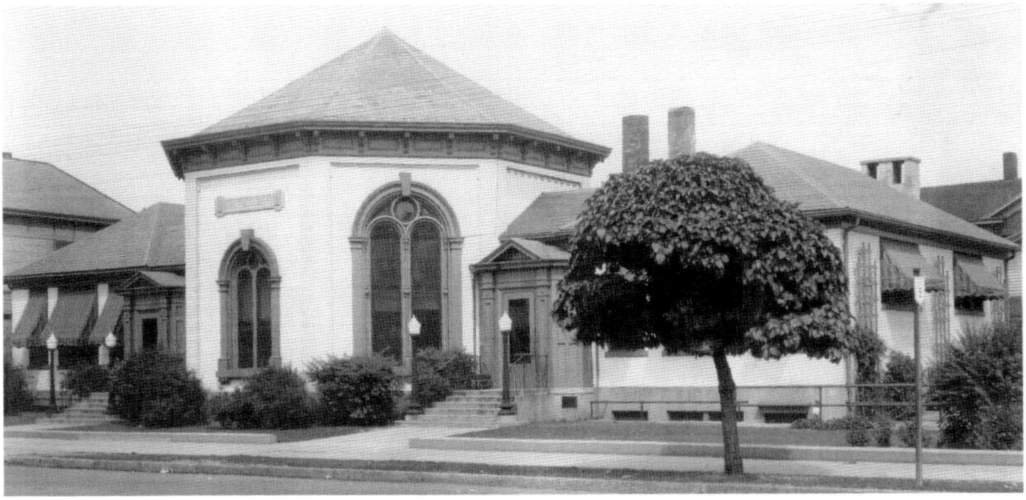

Lane Public Library

The Lane Public Library is seen in this 1936 photograph. The original octagonal building was expanded several times in order to accommodate an increasing collection, space requirements, and library operations. The cupola and its book-and-quill weather vane are missing from the roof in this view. They were returned during a 1996 remodeling of the library.

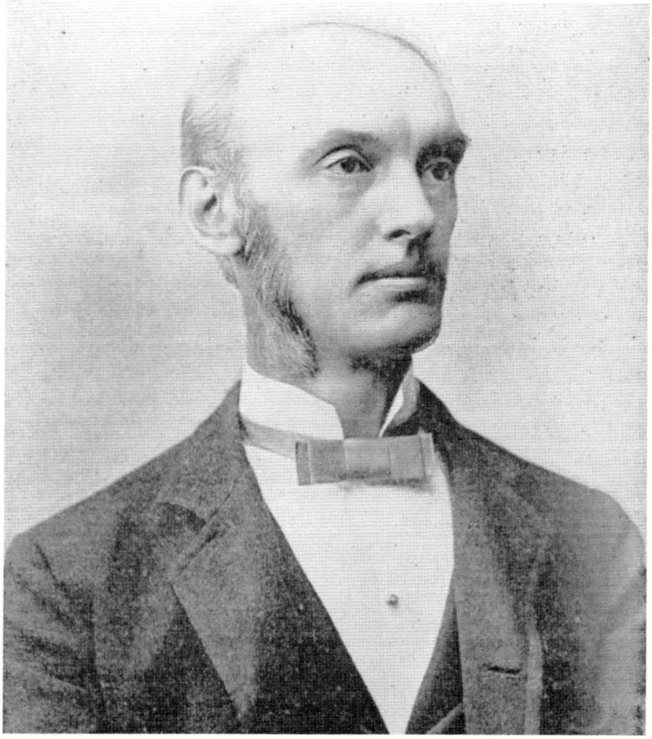

James W. See

During the 1860s, young James W. See (1850–1920) was an apprentice machinist in Missouri and worked in several places before coming to Hamilton in 1874 to be chief engineer for the Niles Tool Company. He started his own business in 1876, invented several devices for telephone systems, and built the first telephone line and the first electric light plant in Hamilton. See, a patent attorney and technical writer, was one of the best-known mechanical engineers and served as an expert witness in more than 300 court cases involving patents. (Courtesy of Lane Library.)

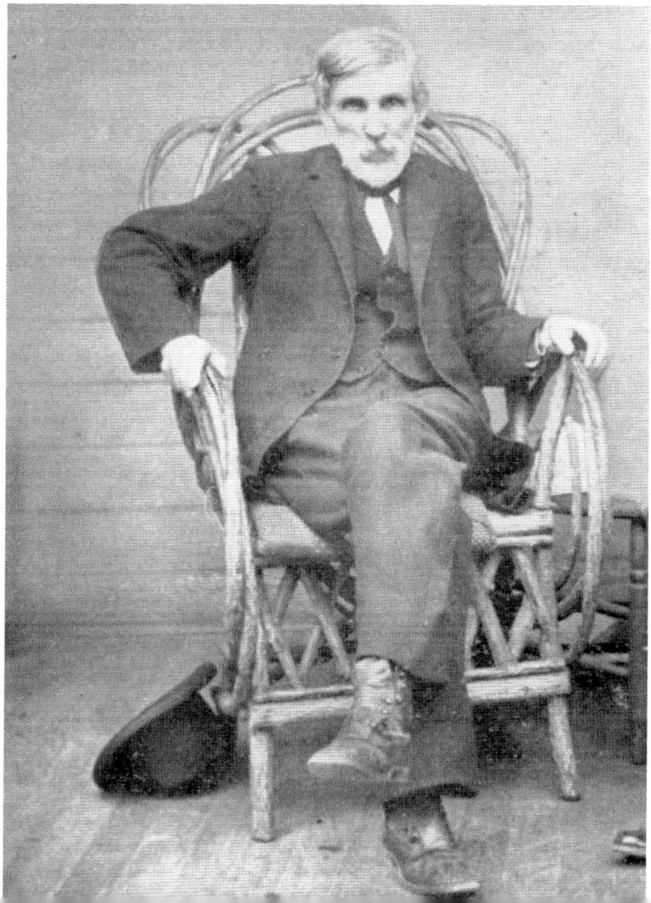

Samuel Z. Gard

Among Samuel Gard's teachers at Antioch College was Horace Mann. Gard (1830–1906) began his law studies in 1856 and was admitted to the bar three years later. Gard and Robert Christy helped establish *Schwildwache*, the first German-language paper in Hamilton, in 1859. He also published the Hamilton *True Telegraph*. Gard was elected Butler County prosecuting attorney, serving from 1862 to 1866 and from 1871 to 1872. He had two sons, Homer and Warren, both of whom were important community leaders. (Courtesy of Lane Library.)

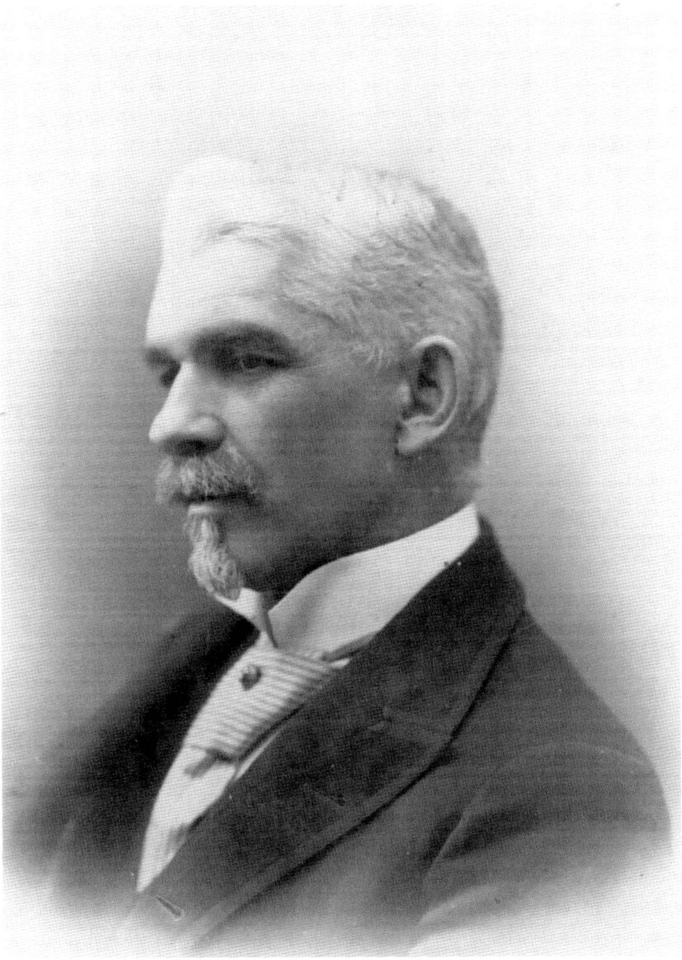

Dr. Dan Millikin

For nearly 40 years, Dan Millikin was one of the most popular, respected, and admired men in Hamilton. He was born in 1845 and was the son of lawyer John M. Millikin and grandson of Dr. Daniel Millikin, the town's first permanent physician. In 1862, he was one of the first three graduates of Hamilton High School. Millikin, who had been tutored by Dr. Cyrus Falconer, earned his doctor of medicine degree at Miami Medical College in Cincinnati in 1875 and immediately began to build his practice in Hamilton. Within a few years, he had a large, lucrative, and important business. In 1884, he joined the faculty of Miami Medical College, holding first the chair of Medical Chemistry, then of Materia Medica and Therapeutics, and finally the chair of Medical Jurisprudence before resigning in 1893. Gov. William McKinley appointed "Dr. Dan" to the Miami University board of trustees in 1891, a position he held until 1900. Millikin served as president of the Ohio Medical Association in 1895 and 1896. He was elected to the Hamilton Board of Education, holding the office of president from 1906 to 1913. Millikin contributed many articles to literary and scientific journals and was a highly effective public speaker. He also wrote several comedies and acted in a variety of locally produced plays and entertainments. Millikin was well liked for his outgoing personality, charming character, geniality, and willingness to help in all sorts of charitable causes. For some of the children he tended, he was known as "Gankie," the grandfather-like man who was the mender of their broken dolls and toys. When Dr. Millikin died in 1914, more than 500 people attended his memorial service, which included a long eulogy by former Ohio governor James F. Campbell and several tributes from prominent local citizens.

CHAPTER TWO

Serving the Community

As the Butler County seat, Hamilton has always been the political and legal center for area residents. Major public servants have traditionally been county prosecutors, sheriffs, auditors, judges, surveyors, and coroners. When the city's charter was granted in 1833, power was invested in a mayor and six trustees. After Rossville and Hamilton merged in 1854, the mayor appointed policemen, subject to the confirmation of the council, which appointed most of the other public servants. For the most part, county sheriffs administered the law until the city created its own police department in 1875, and volunteer firemen protected the community until a professional fire department was created in the 1880s. In 1928, Hamilton adopted a city council–city manager form of government.

William M. Love, George P. Fritz, and John M. Hunker gave all they had, losing their lives while fighting the 1913 Butler County Courthouse fire.

Judge Clarence Murphy, who served on the bench for nearly 30 years; Warren Gard, who represented the area in the US Congress; and Judge John Moser, who with his wife, Shirley, donated the *Hamilton Gateway* sculpture at the Government Services Center, made contributions to the city during their exemplary legal careers. These men did more than just serve in the local courts; they gave back to their community through service and philanthropy.

Attorney John Neilan helped the city recover from the devastating flood of 1913 and worked to form the Miami Conservancy District to make a repeat flood much more unlikely. County engineer Fred Hammerle worked to rebuild roads and bridges ruined by the deluge. Dr. Mark Millikin worked several years as the city's health officer and nearly 25 years as chief of staff at Mercy Hospital. His son, Dr. Neil Millikin, had a 50-year practice and he, too, was a hospital chief of staff.

Policeman James O'Conner streamlined the city's traffic system, and Officer Frank "Pop" Mayer taught Hamilton's youngsters how to operate bicycles safely. Industrialist William Beckett not only served six terms on city council, he was mayor for two terms. Grocer Frank Witt's career was cut short when he died during a council meeting in 1978. Rear Adm. Donald Wulzen had a spectacular military career, including as a commander in South Vietnam.

County coroner Garret Boone handled more than 16,000 cases, including the gruesome murder of 11 members of the Ruppert family. County prosecutor John Holcomb successfully brought James Ruppert to justice for those deaths.

More recently, Jack Kirsch and Hal Shepherd have made great contributions as city managers. Other city government officials who have had a major impact include Mike Fox, Greg Jolivette, and Don Ryan.

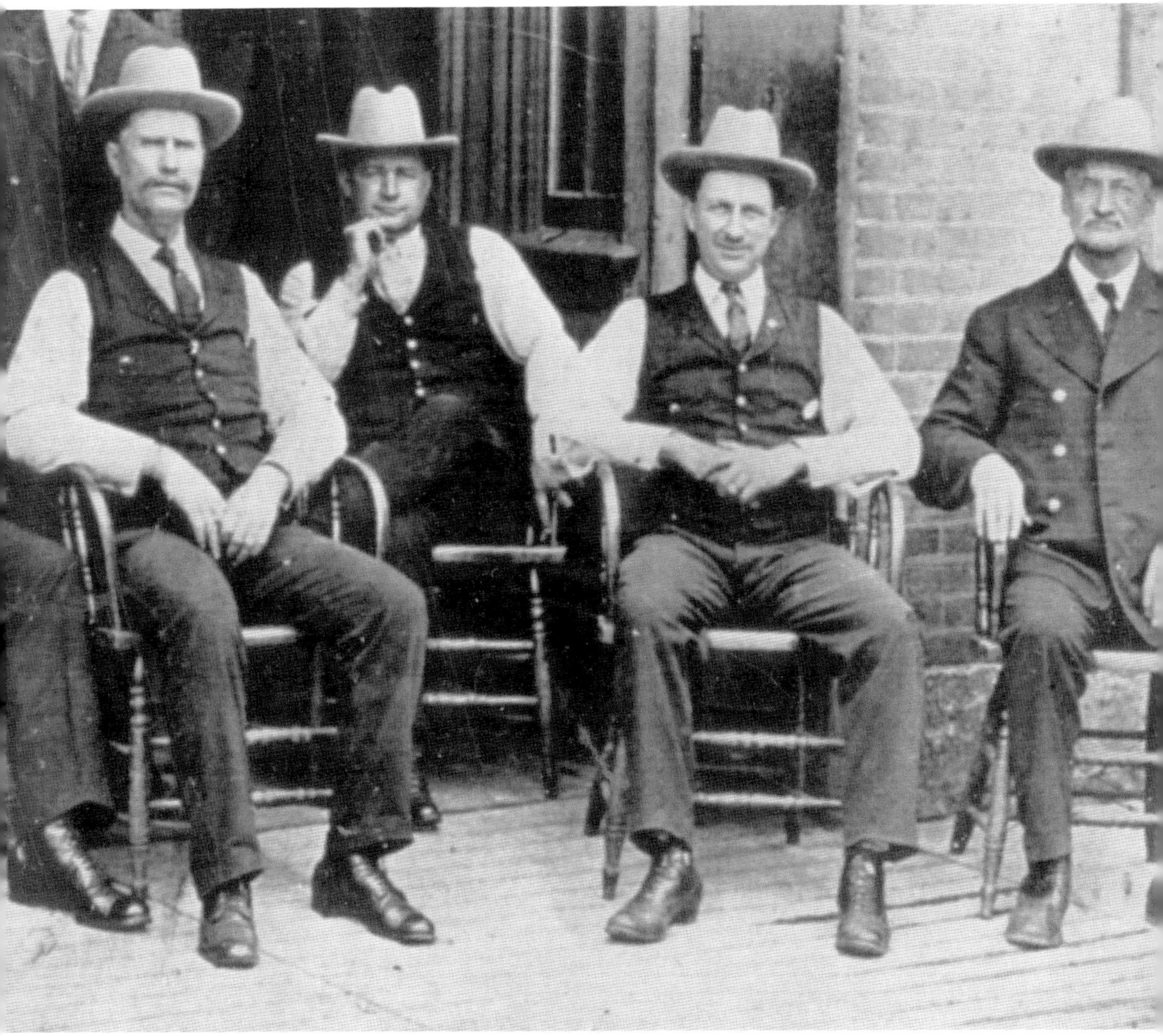

1912 Courthouse Fire Victims

Four members of Hamilton's First Ward Fire Company are seen in this photograph, taken in 1907 or 1908. The men are, from left to right, William M. Love, John C. Smith, George P. Fritz, and Fire Chief William C. Dowty. In 1912, Love and Fritz were fatally injured while fighting the Butler County Courthouse fire. John M. Hunker, a third fireman, also died while battling the blaze. Hunker (1879–1912) was in his first year on the force and died instantly when the courthouse clock tower, dome cupola, and 1,560-pound statue of the Goddess of Justice collapsed. Love (1866–1912), a fireman for eight years, was badly burned and died at Mercy Hospital just five hours after the fire had started. George Fritz (1877–1912) was a 12-year veteran of the department. He died on March 19, five days after the fire. Dowty (1855–1919) had joined the fire department in 1879 as a hoseman and served as a driver for 23 years before being named fire marshal in 1903 and chief in 1905. In 1917, Chief Dowty retired from the department after serving 38 years. Hunker, Love, and Fritz were the first Hamilton firemen killed in the line of duty. They are remembered during several ceremonies every year, and their names appear on plaques at the city building and at the fire department's headquarters. (Courtesy of the George C. Cummins "Remember When" Collection at the Hamilton Lane Library.)

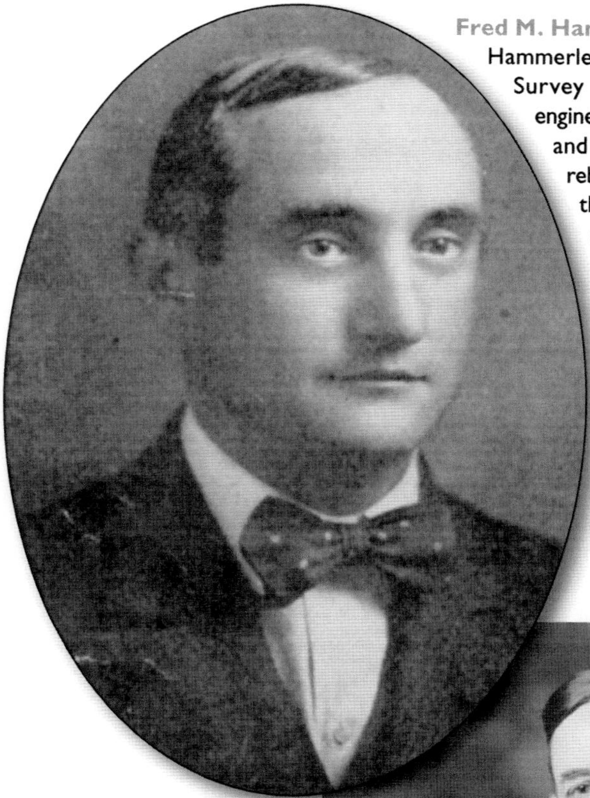

Fred M. Hammerle
Hammerle worked three years for the US Geological Survey before taking a position as assistant city engineer in 1910. He became county surveyor in 1913 and was faced with the massive responsibility of rebuilding the bridges and roadways destroyed by the March 1913 Great Miami Flood. Hammerle (1878–1964) supervised construction of three bridges in Hamilton and one in Middletown, many smaller bridges, and miles of roads. He also was the county's engineer from 1932 to 1948, during which many new roads and bridges were constructed. (Courtesy of Lane Library.)

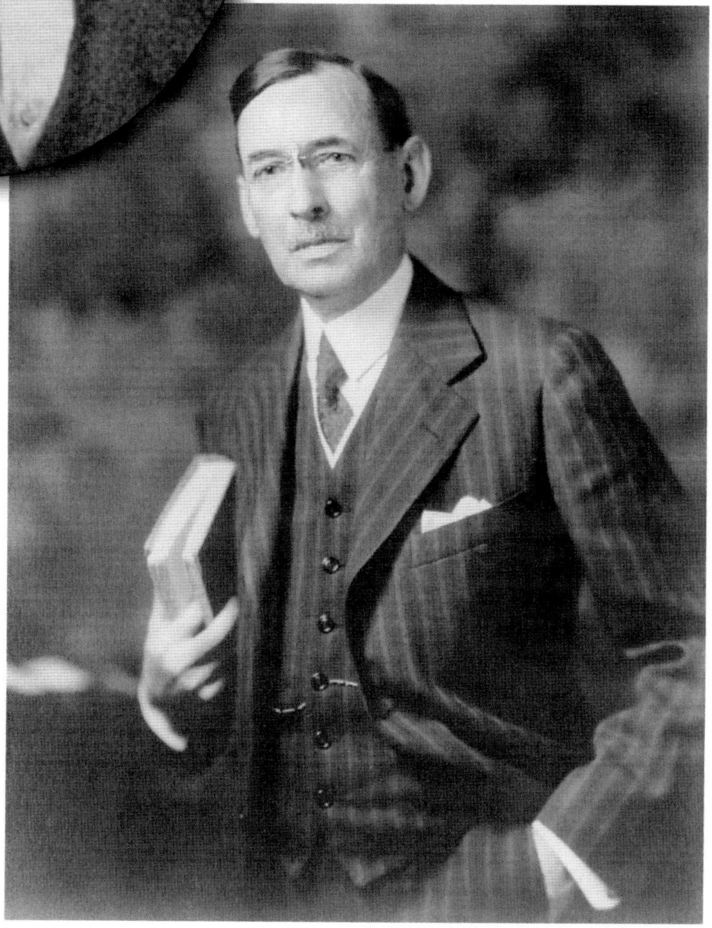

Clarence Murphy
Murphy displayed judicial integrity and impartiality during his years as a probate court judge, from 1894 to 1900, and when he sat on the common pleas court bench, from 1907 to 1929. A highly respected attorney, he practiced from 1889 to 1894 and from 1900 to 1907. Murphy (1862–1939) also was an officer of the Hamilton Dime Savings Bank for many years and sat on the board of the Union Central Life Insurance Company for 43 years, from 1896 to 1939. He was a board member of the chamber of commerce, YMCA, and the community chest.

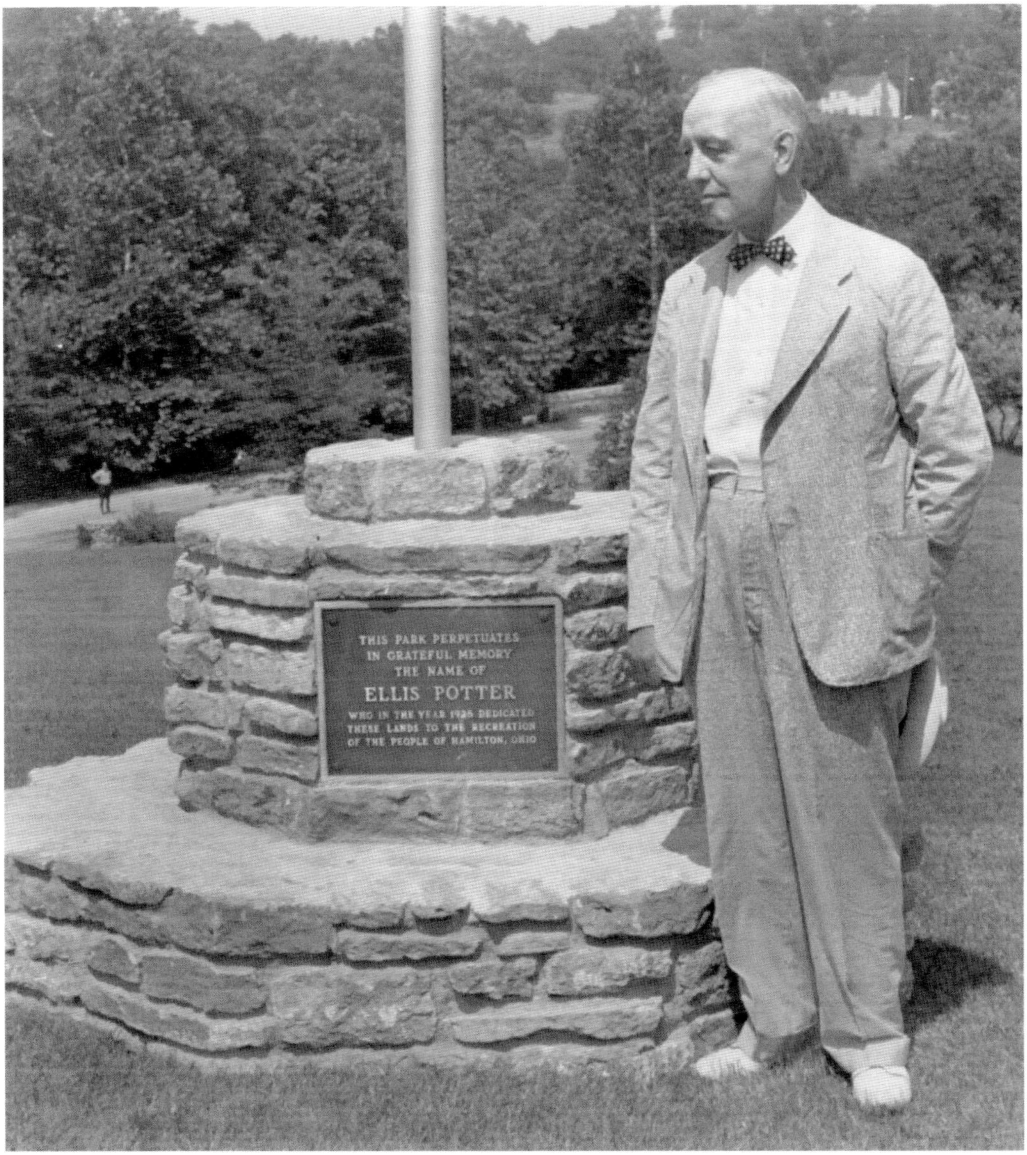

John F. Neilan Jr.

In 1903, Neilan began practicing law in his father's firm and took over the agency four years later. He founded Columbia Federal Savings & Loan Association in 1909. During the crisis brought on by the March 1913 Great Miami Flood, city solicitor Neilan served as "military governor" of the First Ward and directed the affairs of the west side for nearly a month. He supported the formation of the Miami Conservancy District to provide flood protection along the 160-mile river. Neilan (1881–1945) was one of the founders of the Hamilton Welfare Federation in 1920 and was actively involved with the group until 1944, serving as president from 1924 to 1929. He also was chairman of three community chest fundraising campaigns, from 1921 to 1923. During the Depression, Neilan directed Hamilton's relief program and was head of the Civic Works Administration. He helped a variety of other community organizations, including Mercy Hospital and the Hamilton Chamber of Commerce. Neilan Boulevard, completed in 1954, was named in his honor.

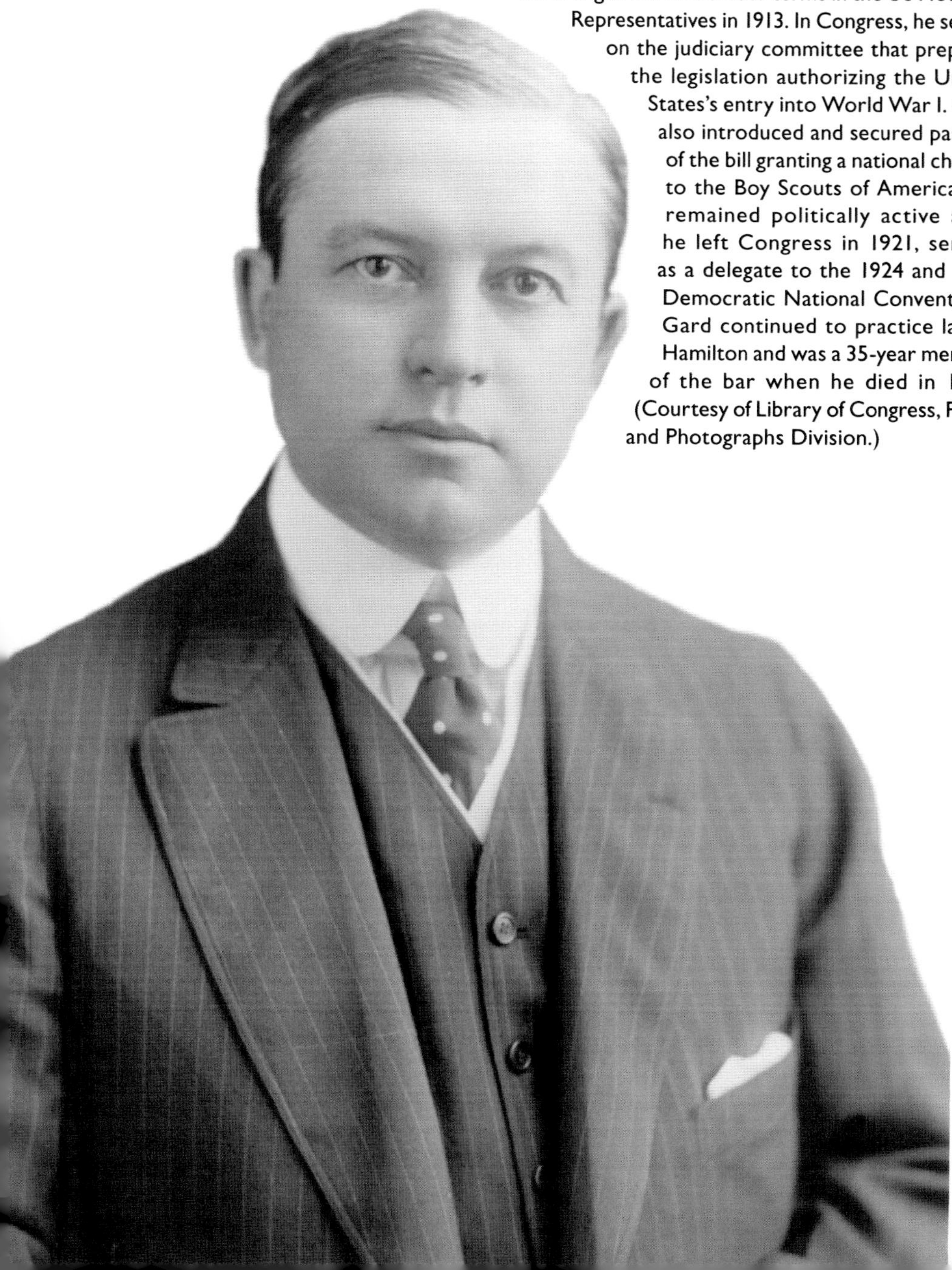

Warren Gard

During the first three decades of the 1900s, Warren Gard was one of the most prominent men in Butler County. He was born in Hamilton in 1873, the second son of Samuel Z. and Mary Duke Gard and younger brother of publisher Homer Gard. Warren graduated from Hamilton High in 1890. He earned his law degree at Cincinnati Law School in 1894 and immediately began his practice. Gard was elected Butler County prosecutor in 1898 and held the position until 1903. He was elected court of common pleas judge in 1907 and served five years. Gard began the first of four terms in the US House of Representatives in 1913. In Congress, he served on the judiciary committee that prepared the legislation authorizing the United States's entry into World War I. Gard also introduced and secured passage of the bill granting a national charter to the Boy Scouts of America. He remained politically active after he left Congress in 1921, serving as a delegate to the 1924 and 1928 Democratic National Conventions. Gard continued to practice law in Hamilton and was a 35-year member of the bar when he died in 1929. (Courtesy of Library of Congress, Prints and Photographs Division.)

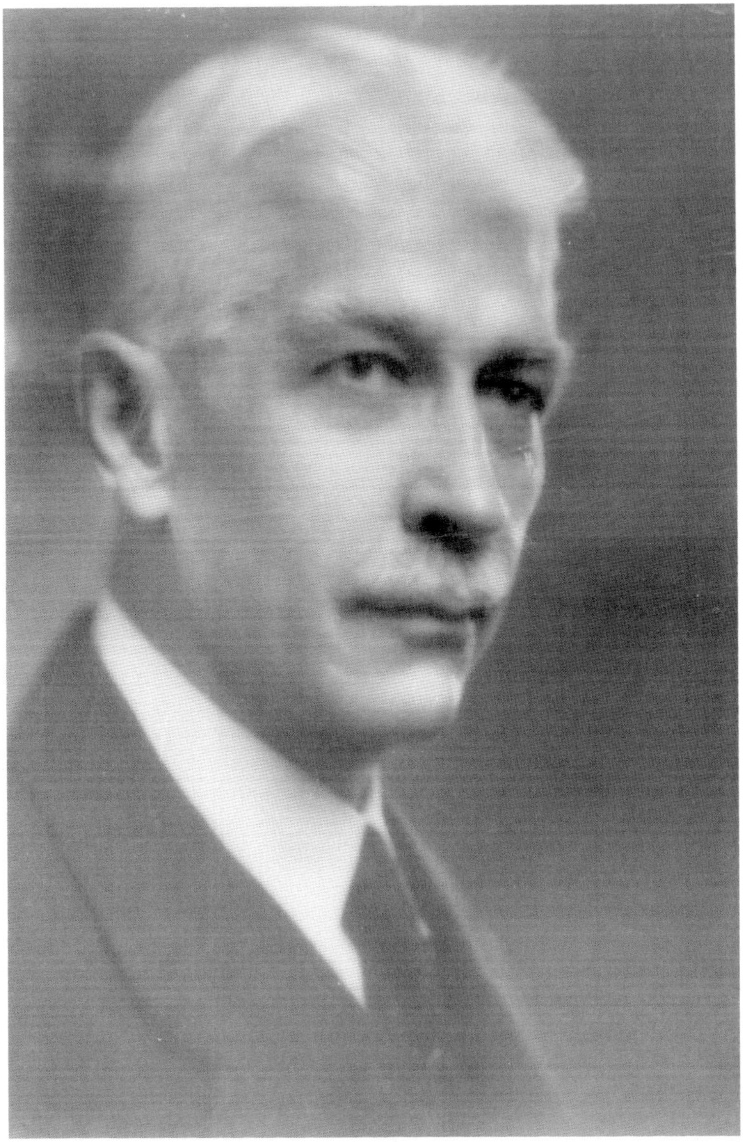

Dr. Mark Millikin

Dr. Mark Millikin began his career in medicine in 1893 when he joined with his father, Dr. Dan Millikin (page 22), to start his practice. He became one of the most prominent physicians in Hamilton, serving the community for more than 50 years before retiring in 1944. Millikin (1868–1945) served as the city's health commissioner from 1904 to 1911 and was the chief of the medical staff at Mercy Hospital from 1920 to 1944. He was a member of the city's first charter commission that tried unsuccessfully to form a city manager government in 1916. In 1926, however, Millikin and the other community leaders on the second commission were able to win voter support for a new city charter. Millikin was elected in 1927 to the first city council under the new charter and was reelected six times, serving from 1928 to 1941, and he was appointed to fill a vacated seat from 1942 to 1943. He served as the chair of the Associated Charities, the forerunner of the United Way, in Hamilton and supported many other local clubs and organizations. In 1945, the city renamed what had been known as the Stahlheber Woods, Millikin Woods, in his honor.

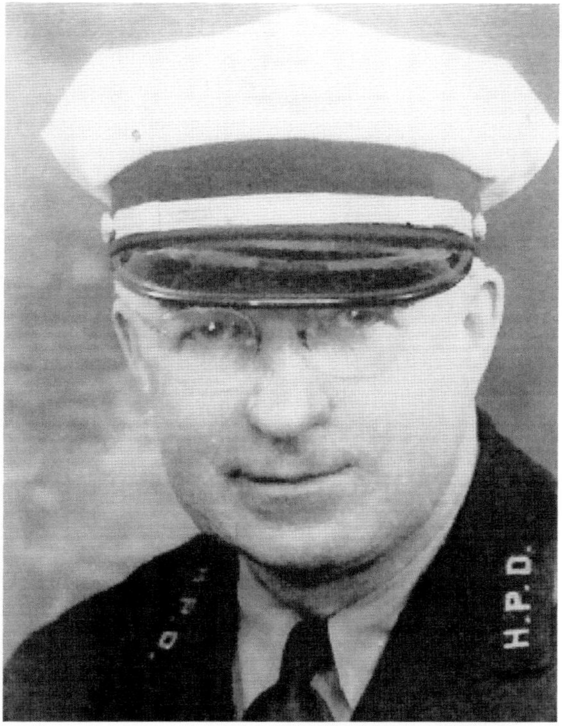

James P. O'Connor
O'Connor joined the Hamilton police in 1921 and walked a beat for the first five years. In 1925, he was operating a semaphore "stop and go" sign at the Second and High Streets intersection when he was struck by an automobile driven by Hamilton mayor Howard Kelley. O'Connor (1894–1959) was appointed the city's first acting traffic sergeant in 1926, a position not made official until 1937. When electric traffic signals were introduced, O'Connor studied downtown traffic patterns to set the timing of the lights to keep traffic moving smoothly. He retired from the force in 1954. (Courtesy of Diane Kuhlmann Beaty.)

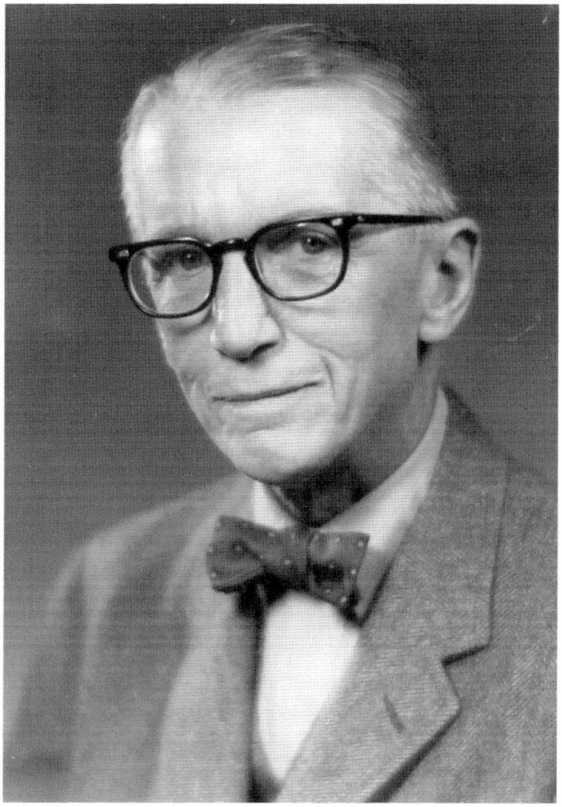

William Beckett
Beckett served six terms as a city councilman between 1940 and 1955, as mayor for two terms, and represented Hamilton in the Ohio Senate in 1956. He worked to raise funds to establish the Miami University–Hamilton campus and was involved in community groups, including the United Appeal, Junior Achievement, YMCA, and Fine Arts Fund. He served as a trustee of Miami University and the Cincinnati Symphony Orchestra. Beckett (1909–1990) was the last member of his family to head the Beckett Paper Company, started by his grandfather in 1848.

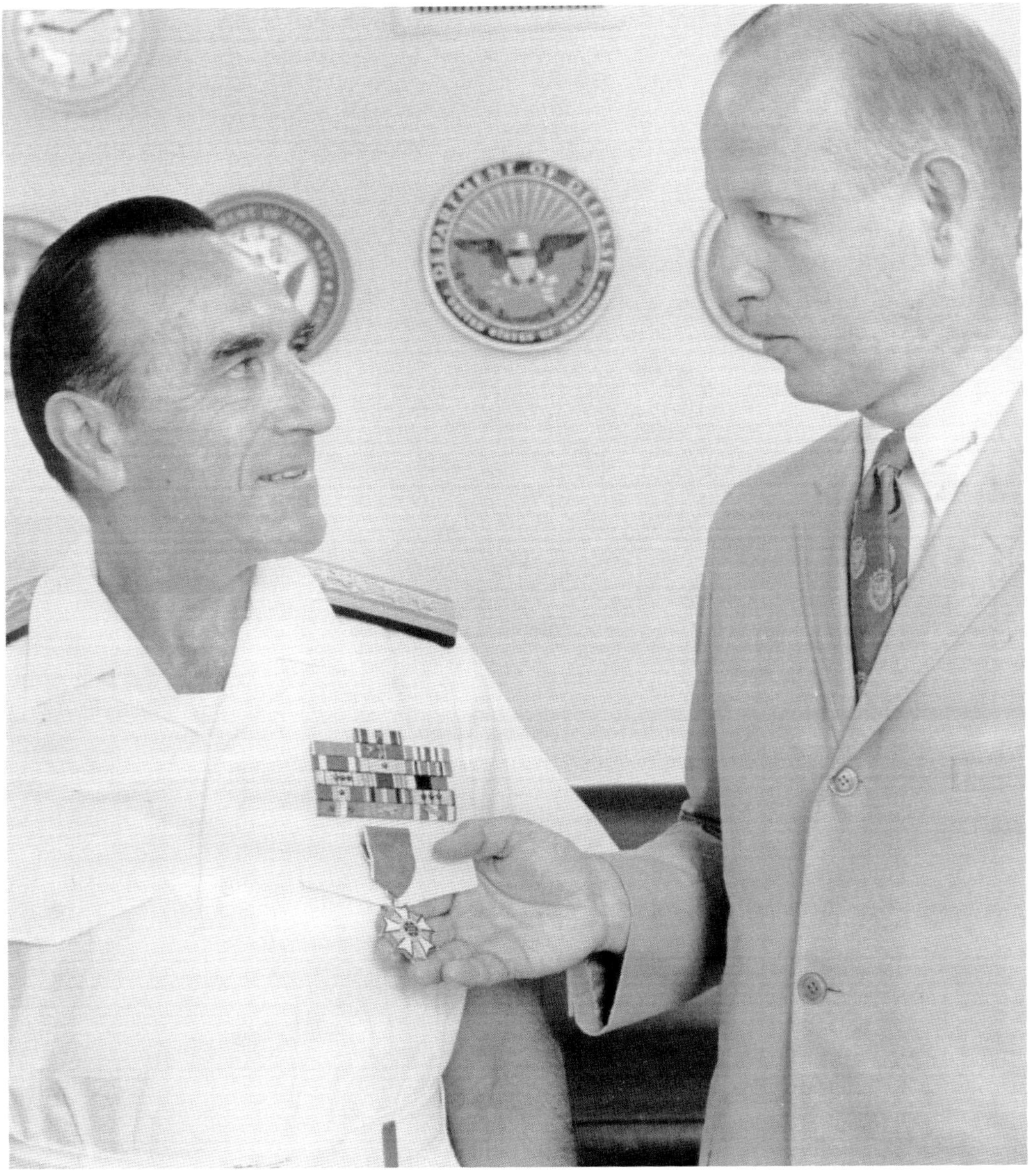

Donald W. Wulzen

Wulzen (1912–1996), a member of Hamilton High's class of 1930, graduated from the US Naval Academy in 1935. During World War II, he was commanding officer of the USS *Porterfield*, a destroyer that participated in strikes on Tokyo, Okinawa, Iwo Jima, and the Ryukyu Islands. Wulzen was awarded two Silver Stars for these actions. He commanded another destroyer, the USS *Warrington*, from 1945 to 1947 and the USS *Copriocornus*, a Spitfire-class cargo ship, from 1960 to 1961. Rear Admiral Wulzen took command of the Seventh Fleet's Amphibious Task Force in 1965 and on March 8, gave the traditional order to "land the landing force" from his flagship, the USS *Mount McKinley*. Upon his order, 5,000 Marines disembarked for Danang, South Vietnam, as the first battalion-sized American combat units deployed ashore in the extended Southeast Asian conflict. Wulzen (left) is seen here receiving the Legion of Merit Award from Robert F. Froehlke, assistant secretary of defense, in 1969. He also received a Gold Star Award in lieu of a second Legion of Merit Award.

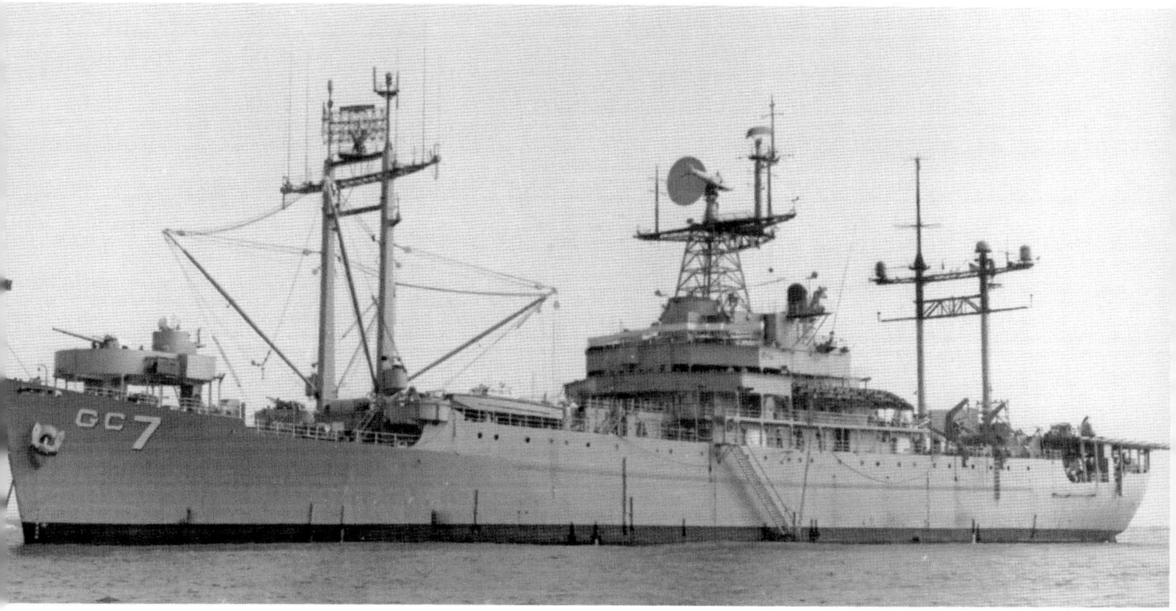

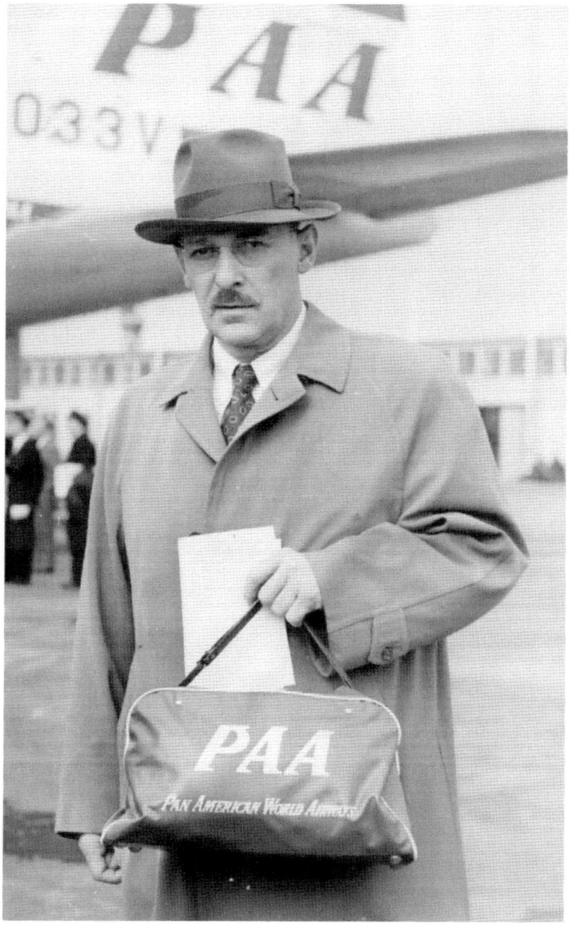

USS *Mount McKinley* (AGC-7)
Rear Admiral Wulzen's flagship is seen anchored in Danang Harbor in 1965. It had previously served as the command ship for the atomic bomb tests at Bikini Atoll and Eniwetok in 1947 and 1948. In 1950, Gen. Douglas MacArthur directed the amphibious assault on Inchon, Korea, while aboard the ship. After the Korean War, the *Mount McKinley* was deployed for several tours in the Mediterranean for NATO service. In 1962, the ship took part in the Cuban missile crisis quarantine. It was decommissioned in 1970.

Dr. Neil Millikin
Dr. Neil Millikin (1900–1981), son of Dr. Mark Millikin, was a general practitioner in Hamilton for more than 50 years. In 1962, Millikin was elected chief of staff at Mercy Hospital, a position held by his father and grandfather, Dr. Dan Millikin. He also was the chief of staff at Fort Hamilton–Hughes Memorial Hospital. For three decades, Millikin provided medical care to the local US Selective Service board without pay. He was a founding member of the Hamilton Community Foundation and a board member of the county Children's Home for 33 years.

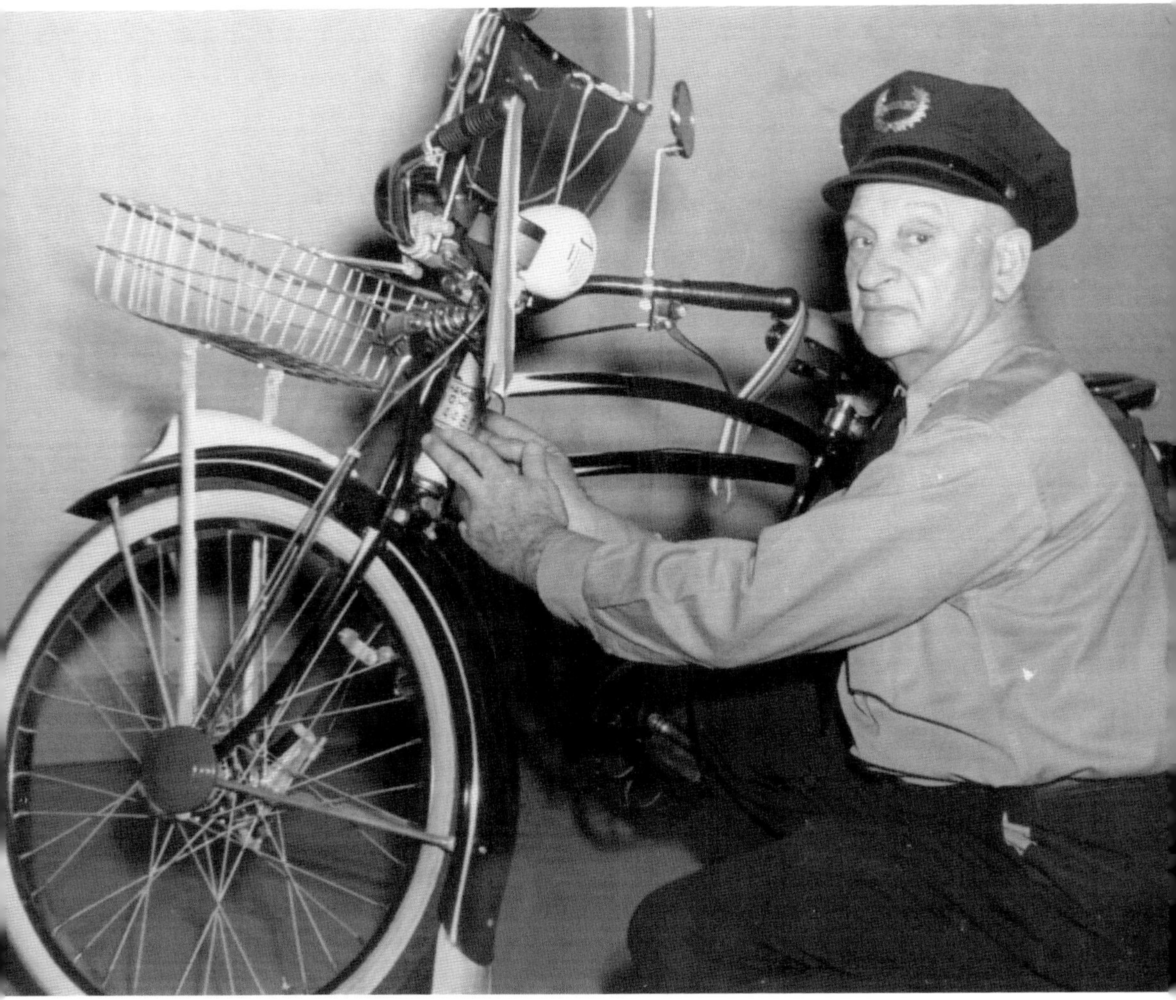

Frank "Pop" Mayer

Nearly every youngster in Hamilton knew Officer "Pop" Mayer. For many years, Mayer (1887–1971) was in charge of inspecting and licensing bicycles. He would test each bicycle's braking power, wheel alignment, horns, lights, and other parts before registering it and placing the coveted safety sticker on the bicycle's rear fender. Mayer also gave safety talks to youngsters in city and parochial schools as well as at the teenage bicycle court. He acquired the name "Pop" from a seriously injured little girl he had removed from an automobile wreck. Mayer had taken extra care and tenderly transferred the girl to a stretcher for transportation to the hospital. After her dismissal from the hospital two months later, the girl and her parents visited police headquarters to find Patrolman Mayer. She threw her arms around him and said, "I'll never forget the way he treated me at the accident. He was just like a poppa to me." Mayer joined the police department in 1923 and served the community for 38 years. He was a driver for 20 years and spent many hours reloading used .38 Special cartridges for policemen to use during shooting practice. Over the years, Mayer reloaded nearly 75,000 rounds of ammunition. In 1974, the Hamilton Police Department named its new pistol range the Frank "Pop" Mayer Firing Range.

Garret J. Boone
Dr. Boone was appointed to the county coroner's office in 1938 and, beginning in 1946, was elected to nine consecutive four-year terms until his retirement in 1980. He served as president of the Ohio State Coroner's Association in 1971 and 1972 and worked to improve the ways county coroners handled details at the scene of major disasters. Boone (1902–1980) worked an estimated 16,000 coroner cases during his career, including the investigation of the Ruppert family murders in 1975.

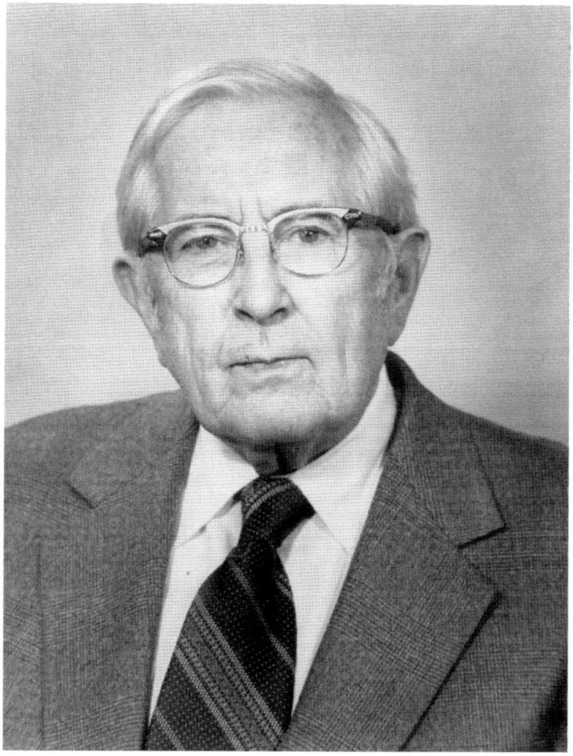

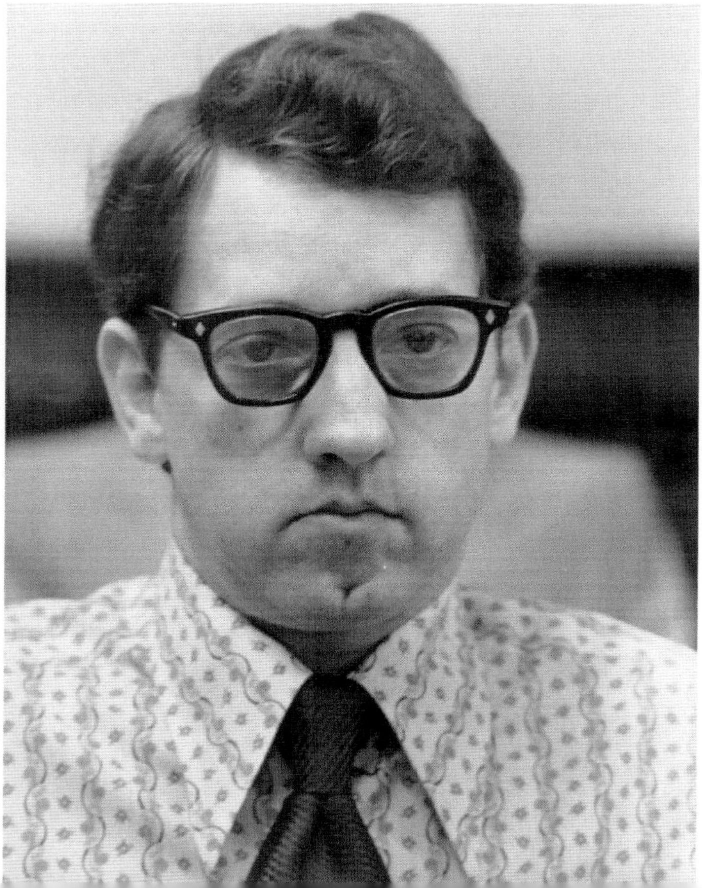

James U. Ruppert
On Easter Sunday, March 30, 1975, James Ruppert walked through his mother's house and committed America's largest family mass murder. He methodically gunned down his mother, brother, sister-in-law, and their eight children, aged 4 to 17. Ruppert was sentenced to 11 consecutive life terms at his 1975 trial, but the decision was overturned. A three-judge panel found him guilty of first-degree murder on two counts, but not guilty by reason of insanity for the deaths of the children. In 1995, the Ohio Parole Board denied his request for parole and ordered him to serve 40 more years before seeking parole again.

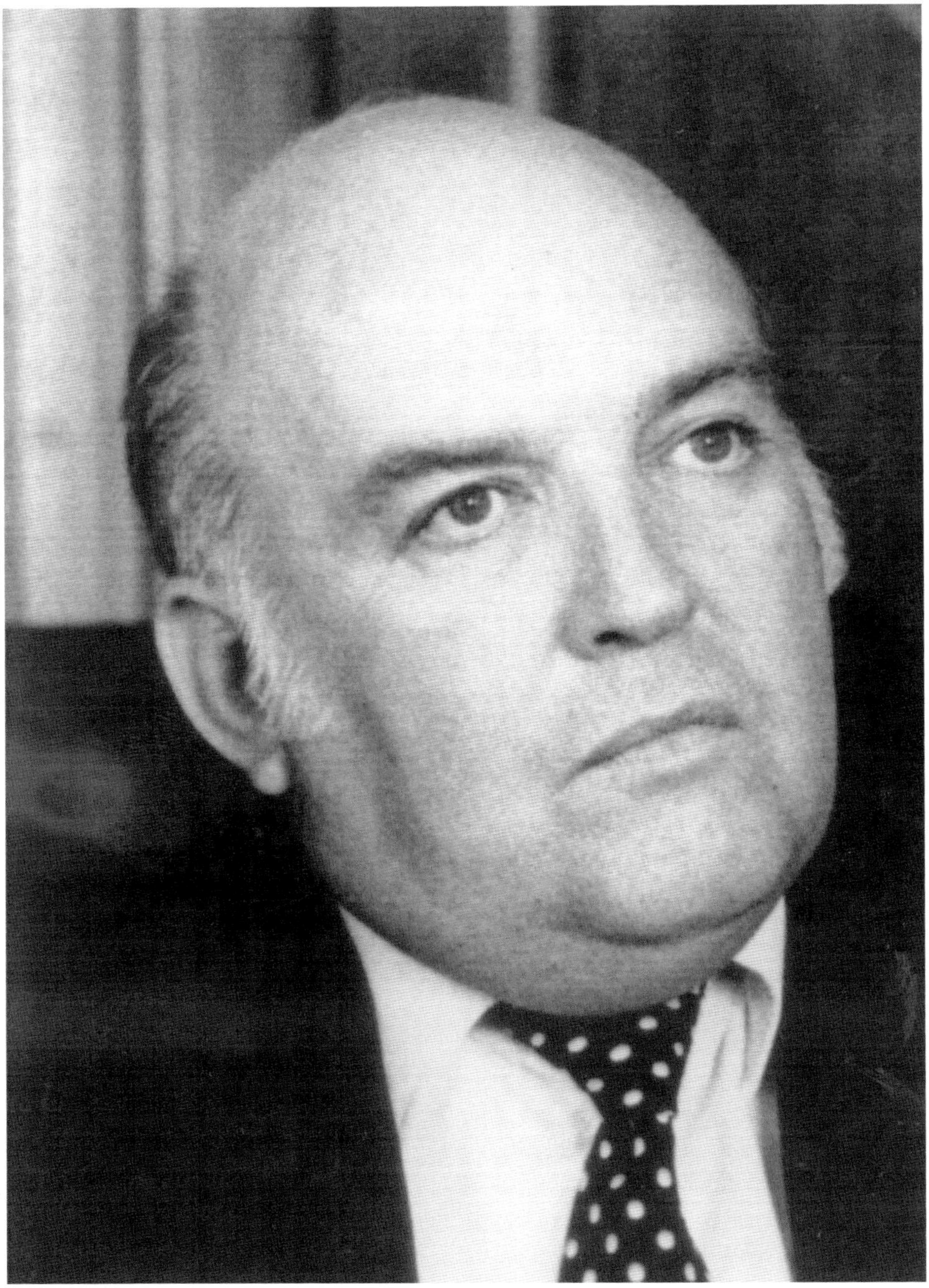

John F. Holcomb

Holcomb was a member of Hamilton High's 1954 state championship basketball team. After seven years as a letter carrier, he became an assistant prosecutor, serving from 1965 to 1972. In 1973, he was elected county prosecutor, a position he held until his death. Holcomb (1937–2000) was named Ohio Prosecuting Attorney of the Year in 1998. He successfully prosecuted several high-profile cases, including the Ruppert family murders of 1975, the dismemberment of a Fairfield woman by a Satanist in 1987, and a Liberty Township crossbow murder conspiracy in 1993.

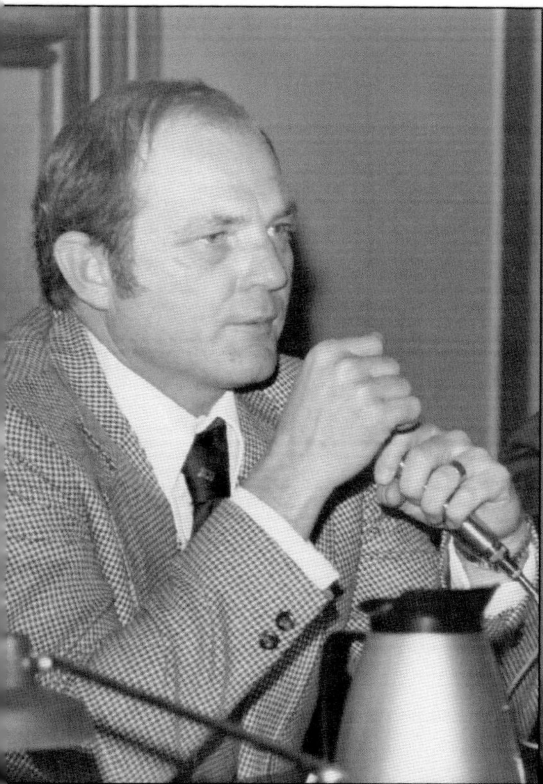

Frank D. Witt
In 1978, Mayor Witt collapsed during a city council meeting and died. He owned and managed the Five Points Super Market when, in 1971, he was first elected to the city council and, being the top vote-getter, became the mayor. Witt (1935–1978) was active in a variety of community organizations and was president of the Hamilton Safety Council and trustee of the Fort Hamilton Hospital and Children's Home. In 1975, during his third of four terms as mayor, the Rossville Historic District was placed in the National Register of Historic Places.

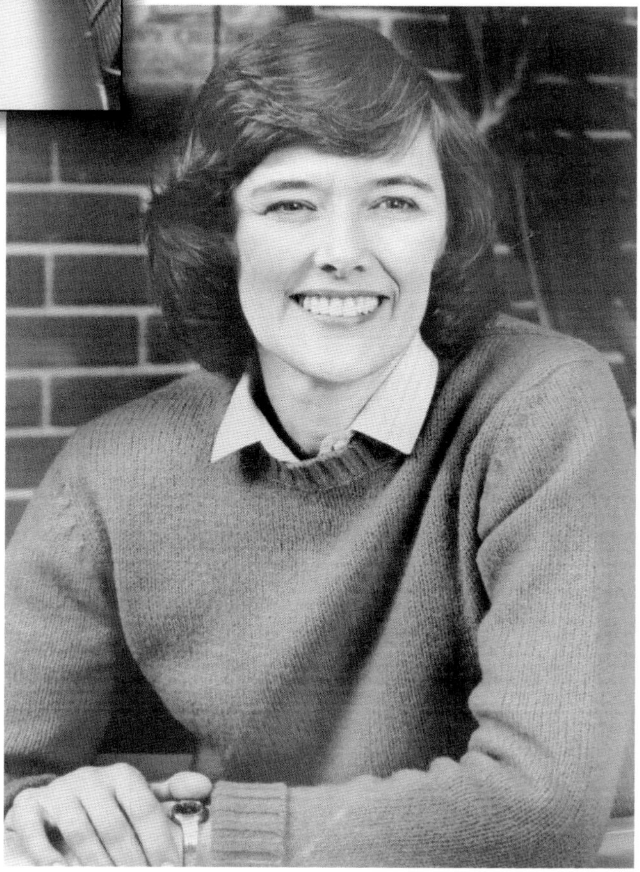

Patricia Scott Schroeder
Schroeder attended Wilson Junior High from 1952 to 1955 and took part in glee club, Honor Scouts, Y-Teens, and served on the *Reflash* yearbook staff. She served in the US House of Representatives from 1973 to 1997 and was the first woman elected to Congress from Colorado. Schroeder (1940–) was known for coining the phrase "Teflon President" to describe Ronald Reagan and for writing the 1993 Family and Medical Leave Act, signed into law by President Clinton. She was named to the National Women's Hall of Fame in 1995.

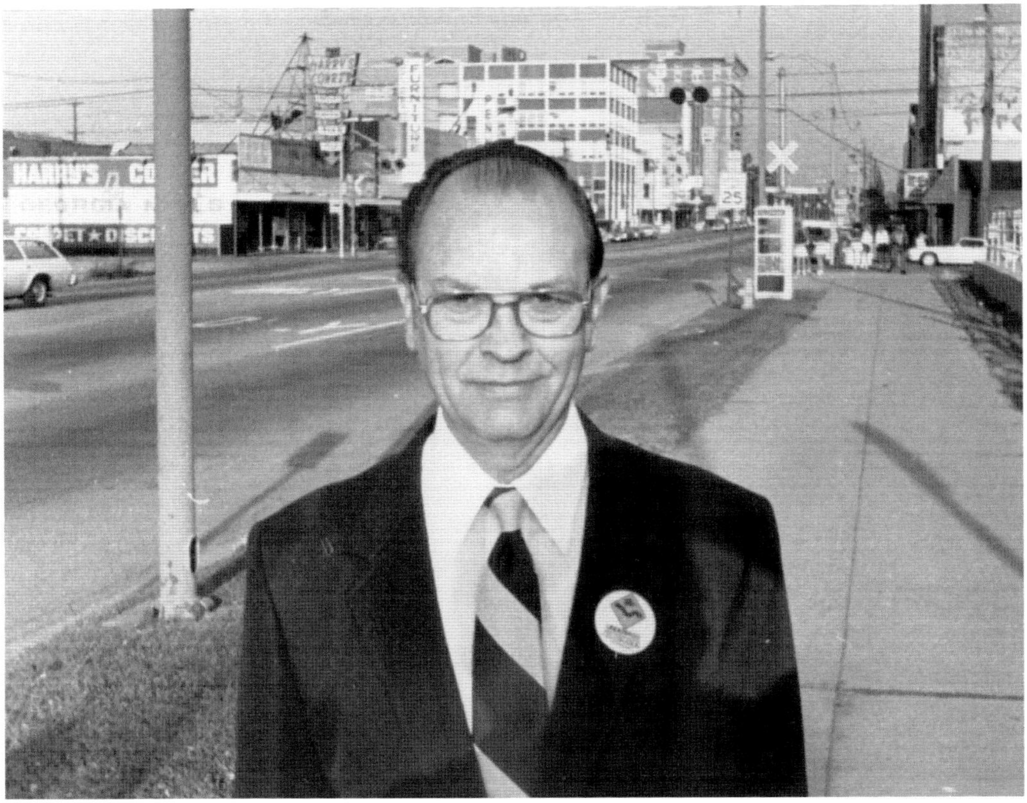

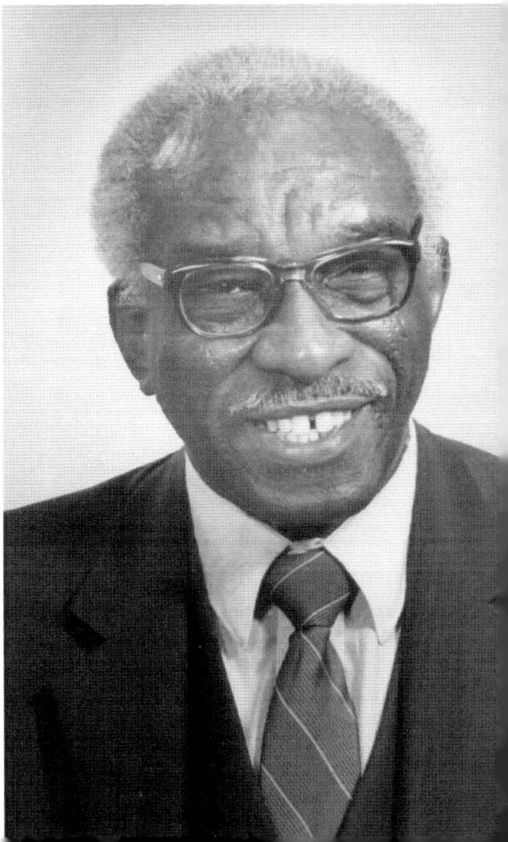

Bernard "Jack" Kirsch

Kirsch was chief deputy engineer for Butler County for eight years before taking over the city's public works department in 1958. He served in that position until he was named city manager in 1975. Kirsch (1926–) dedicated much of his effort toward making the downtown High Street railroad underpass a reality. Construction of the underpass, first proposed in 1919, began in 1981. The first traffic passed under the railroad tracks in 1983, the year Kirsch left his city manager position. In 2003, the city named the underpass in his honor.

Nathaniel D. Sherman Jr.

For many years, Sherman (1925–1999) made an impact with his leadership and work at the Hamilton Human Relations Commission. He labored to improve minority housing opportunities, race relations, fair employment practices, and educational opportunities. He helped improve the Booker T. Washington Community Center and was president of the local chapter of the National Association for the Advancement of Colored People during the turbulent 1960s.

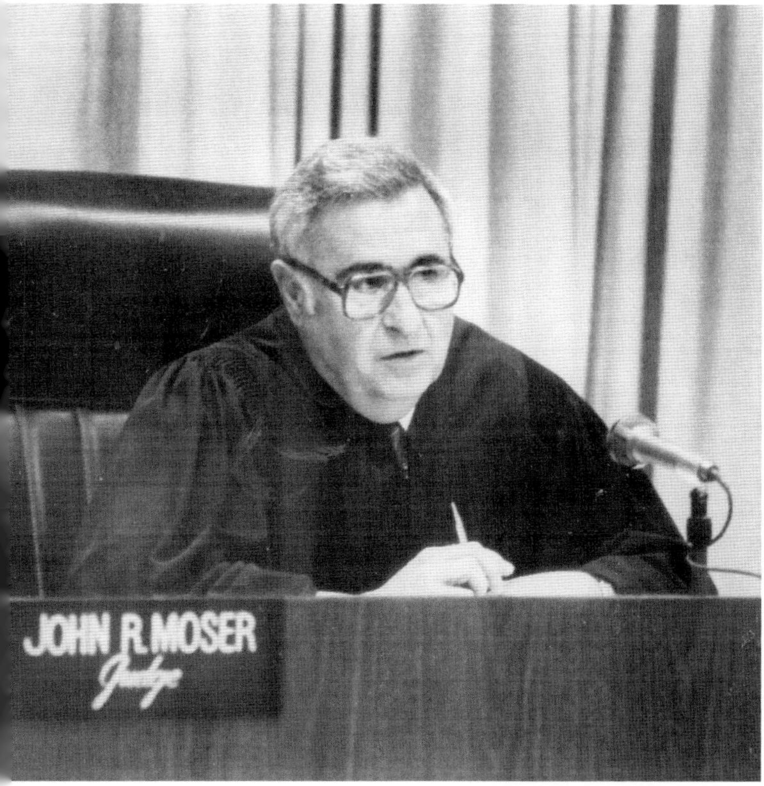

John R. Moser
Moser, a 1945 graduate of Hamilton High, practiced law from 1953 until 1979 and served as an assistant prosecutor for eight years, from 1956 to 1964. He was elected to the court of common pleas bench in 1979 and presided for 20 years. Moser (1927–), a master gardener, received the Butler County Bar Association's James S. Irwin Award for Professionalism in 2003. He and his wife, Shirley, funded *The Hamilton Gateway*, the large sculpture in the plaza of the Government Services Center.

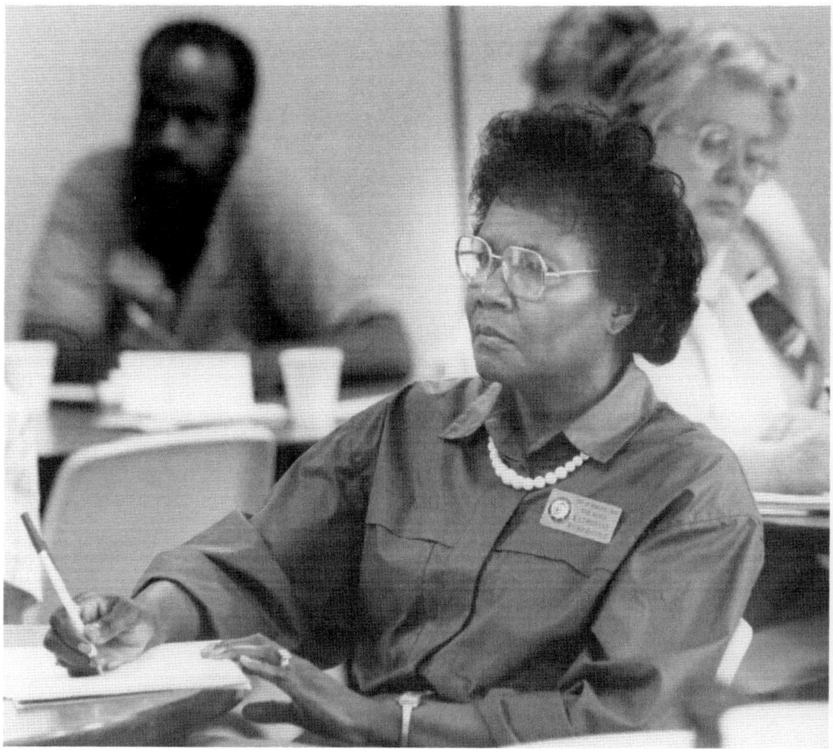

Katherine Rumph
Rumph was the first African American councilwoman in Hamilton's history. She served 12 years on the council, from 1984 to 1995. Starting in 1989, she was known as Katherine Rumph-Cole. She was a strong supporter of the Booker T. Washington Community Center and many other Second Ward developments. In 1996, Rumph-Cole (1928–) moved to New Miami, remarried, and was elected to the town council as Katherine Rumph-Butler. She became mayor of New Miami in 2003.

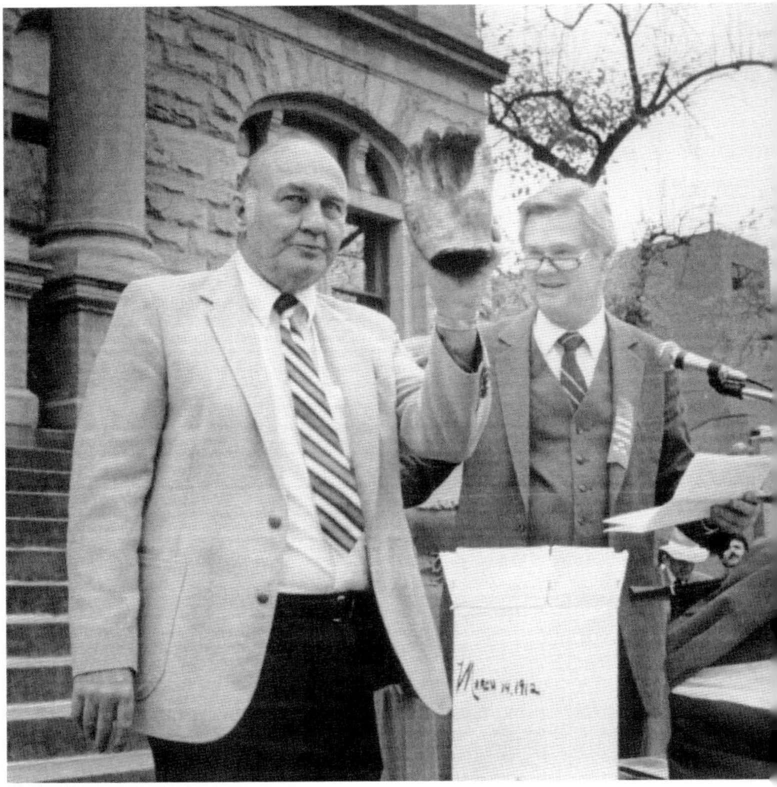

Robert R. Walton and James S. Irwin

County sheriff Robert R. Walton (left) and James S. Irwin display the hand of the Goddess of Justice statue that crowned the county courthouse dome when fire damaged the building in 1912. Walton (1925–1999) was a Middletown policeman from 1950 to 1976 and the Butler County sheriff from 1976 to 1988. Irwin (1933–), a trustee of the courthouse historical society, was a lawyer with the Millikin & Fitton firm for 34 years, from 1963 to 1997. The Butler County Bar Association created the James S. Irwin Award for Professionalism in 2003 in his honor.

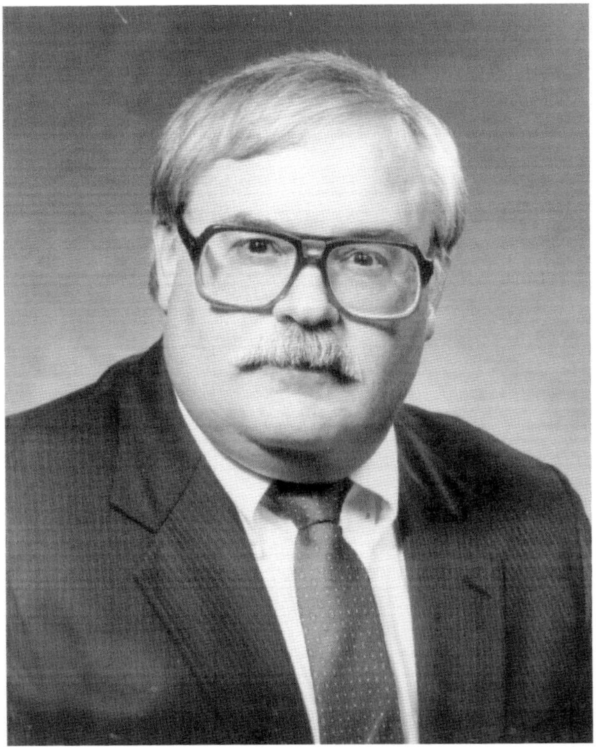

Harold "Hal" Shepherd

For 27 years, Shepherd (1944–) had a hand in managing the city of Hamilton. Between 1972 and 1989, he was an assistant city manager and then served as city manager for 10 years. Under his watch, Hamilton celebrated its bicentennial, built the Fitton Center for Creative Arts and One Renaissance Center, established TV Hamilton, and underwent many major improvements. In 1999, the year Shepherd began an eight-year term as city manager of Cortez, Colorado, Hamilton named its new fire department headquarters in his honor.

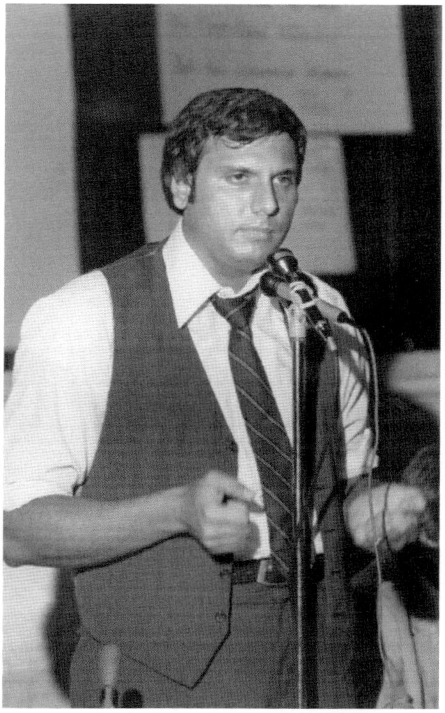

Michael A. Fox

"Mr. Butler County" represented Hamilton and Fairfield in the Ohio State Legislature from 1975 to 1997 and then became a Butler County commissioner, serving from 1997 to 2007. Fox then served as the director of the county's children's services department until 2009. Some of Fox's achievements included the founding of the county Transportation Improvement District and construction of a new jail and the Government Services Center. Fox (1949–) was indicted on federal charges in 2009 and pled guilty, resulting in a four-year prison sentence in 2012.

Gregory V. Jolivette

Jolivette (1951–), seen behind the counter of his seasonal root beer stand, began his political career when he was elected in 1981 to Hamilton's city council. He served six two-year terms from 1981 to 1990 and from 1995 to 1997, including eight years as mayor. Jolivette next represented Hamilton in the Ohio House of Representatives from 1997 to 2004, and then became a Butler County commissioner from 2004 to 2010. Jolly's, the root beer stand begun by his father, has been in business for more than 65 years.

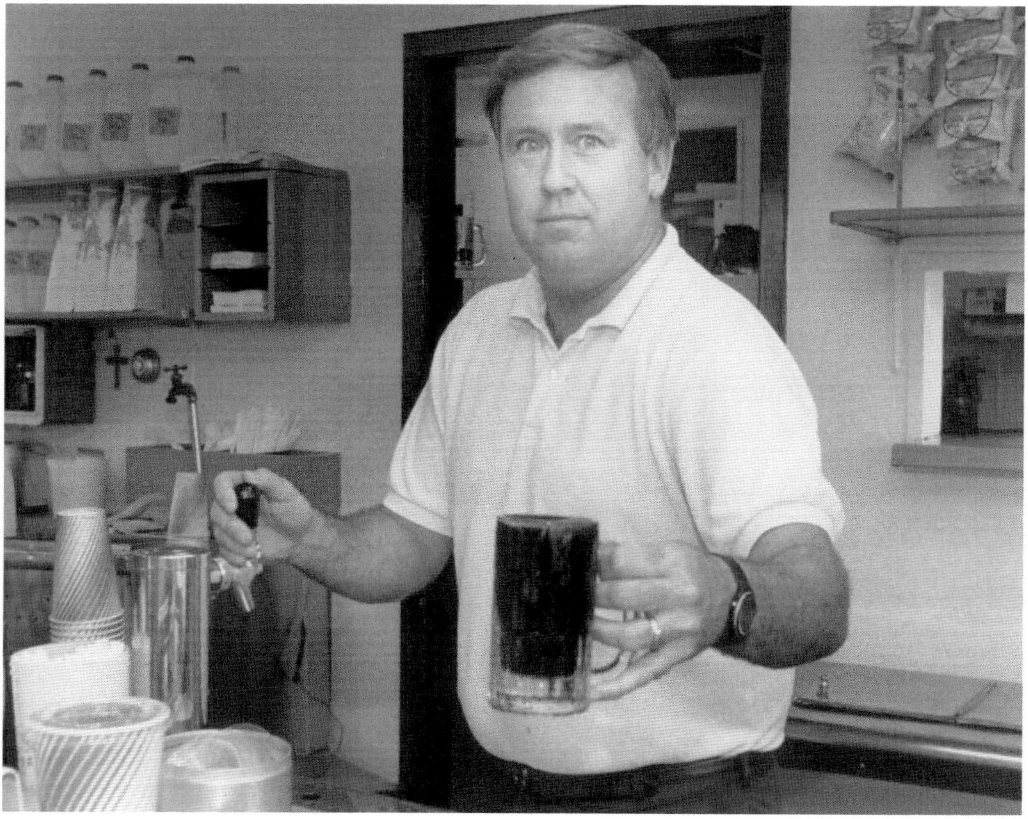

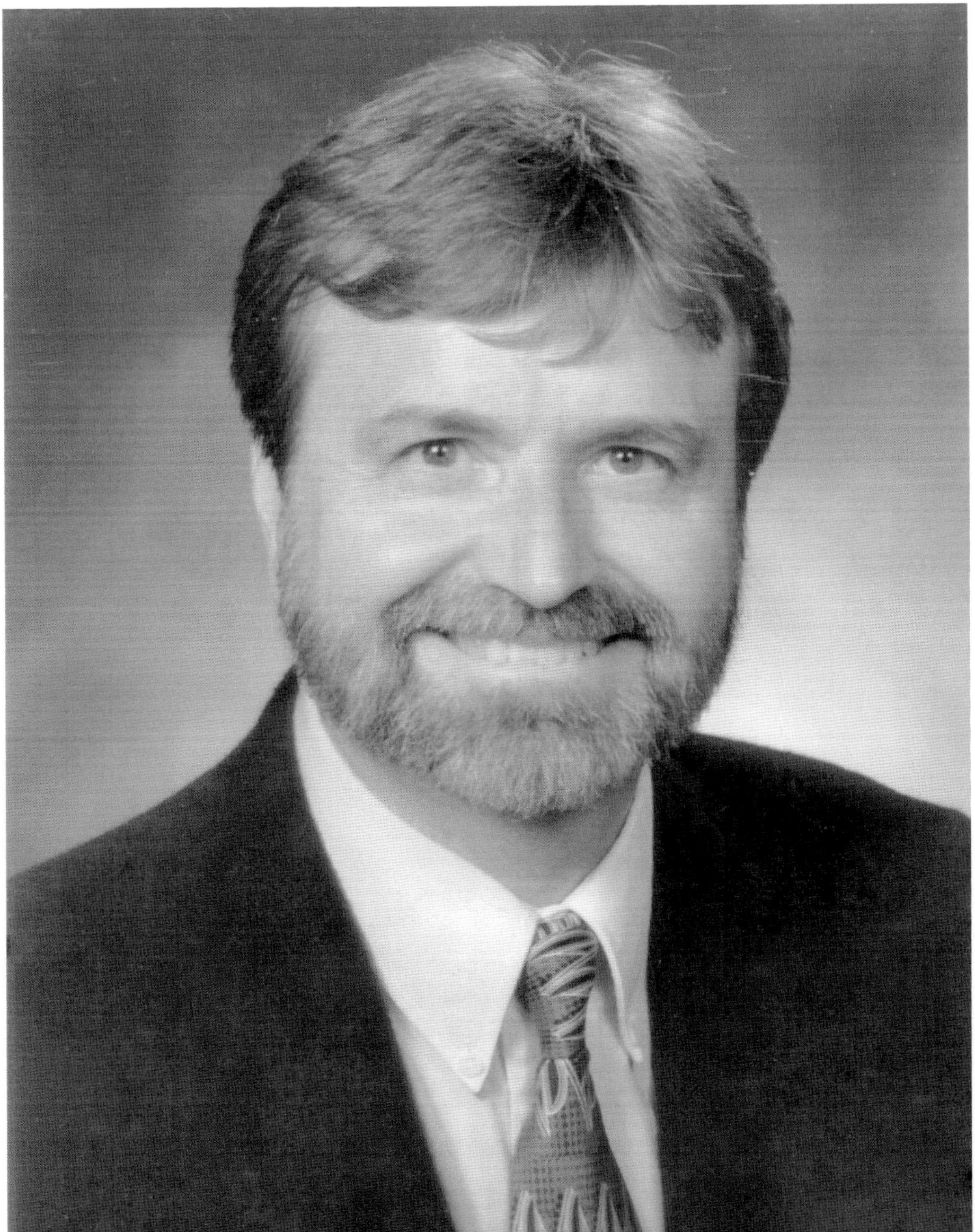

Donald V. Ryan

Ryan joined Hamilton's city council in 2000 and served as mayor from 2002 to 2010. Known as Hamilton's most positive supporter, he worked to make the city a more attractive place in which to live and operate a business. Ryan (1948–), several city staff members, and a 40-citizen committee created and implemented the Vision 2020 plan for Hamilton's future. He operates three metal fabricating and manufacturing businesses and opened Ryan's Tavern on High Street in 2008. Ryan was named Citizen of the Year in 2011.

CHAPTER THREE

Building Sound Minds

The Hamilton school district had a modest beginning in 1851, when Ohio first allowed localities to centralize several township school districts under one school board. The district began with two buildings, little more than elementary schools, where all pupils were taught in one room by a single teacher and studied the same subjects with no systematic gradation of work. In 1854, Hamilton and Rossville were unified into one town consisting of three political wards, each with a school building. As the city developed, grew, and annexed land, the district constructed 46 permanent school buildings. The list of the men and women who have served as school board members reads like a who's who of Hamilton business, industry, and professions, and the district has benefited from excellent superintendents, principals, and teachers.

Among the dominant superintendents was Alston Ellis, who, after serving 13 years in Hamilton, became president of Colorado State University and Ohio University. Darrell Joyce administered the district for 26 years, and D.R. Baker was able to keep the schools open and functioning throughout the Great Depression. Terry Wickham led the district during World War II and then served as president of Heidelberg University for 21 years. More recently, Robert Quisenberry and Lester Dickey supervised the schools during 30 turbulent years. Janet Baker, the district's first woman superintendent, spearheaded the construction of state-of-the-art school buildings.

Soldier and businessman August Margedant was a board member for 15 years. More recently, George Jonson, Glenn Stitsinger, and Larry Bowling were on the board for more than 25 years and worked with Superintendent Baker to build the district's newest schools.

The district's longtime teachers included naturalist Will Harbaum, who taught 28 years and initiated the area's Christmas bird count; elementary school teacher Elisabeth Schwarz (49 years); Will Lebo (33 years), who taught music and band to hundreds of students; and popular history teacher Ella Mae Cope (49 years), who brought nationally known speakers to Hamilton. James Grimm (38 years) developed physical fitness programs in the schools and supervised the city's recreation programs. Joe DeAngelo has taught marketing education and career technology courses at Badin High for nearly 50 years.

Hamilton High principal Horace Townsend became the first commissioner of the Ohio High School Athletic Association. William Cope served as principal of the high school for 24 years. Fr. Francis Miller was the founding principal at Badin High, and Kathleen Daulton administered Queen of Peace School for 12 years.

Dr. Bernie Phelps, legendary communications professor at Miami University, worked to raise the funds needed to start the Hamilton campus and served as the director of its programs during its initial years.

Raymond Bisplinghoff taught at the Massachusetts Institute of Technology for several years. As a director of research at NASA, he planned several Apollo missions, including the Apollo 11 moon landing of July 1969.

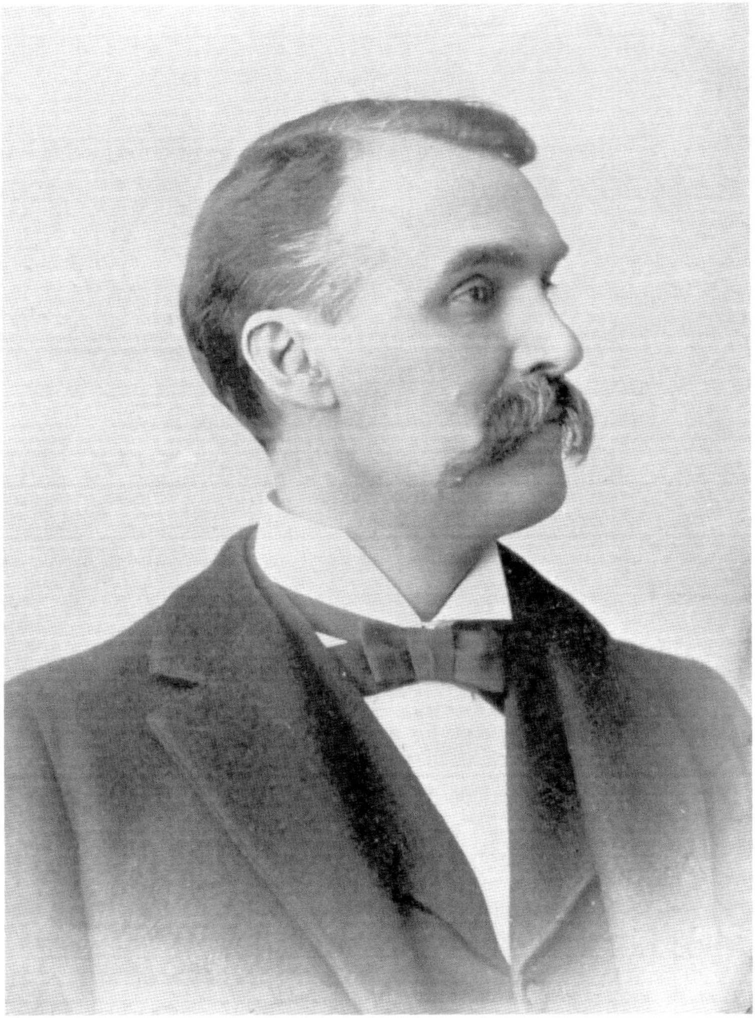

Alston Ellis

Ellis (1847–1920) served a total of 13 years during two separate terms as superintendent of Hamilton's schools. His first appointment ran from 1871 to 1879, and his second was from 1887 to 1892. Between his two terms in Hamilton, he headed the Sandusky, Ohio, public schools. Ellis left his Hamilton position in 1892 to become the third president of Colorado State Agricultural College in Fort Collins, serving there until 1899. He returned to Ohio and assumed the presidency of Ohio University in Athens from 1901 until his death in 1920. During his tenure in Hamilton, Ellis worked to raise academic standards and to improve the district's school buildings. While he was Hamilton's superintendent, the district built the first Fourth Ward School, renamed Jefferson School in 1909, and the Third Ward, or Washington, School. He also created the district's 1890 school-building plan, out of which was constructed Hamilton's Central High School and the Columbian (Jackson) and Straub (Monroe) elementary schools. Ellis was a "bricks and mortar" president at Colorado State as well, building six new structures, and at Ohio University, which added a dozen new buildings under his leadership. Even though Ellis was considered arrogant, egotistical, and outspoken, he was a nationally recognized leader in public school education. He earned bachelor's (1867) and master's (1872) degrees at Miami University, and doctor of philosophy degrees from College of Wooster (1979) and Ohio State University (1888), as well as a doctor of laws degree from Ohio State (1890). (Courtesy of Rob Wile.)

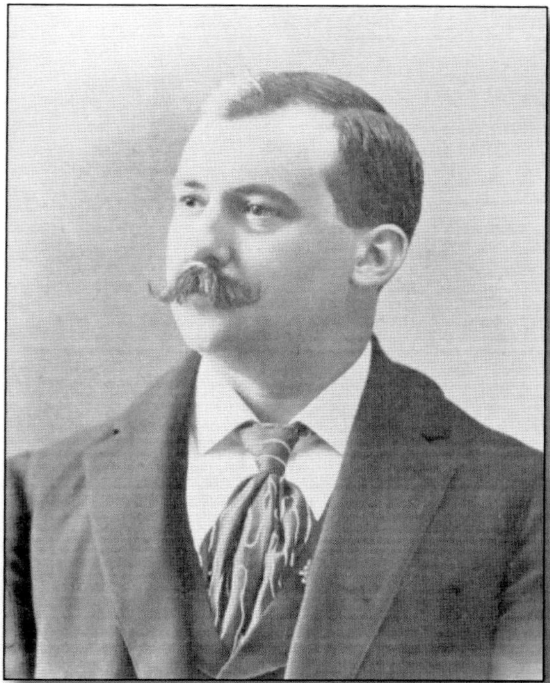

Samuel L. Rose
Prior to serving as principal of Hamilton's Fourth Ward School from 1889 to 1894, Rose (1865–1903) had worked as a teacher, clerk of courts, and school building principal. He resigned in 1894 to become managing editor of the Hamilton *Daily Democrat* newspaper but returned to the district to serve as superintendent from 1895 until his death in 1903 from what the doctor called "brain exhaustion." Rose created a better high school curriculum that allowed students to take either a classical or scientific business course of study. (Courtesy of Rob Wile.)

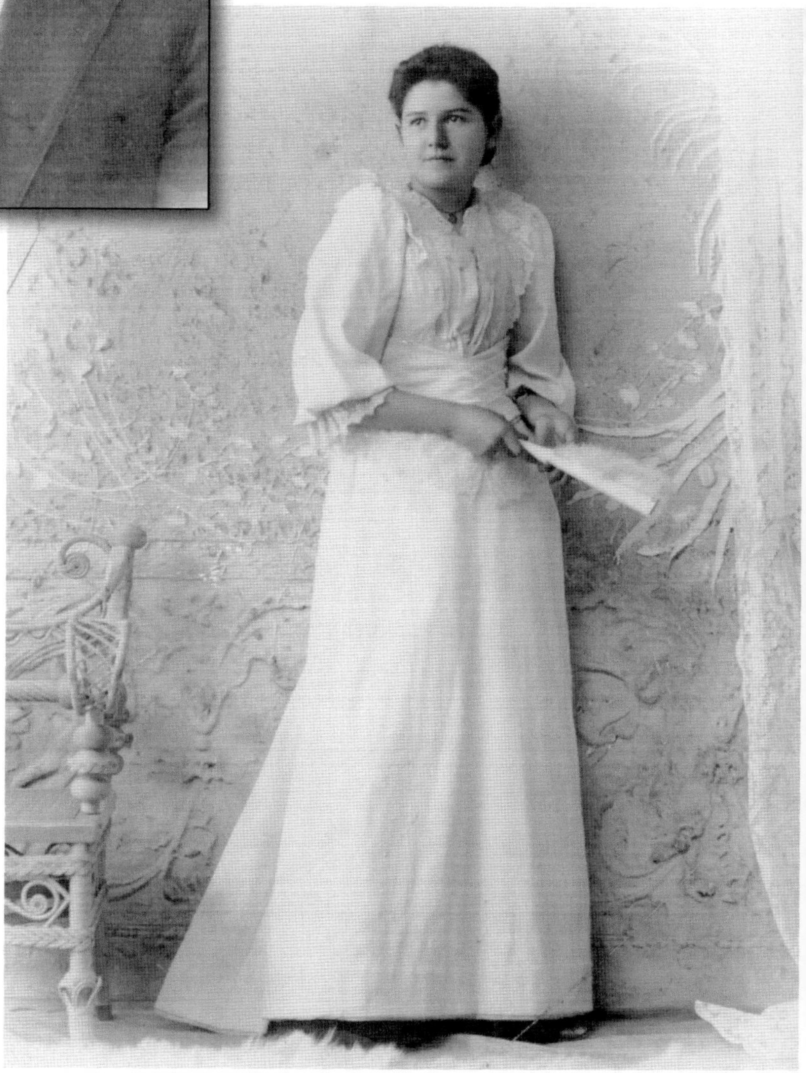

Margaret Elisabeth Schwarz
Schwarz (1874–1951) graduated from Hamilton High in 1892 and began teaching in 1894 at the Fifth Ward School, which was renamed Madison School in 1909. Schwarz, seen here in her college graduation dress, usually taught fourth-grade students during her 49-year career in the district. She frequently trained her students to give dramatic readings to younger students, such as when they interpreted Dickens's *A Christmas Carol* for Stella Weiler Taylor's second-grade class in December 1932. (Courtesy of Jackie Freyberg.)

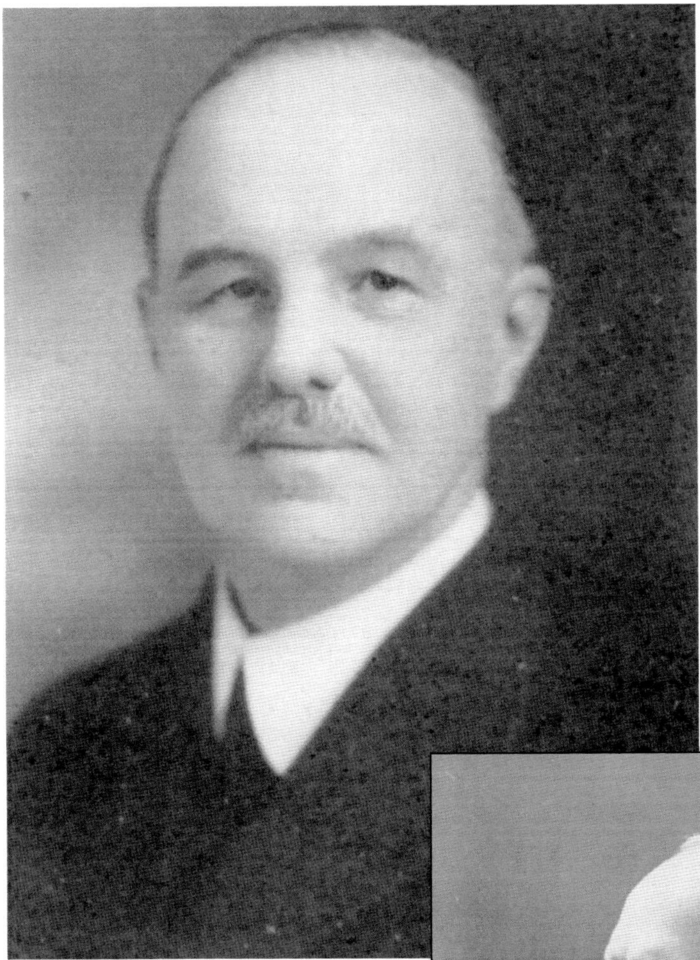

August W. Margedant

Margedant (1869–1927) was one of the handful of persons who served 12 years or more on the Hamilton Board of Education. He was board vice president from 1905 to 1909, president from 1914 to 1923, and board member from 1926 until his death in 1927. Margedant, who was also the city's public safety director, had a distinguished military career, serving from 1891 to 1900 and fighting in the Spanish-American War. He was president of Bartel & Margedant, makers of woodworking machinery, from 1900 until 1918, when the business was sold. (Courtesy of Hamilton City School District.)

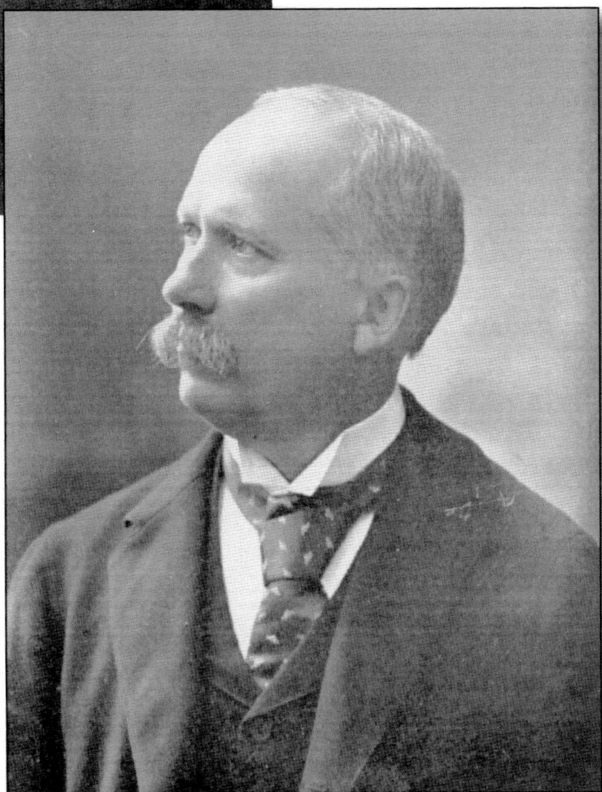

William P. Cope

W.P. Cope (1850–1915) was principal of Hamilton High from 1885 to 1909. His tenure ranged from the days when all classes were taught on the third floor of the First Ward School, into the era of Central High School, which was constructed in 1892. He was a Lane Library trustee and worked to build a library of 1,000 volumes at the high school. In 1903, when his daughter Ella Mae was a senior at Hamilton High, he acted as superintendent for four months after the death of Samuel L. Rose.

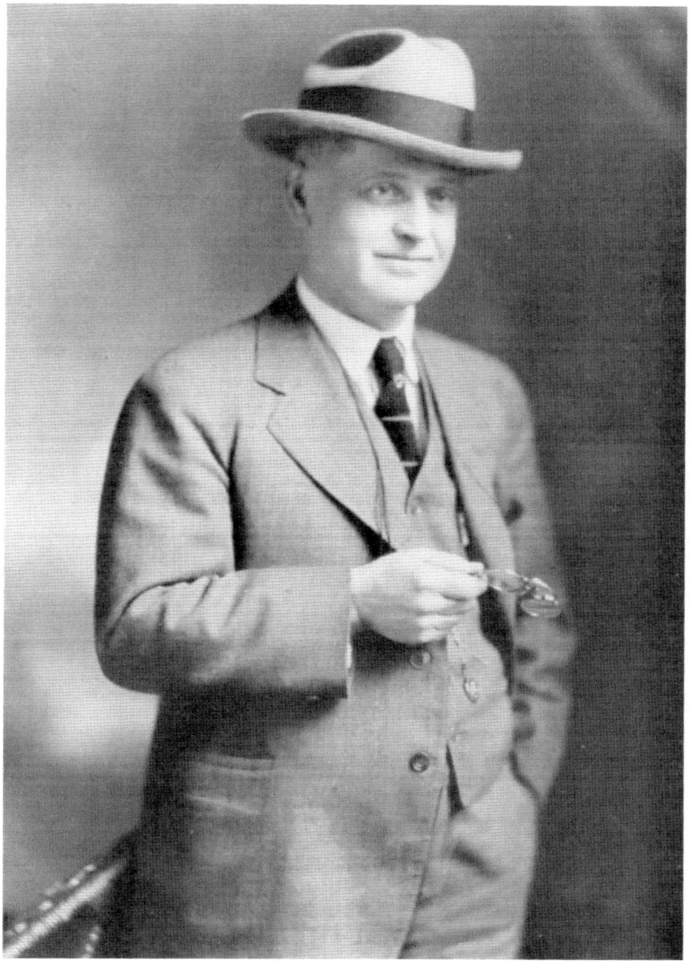

Will H. Lebo

Prof. Will Lebo (1866–1946) joined the Hamilton School District as supervisor of music in 1900 at an annual salary of $1,000. Lebo developed the music education curriculum in both the elementary and high schools, introduced music texts in classes, trained thousands of young people in singing, established a music library of hundreds of vocal selections and instrumental arrangements, organized the high school band in 1920, and produced many concerts for the community. In 1903, he presented a chorus of 1,600 schoolchildren and the combined bands of the city in a program at the courthouse celebrating the county's centennial. For that special occasion, Lebo wrote the "Fort Hamilton March" for one of the town's military bands. He staged other large-scale productions, including one in 1914 during which all students from the fourth grade through high school performed when the Liberty Bell was brought to Hamilton. In 1918, he organized another community celebration with several thousand children performing at the Butler County fairgrounds in honor of the military. Lebo also directed the music activities for the celebration of the 125th anniversary of Hamilton in 1916, including writing the song "My Hamilton," with lyrics by Stella Weiler Taylor. In the schools, Lebo's students participated in several marching bands, at least three orchestras, frequent operetta productions, several glee clubs, and a number of junior orchestras and choruses in the elementary grades. He retired from the classroom in 1933 and was elected to the district's board of education, serving from 1934 to 1938. The exceptionally talented Lebo played in several military bands; gave private instruction in voice, piano, cornet, and clarinet; and for many years served as choir director and organist at the First Methodist and First Baptist churches. (Courtesy of Hamilton City School District.)

Darrell Joyce

The influence of Darrell Joyce on the Hamilton schools was enormous. Joyce (1874–1936) was the principal of the Columbian School in 1902 when he was a senior at Miami University. He had six years of experience as a teacher and superintendent of Ross's schools before entering the university in 1900. In 1903, Joyce was named Hamilton's superintendent and served in the position until he resigned in 1929 due to ill health. He worked to improve the district's curriculum, raise academic standards, improve student discipline, and increase teacher salaries, and he was responsible for adding industrial arts, home economics, physical education, and military training programs. During Joyce's tenure, the district constructed Tyler School (1904), acquired Polk School through annexation (1908), built Taylor (1909), Lincoln (1909), Hamilton High (1915), the Hamilton High gymnasium (1924), and two expansions of the Van Buren School (1913 and 1921). He also provided the leadership for the successful 1927 bond issue campaign that funded the construction of three elementary and two junior high schools. Joyce was named to the Miami University Board of Trustees in 1910 and served until 1932. In 1910, he worked to help organize the Hamilton Chamber of Commerce. He also helped in the development of the Hamilton District War Chest in 1918 and the Hamilton Community Chest, organized in 1920. In 1955, Henrietta Joyce, his widow, donated more than 225 acres of land that became the foundation of the community park named in his honor. (Courtesy of Hamilton City School District.)

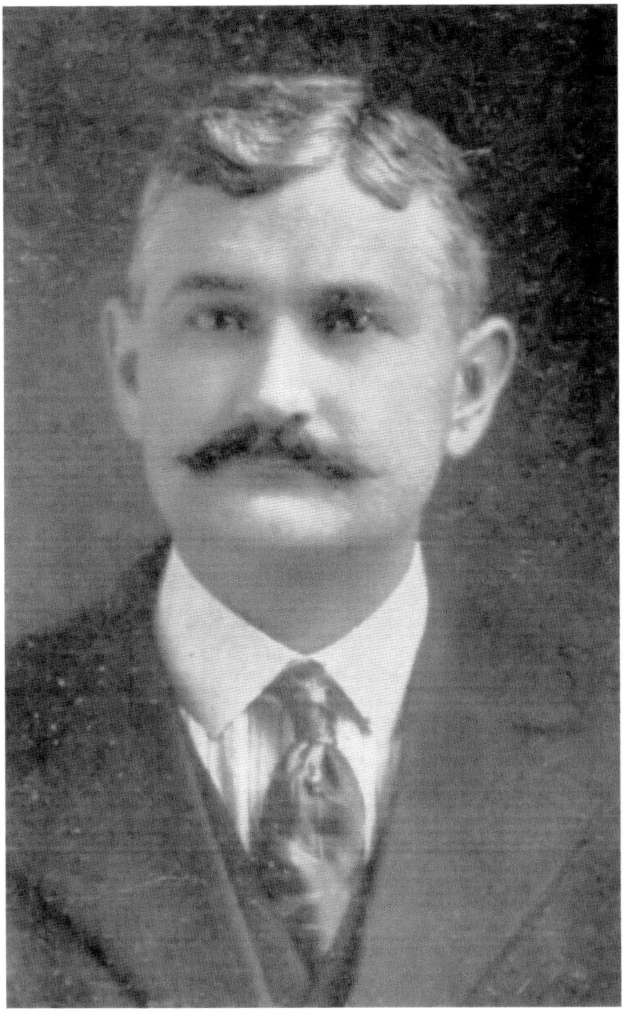

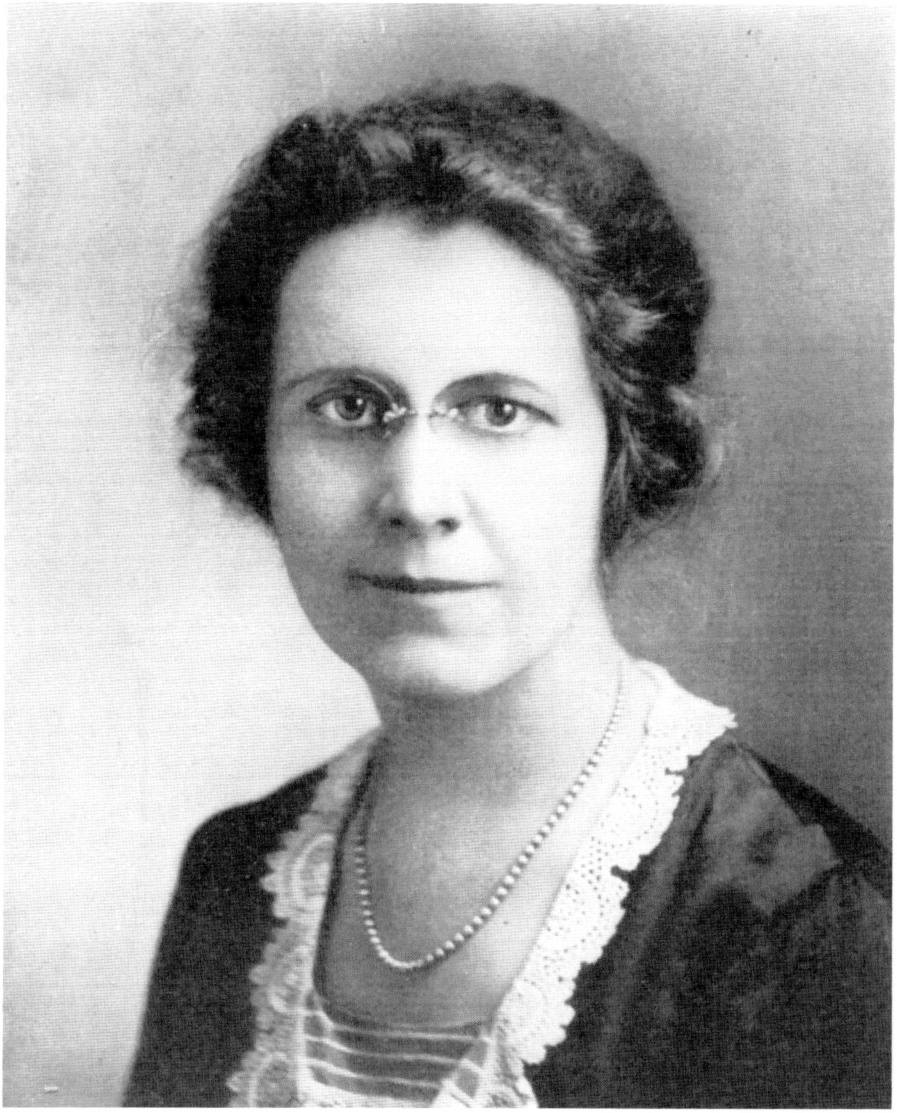

Ella Mae Cope
In 1956, Ella Mae Cope retired after a distinguished 49-year teaching career at Hamilton High. She had taught American history to thousands of students and had taken hundreds of them on more than 20 class trips to Washington, DC. Cope (1884–1972) also taught a night-school adult citizenship class for more than 30 years to an estimated 2,000 immigrants. In 1925, Cope and colleague Marjorie Grafft organized the American History Club, an outstanding student organization that brought many prominent speakers, such as Lowell Thomas and Eleanor Roosevelt, to Hamilton. The club earned $289 sponsoring a 1928 visit by Will Rogers, which was augmented by a $100 gift from Rogers. The money was used to buy a white carrera marble statue of Venus de Milo for the high school auditorium. In 1925, Cope was one of two women elected to the city charter commission, the 15-person group that created Hamilton's city-manager form of government. Cope's retirement in 1956 brought to a close more than 70 consecutive years of service to Hamilton High School by Cope and her father, William P. Cope. The *Hamilton Journal News* wrote upon her retirement that "she represented the epitome of a good teacher." (Courtesy of Hamilton City School District.)

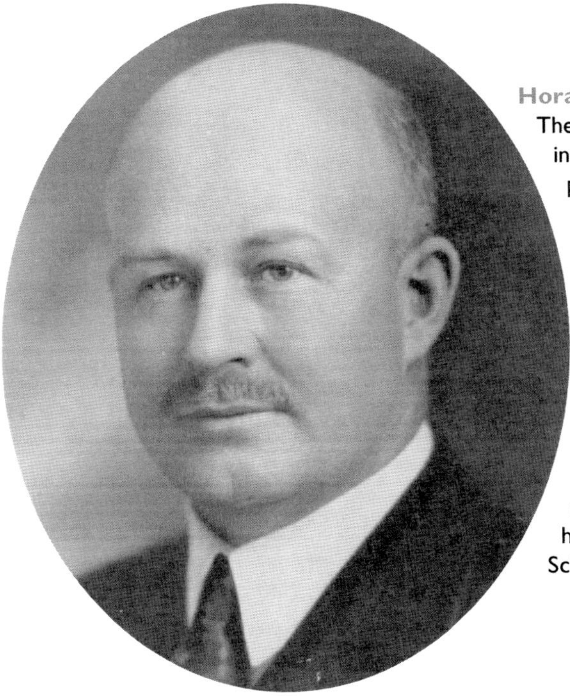

Horace R. Townsend

The new Hamilton High School was built in 1915, and Townsend became its first principal. He administered the building from 1916 to 1925. He was involved in planning the construction of the school's gymnasium, which opened in 1924. Townsend (1883–1944) left the district when he became the first commissioner of the Ohio High School Athletic Association, serving from 1925 until his death in 1944. Wilmington College, where Townsend did his undergraduate study, named its football field in his honor. (Courtesy of Hamilton City School District.)

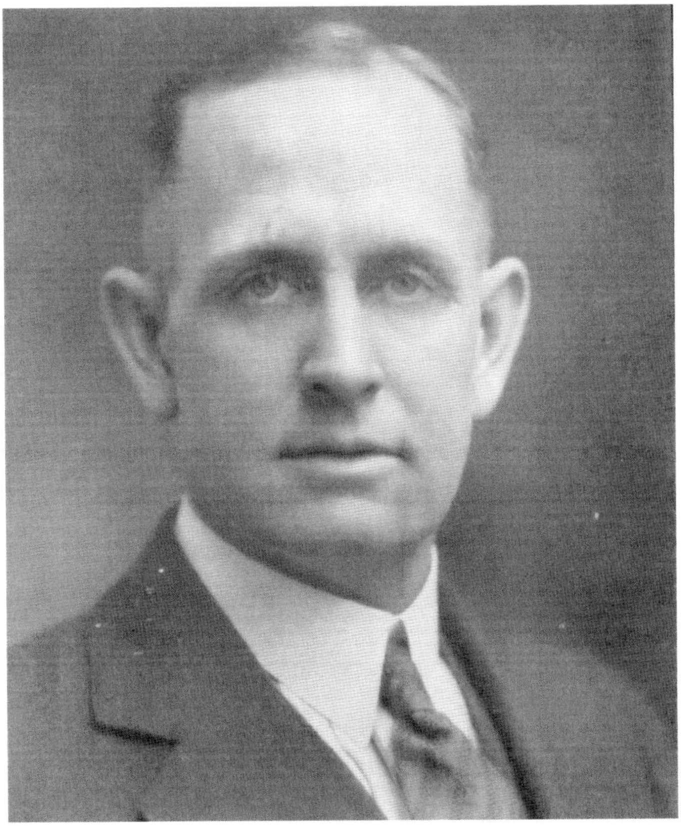

Clyde W. White

White (1883–1943) replaced H.R. Townsend as principal of Hamilton High in 1925, holding the position until 1938. He was appointed district superintendent in 1939 when D.R. Baker left the school system. White resigned his office during the June 29, 1943, meeting in which the school board had offered him a one-year contract instead of the two-year agreement it usually gave superintendents. White died suddenly on August 2, only three days after his contract with the district ended. (Courtesy of Hamilton City School District.)

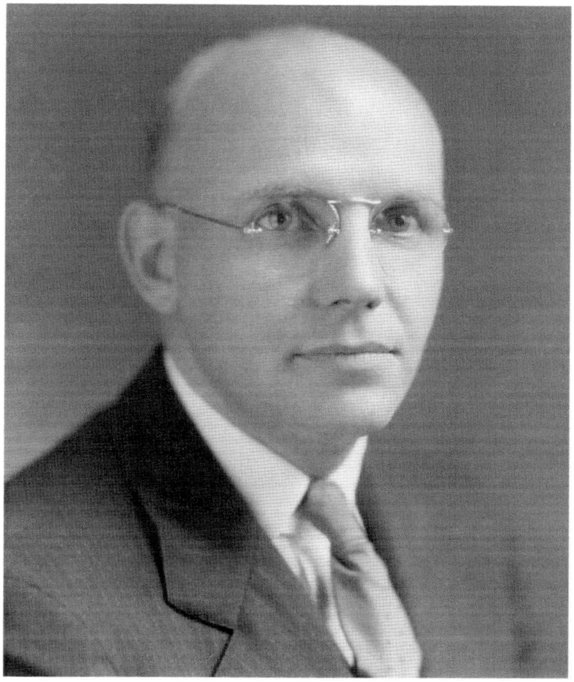

D.R. Baker
Baker served as superintendent in the Depression era, from 1929 to 1939. He had been a Hamilton High physics teacher for four years and a building principal for seven years. Baker (1892–1986) kept the schools open and financially stable even though district revenues were reduced by 40 percent due to low property appraisals and closed businesses. All staff received a 20-percent cut in pay, and the district operated with a shortened school year. Still, Baker opened the Buchanan, Fillmore, and Pierce schools in 1929, Roosevelt Junior High in 1930, and Wilson Junior High in 1934. (Courtesy of Hamilton City School District.)

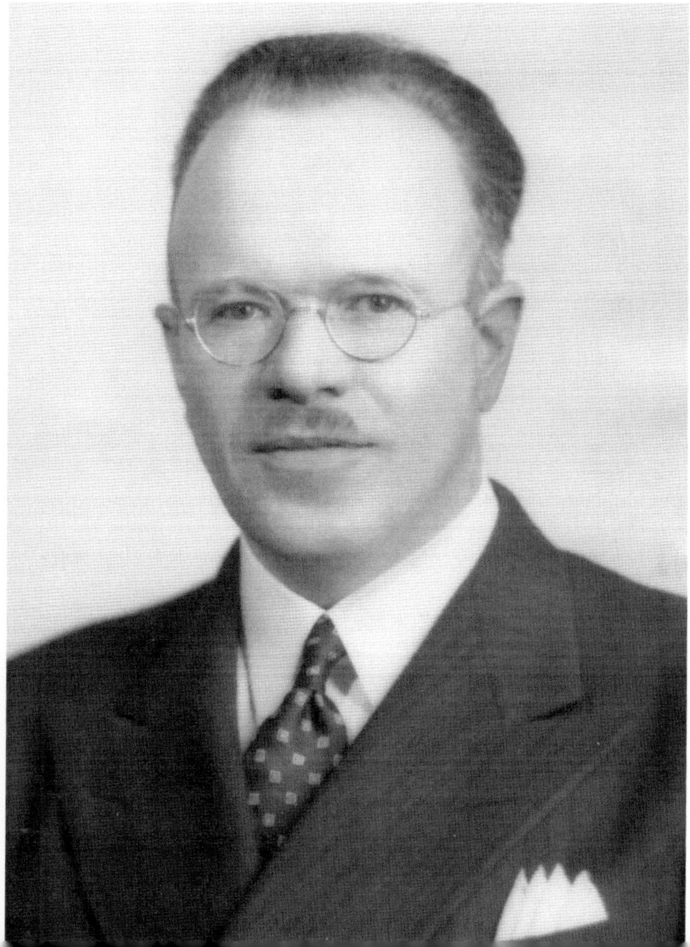

W. Terry Wickham
Superintendent Wickham (1899–1988) headed the successful campaign for a $4.29-million bond issue in 1947 that funded construction of the new Jefferson, Harrison, and Adams schools and classroom additions at the old Fillmore and Pierce buildings. His tenure in Hamilton was from 1943 to 1948, a difficult time characterized by wartime problems. In 1948, Wickham was appointed the 10th president of Heidelberg University in Tiffin, Ohio, a position he held for 21 years until his retirement in 1969.

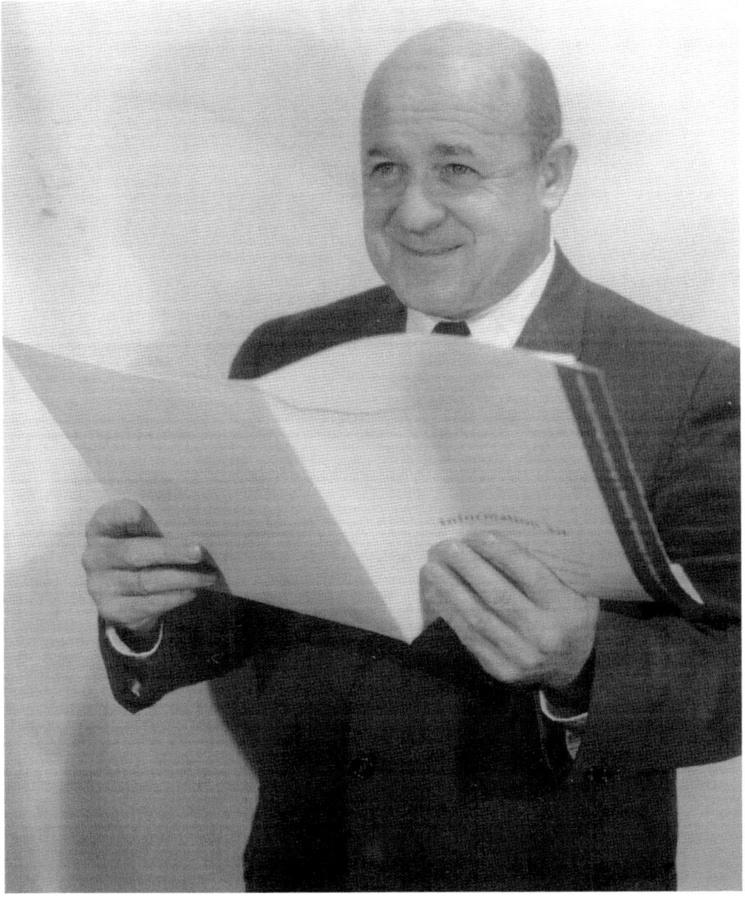

James W. Grimm

Jim Grimm's (1906–2003) visionary teaching techniques and approach to physical fitness and health advocacy earned him national recognition. His 38-year career in the Hamilton schools ran from 1934 through 1972. He was a physical education teacher at Wilson Junior High and Hamilton High and later became the health and physical education director for the entire school district. Grimm coordinated the district's physical education program throughout all grade levels. He developed several popular programs for students, including the Wilson Circus, Saturday Morning Open Gym, and the Big Blue Flip Twisters tumbling team, which entertained at high school sporting events and won gymnastics tournaments throughout the 1950s and 1960s. He served several years as the director of parks and playgrounds for the City of Hamilton. As city recreation director, he originated a wide variety of playground programs such as Little Fish, Indian Pow-Wow, Hobo Campfires, and the Operation Pumpkin Halloween program. He developed the Rotary Show Wagon and coached the Rotary Swim Team. Grimm received a Kennedy Foundation Grant to build Cliffview, an outdoor nature park and bike trail to serve as a work and learning project for mentally challenged youngsters. He also served on the first committee for the Special Olympics. Grimm was instrumental in the development of the Booker T. Washington Community Center and the Murstein Center for Senior Citizens. He served as a chairman of the 1976 bicentennial celebration and initiated the effort to obtain a replica of the Liberty Bell for the city. After Grimm retired, he continued to foster physical fitness by working in the Nautilus and health room at Hamilton's Central YMCA. His work was honored when he was inducted into the Butler County Sports Hall of Fame in 1991 and the Junior Achievement Hall of Fame in 1997. Jim Grimm served countless youngsters as an educator, coach, and, more than anything else, an excellent role model.

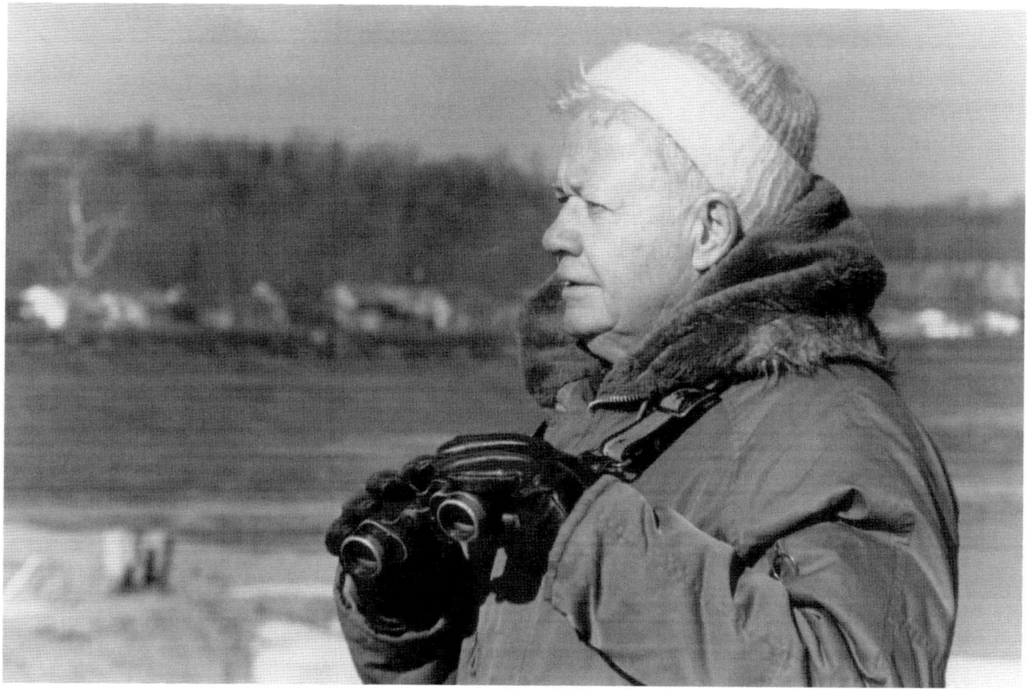

Will H. Harbaum
Biology teacher Will Harbaum (1921–2006) had a 28-year career serving students at Roosevelt, George Washington, and Taft before his retirement in 1976. He was a recognized authority on nature and conservation and wrote for outdoors magazines and area newspapers. After his father died in 1973, Harbaum continued the tradition of the annual Hamilton-Fairfield Christmas bird count that his father had started in 1919. In 2000, the Butler County Metroparks named the Will Harbaum Wetland Education Area at Gilmore Ponds in his honor.

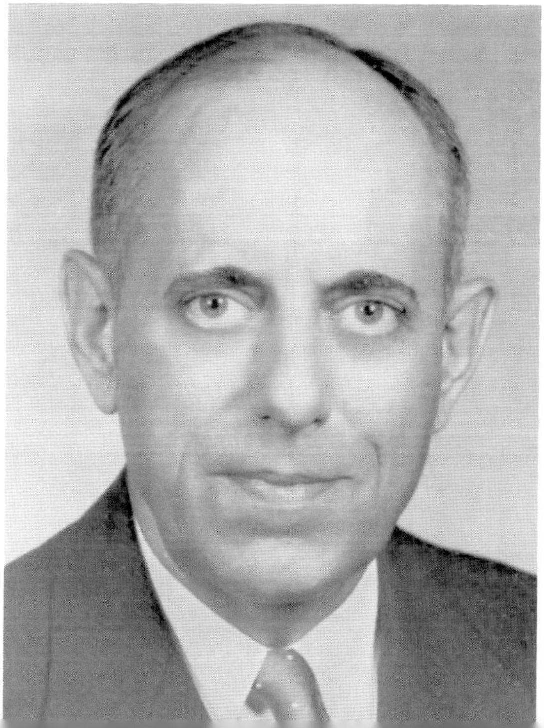

Lester L. Dickey
Dr. Dickey was superintendent from 1953 to 1970, a period when the district built 10 new schools. Between 1954 and 1957, Grant, Madison, Van Buren, McKinley, and George Washington schools were opened. In 1956, Dickey (1902–1992) won voter support for a $6.48-million bond issue that funded five additional schools: Cleveland, Monroe, and Hayes elementary schools and Garfield and Taft high schools. These were the last schools the district would build for nearly 50 years. Dickey retired from Xavier University, where he had been an associate professor from 1970 to 1977. (Courtesy of Hamilton City School District.)

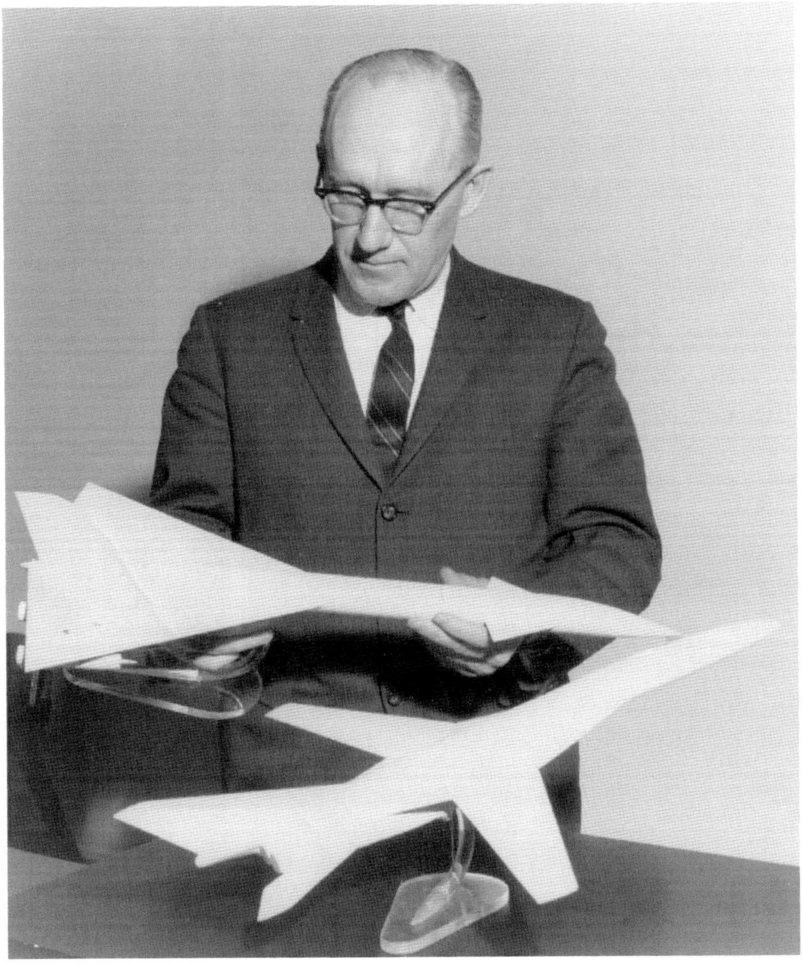

Raymond L. Bisplinghoff

After graduating from Hamilton High in 1934, Bisplinghoff (1917–1985) became an educator, a world-renowned aeronautical engineer, and a national policymaker in the fields of science and engineering. He earned bachelor's and master's degrees at the University of Cincinnati before joining the Navy Bureau of Aeronautics in 1943. Bisplinghoff became an assistant professor of aeronautics at the Massachusetts Institute of Technology (MIT) in 1946 and was promoted to full professor in 1953. While at MIT, he earned a doctoral degree in physics at the Swiss Federal Institute of Technology in 1956. In 1962, he took a leave of absence to serve as director of advanced research and technology at the National Aeronautics and Space Administration (NASA) in Washington, DC. Bisplinghoff returned to MIT as head of the Department of Aeronautics and Astronautics in 1965 and became the dean of the College of Engineering in 1968. He returned to Washington in 1970 to serve as deputy director of the National Science Foundation. The University of Missouri at Rolla hired Bisplinghoff to serve as chancellor from 1974 to 1977. From 1977 until his retirement in 1984, he was senior vice president for research and development at Tyco Laboratories in Exeter, New Hampshire. Bisplinghoff wrote three textbooks and was involved in planning five NASA Apollo missions, including the Apollo 11 moon landing mission of July 1969. During his lifetime, he received many awards, including the Exceptional Civilian Service Medal by the US Air Force, the Distinguished Service Award by the National Science Foundation, the Extraordinary Service Medal by the Federal Aviation Administration, and the Distinguished Service Medal by NASA. (Courtesy of Timothy L. Gillespie.)

Bernard F. Phelps

Bernie Phelps played a major role in bringing the opportunity for higher education to Hamilton's residents. He was a second lieutenant and Marine Corps aviator during World War II, serving in Washington, DC, and two tours in the Pacific. Phelps (1921–) graduated from Indiana State University and moved to Butler County in 1946 to attend Miami University as a graduate assistant in the speech department. In 1947, he earned the first master of arts in theater degree ever awarded by the university and was appointed to a faculty position in the speech department the following year. He completed his doctoral degree at Ohio State University in 1957 and became a full professor and one of the most popular teachers at Miami. For years, Phelps served as parliamentarian for the Miami University faculty senate, public address announcer during football games at Miami Field, and a greatly respected mentor of younger staff members. He also was elected mayor of Oxford, serving from 1965 to 1968. Phelps was appointed the director of the Miami University–Hamilton campus 15 months before it opened. In 1966, working with Peter E. Rentschler, he helped lead the successful campaign to raise the money needed to match the $1.8 million the Ohio general assembly had given for campus buildings. Ground-breaking ceremonies for the campus were held on June 20, 1967, but strikes delayed the opening and official dedication until September 26, 1969. Dr. Phelps, as campus director from 1968 to 1976, was involved in selecting faculty members, establishing programs and curriculum, and recruiting a student body. Phelps Hall, the Miami University–Hamilton technical education building, was named in his honor. Bernie had one other strong tie with Hamilton: Bill Phelps, one of his sons, was a longtime director of the Hamilton Parks and Recreation Department. Bernie Phelps was named Professor Emeritus of Communication following his retirement in 1986. The author of this book benefited greatly from having been a friend and colleague of this wonderful man.

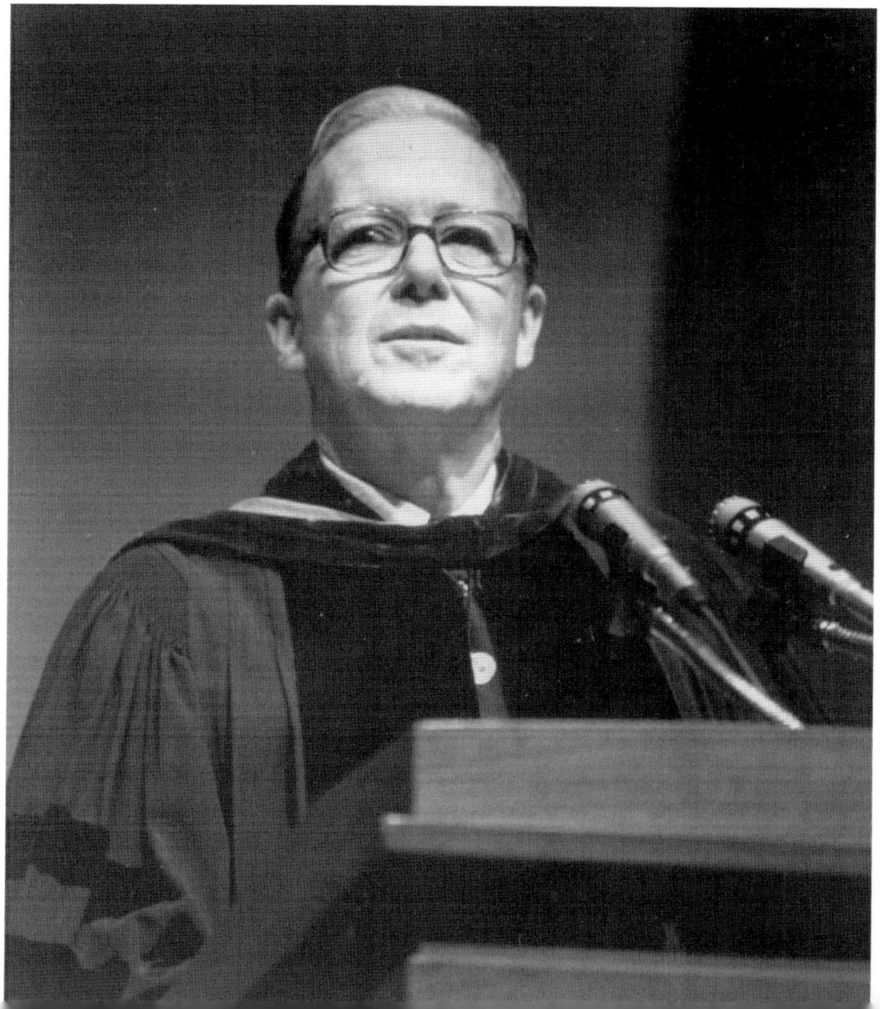

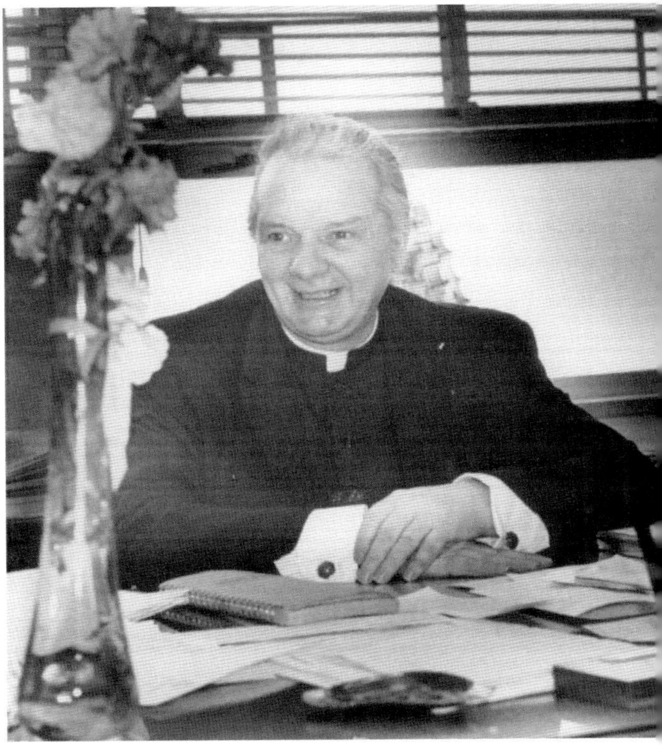

Fr. Francis J. Miller
Father Miller began his ministry as a pastor in several area parishes. He was a faculty member at Seton Hall High School and Mount St. Mary's Seminary from 1956 to 1964 before coming to Hamilton. Miller (1924–2010) played a major role in the planning and construction stages of the Stephen T. Badin High School and became the founding principal, serving from 1965 to 1975. He was pastor of St. Mary Parish from 1965 to 1982 and then became the pastoral counselor for Catholic Social Services of Southwestern Ohio, serving until 1986.

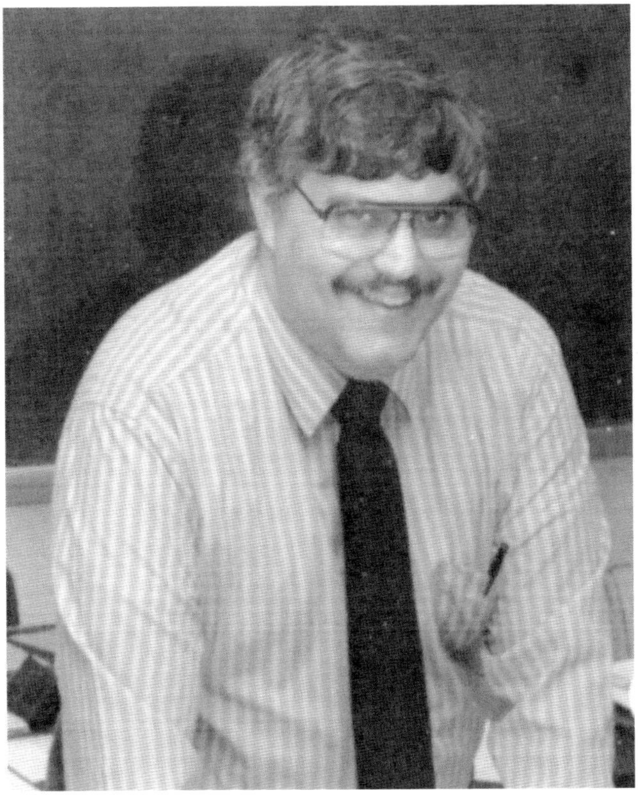

Joe DeAngelo
DeAngelo (1945–) joined the faculty at Stephen T. Badin High School in 1967, the school's second year of existence. During his early years at the school, he was a swimming and track coach and even produced the school's variety show for 19 years. DeAngelo developed Badin's marketing education and career technology courses and the school's highly successful DECA program in 1968. He has been named Ohio's Vocational Education Teacher of the Year and has received other awards for his service to students. (Courtesy of Lane Library.)

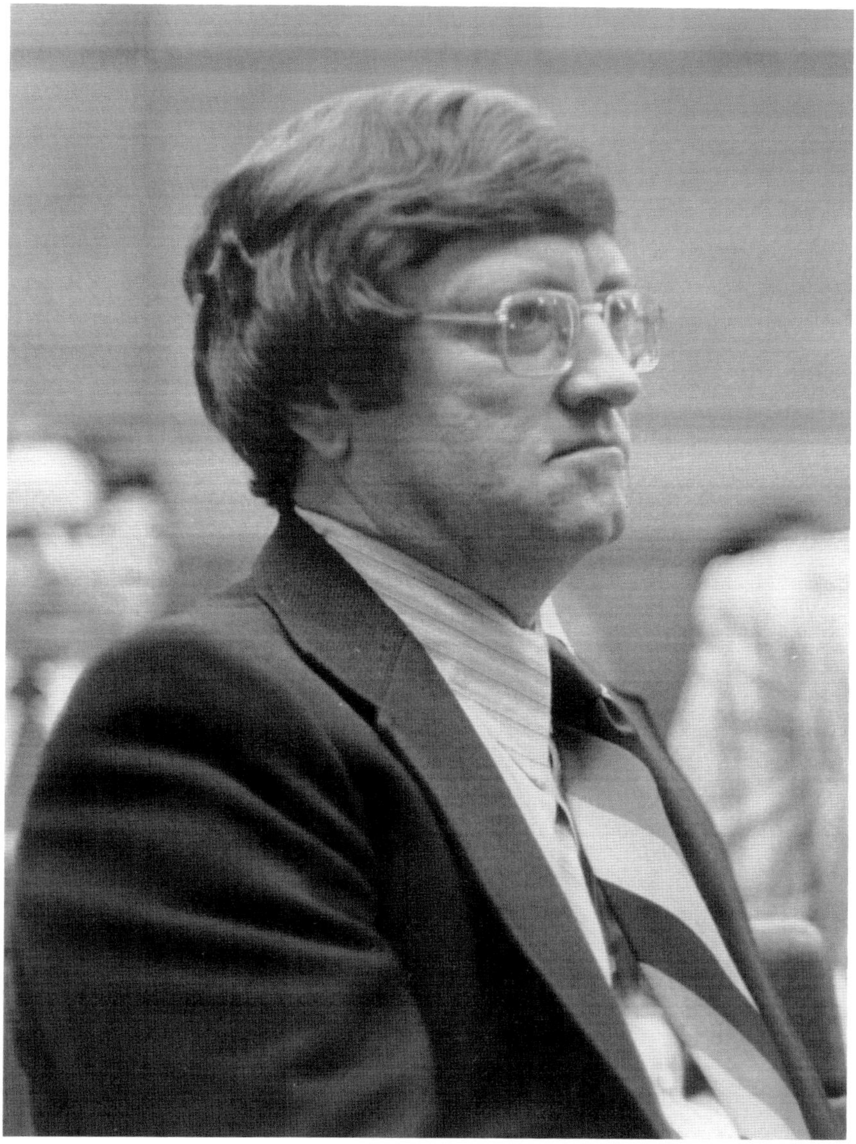

Robert R. Quisenberry

Superintendent Quisenberry was a strong advocate of "back-to-basics" academic programs and firm student discipline during his administration of Hamilton's schools from 1977 to 1990. He began his service in the district as a teacher at Fillmore Elementary School, followed by other administrative assignments at Roosevelt and Garfield schools. As Quisenberry (1935–2006), principal of George Washington Junior High, was attending the June 6, 1977, meeting in which the Hamilton Board of Education named him superintendent, young Wade Allen Swank drowned in a gravel pit near the school while playing hooky. Sadly, Quisenberry's first act as the district's superintendent was to stand beside the pit as rescue workers searched for the student's body. He worked to create the $4.5-million Job Development Center, a cooperative venture of Miami University–Hamilton and the city schools to provide job training for high school and college students and local adults. The new vocational education center was built adjacent to Hamilton High and dedicated in 1985. Quisenberry also served the community as a member of the boards of the YMCA, Junior Achievement, and the Hamilton Economic Development Corporation.

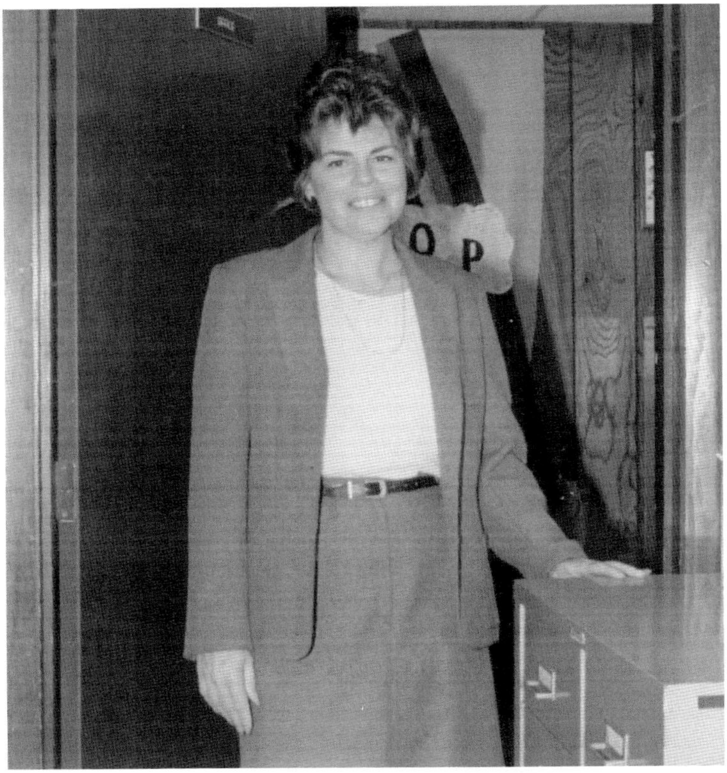

Kathleen M. Daulton
Daulton was principal of Queen of Peace School from 1986 to 1998. She worked with Fr. Norbert McCarthy to build the new school, which opened in 1992. Daulton (1945–) has served 46 years in education, including 34 years in the Cincinnati archdiocese. She was one of 12 principals out of 6,000 named a distinguished principal by the National Catholic Educational Association in 1996. Since 1999, Daulton has continued her ministry as principal of the St. Viator School in Las Vegas, Nevada.

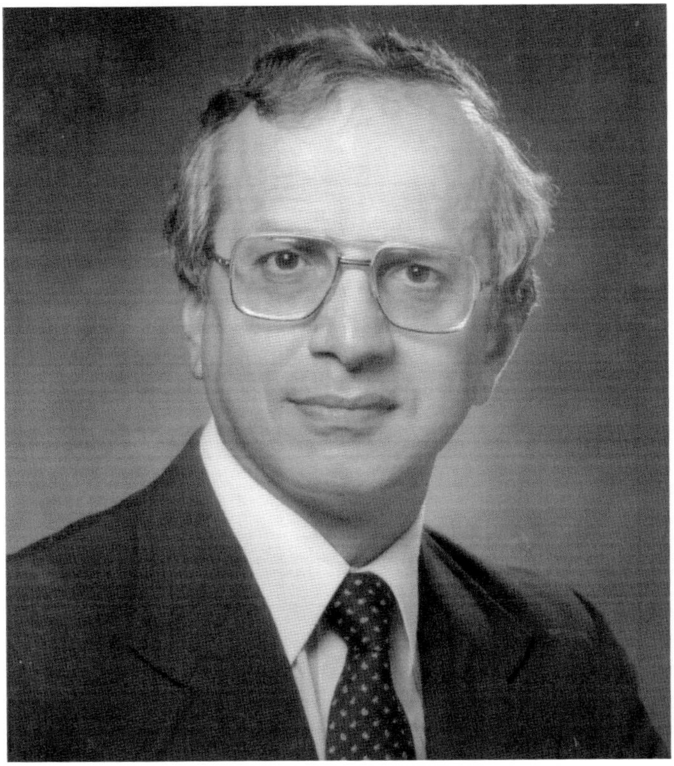

George Jonson
Jonson, a 1952 graduate of Hamilton High who attended Ohio State and the University of Cincinnati law school, started his law firm in 1962. He was elected to Hamilton's city council, serving five terms from 1964 to 1973. Jonson (1934–) is a member of the district's athletic hall of fame and has served on the board of education since 1982. He was deeply involved in developing the three-phase Master Facilities Plan, which led to the construction of nine new district school buildings and the improvement of several others.

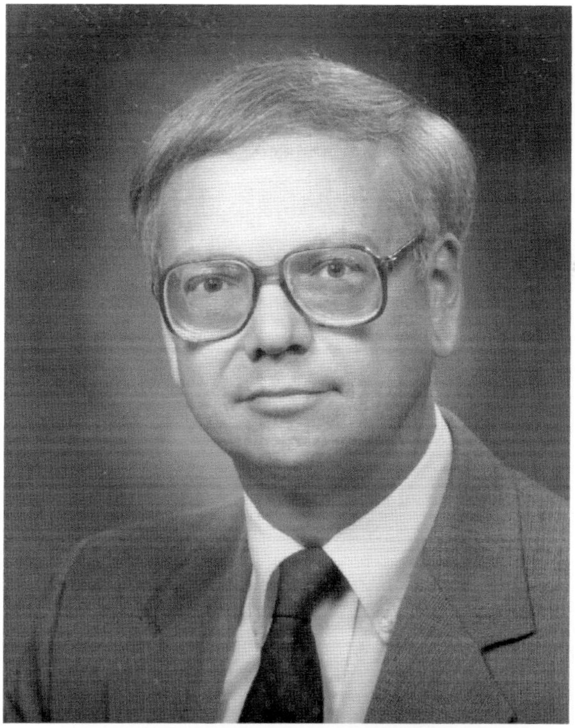

Glenn Stitsinger
Dr. Stitsinger attended the Ohio State University College of Dentistry after he graduated from Hamilton High in 1958. He maintained a successful private practice for 36 years before his retirement. Stitsinger (1940–) has been on the board of education since 1986, working to create the Master Facilities Plan to build, rebuild, and renovate district school buildings. He also has served on the boards of several community organizations, including the Hamilton Chamber of Commerce and Fort Hamilton Hospital.

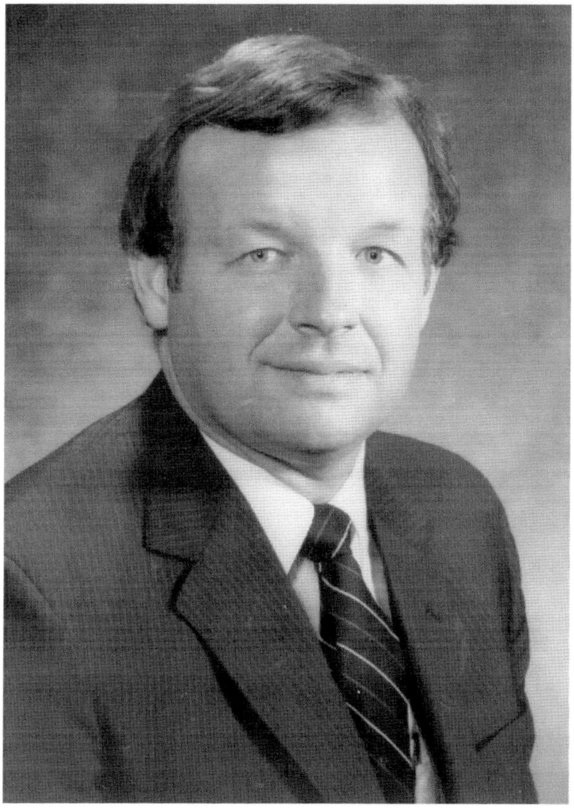

Larry Bowling
Bowling was a 1964 Garfield High graduate who earned a bachelor's degree at Indianapolis University. He has operated a financial services agency for years. Bowling (1946–) has been a member of the board of education since 1988 and has been actively involved in creating the district's Master Facilities Plan. He was named Hamilton's Citizen of the Year in 2006 by the Greater Hamilton Chamber of Commerce. Bowling is also a member of the school district's athletic hall of fame.

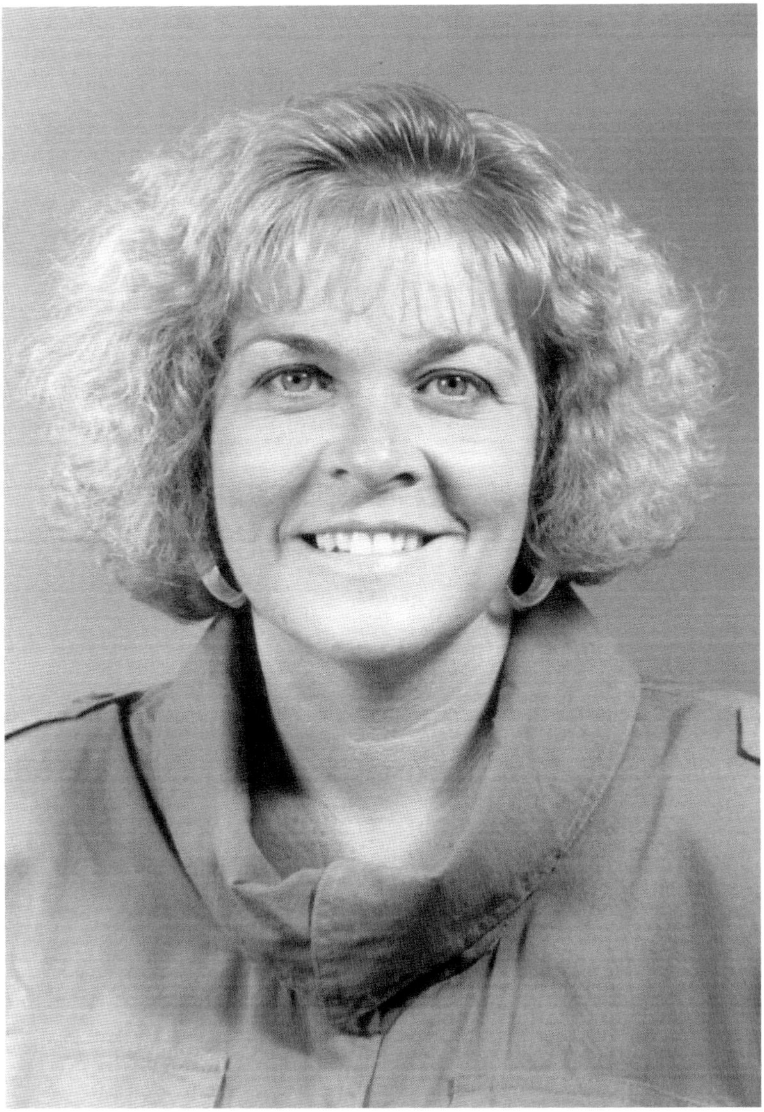

Janet Baker
Baker started her career in Hamilton's schools in 1970 as a grade-school teacher. She also served as a librarian, principal, director of elementary education, and central office administrator before she became the district's first woman superintendent in 1992. Baker worked with the board of education to create the district's Master Facilities Plan in 1997. She spearheaded the school board's efforts in 1999 and 2006 to pass two local bond issues to raise $114 million. Passage of the bonds meant an additional $120 million from the Ohio Schools Facilities Commission to enable the district to build eight state-of-the-art elementary school buildings, a freshman school, rebuild a middle school, and make additional improvements at Hamilton High. Baker (1946–) was named Ohio's Superintendent of the Year in 2000 by the Buckeye Association of School Administrators. In 2002, she received one of the first five Vision Awards given by the Vision 2020 Committee. In 2005, Baker made the policy decision to require the inclusion of character education in all schools and have students take part in character-building programs. As a result of the staff's efforts, the district received the Ohio District of Character Award in 2010 and 2011 and was named a National School District of Character in 2012 by the Character Education Partnership.

CHAPTER FOUR

Industrial Artisans and Manufacturers

The stimulus for much of Hamilton's early industrialization was the cheap power that was provided by the city's hydraulic system. In 1845 and 1846, two water races from the Great Miami River were built to flow through the town such that they could be used to power mills and factories. Many of the earliest manufacturing concerns were located along the hydraulics. Other factors that attracted early industries to Hamilton included the proximity of the Miami and Erie Canal and the availability of excellent rail services.

Hamilton's industries became leaders in many lines of products. There were highly successful papermaking mills, such as the Beckett Paper Company and Champion Coated Paper. The Niles Tool Works was one of the largest machine tool plants in the world. Nearly half of all safes and vaults were made at Mosler Safe & Lock Company and Herring-Hall-Marvin Safe Company, making Hamilton the "safe capital of the world." Several large foundries turned out castings of all sorts. Many other types of manufacturing and industrial concerns did business in the town. The slogan the local chamber of commerce aptly used for many years was "the greatest manufacturing city of its size in the world."

Most of the men who led Hamilton's industries resembled that era's model of corporate leadership. They administered their companies, worked to meet community needs, and, in many cases, looked after their employees and their well-being. Those featured here were among that group of leaders.

One family stands out as having perhaps the greatest impact on manufacturing and industry in Hamilton. George A. Rentschler headed several companies, including the Hooven, Owens, Rentschler Company and Hamilton Foundry & Machine Company. One son, Gordon Sohn Rentschler, became head of the National City Bank. A second son, Frederick Brant Rentschler, formed the Pratt & Whitney Aircraft Company and United Airlines. Walter A. Rentschler and Peter E. Rentschler, two grandsons, continued the family oversight of the Hamilton Foundry & Machine Company. Several fourth-generation industrialists continued the family traditions in various manufacturing concerns.

Key leaders in other industries included Thomas Beckett, Peter Thomson, and Reuben Robertson in papermaking firms. Asa Shuler and John Benninghofen made excellent products in their woolen mill. Lazard Kahn's Estate Stove Company and Moses Mosler's safe and lock company were leaders in their product lines.

More recent business leaders featured here include retailer William Murstein, insurance executive Howard Sloneker, funeral home owner Donald Jordan, and restaurant owner Joel Schmidt.

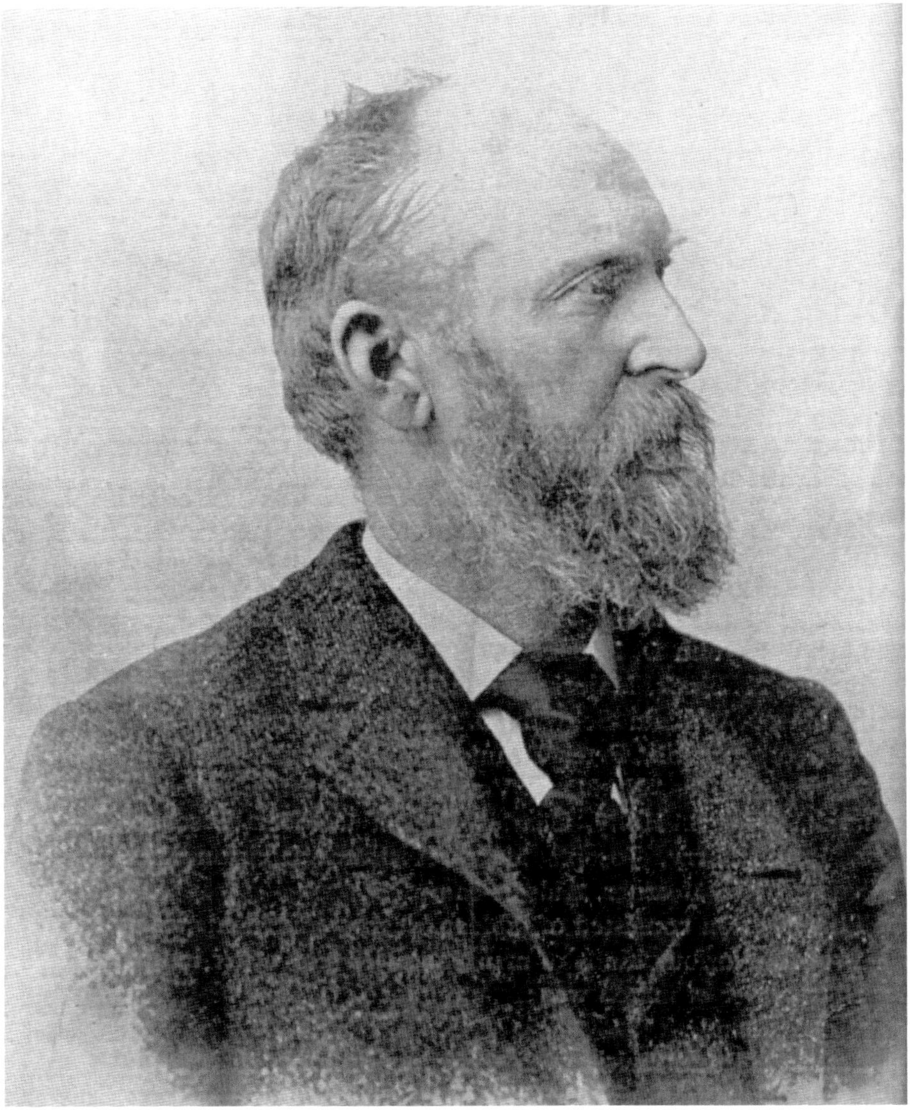

Peter Schwab

Schwab's community involvement and marketing skills made him the most famous local brewer. He bought his brewery in 1875, changed its name to the Cincinnati Brewing Company, and marketed his "Pure Gold" branded lager as "the beer that made Milwaukee jealous." When he incorporated his company, it had a daily brewing capacity of only 50 barrels. Within 15 years, his brewery was one of the industry's leaders in the central states and his product was sold from Washington to St. Louis. Schwab (1838–1913) was president of Hamilton's city council for two years and served on the board of education for 12 years, from 1882 to 1894, including eight years as president. Among his many real estate holdings was the music hall, which he sold to the school board in 1899 for $22,000. The remodeled building became the district's Second Ward School, which was renamed Harrison School in 1909. Schwab had a great deal of influence in the community and region and was considered a political dictator. He strongly supported building electric interurban railroads throughout the county. Schwab was a trustee of Mercy Hospital, and he provided the hospital with ice from his plant on a daily basis from 1892 until his death in 1913. (Courtesy of Diane Kuhlmann Beaty.)

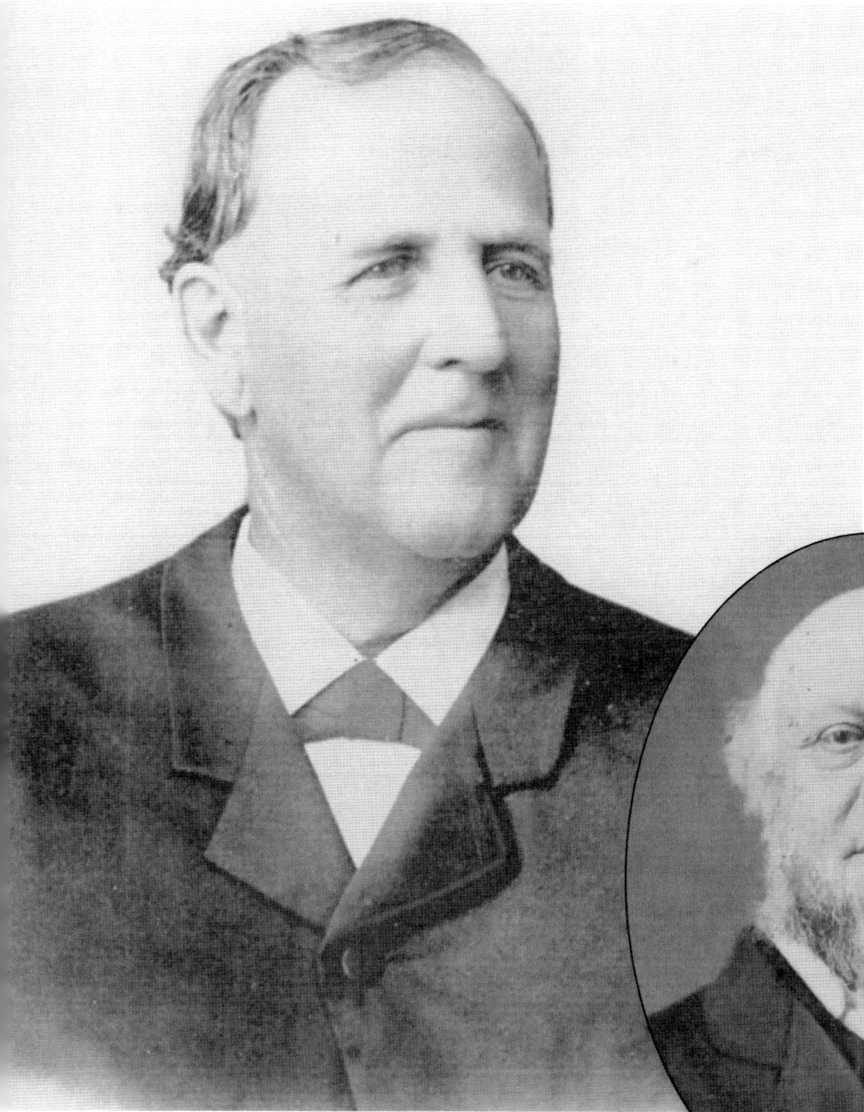

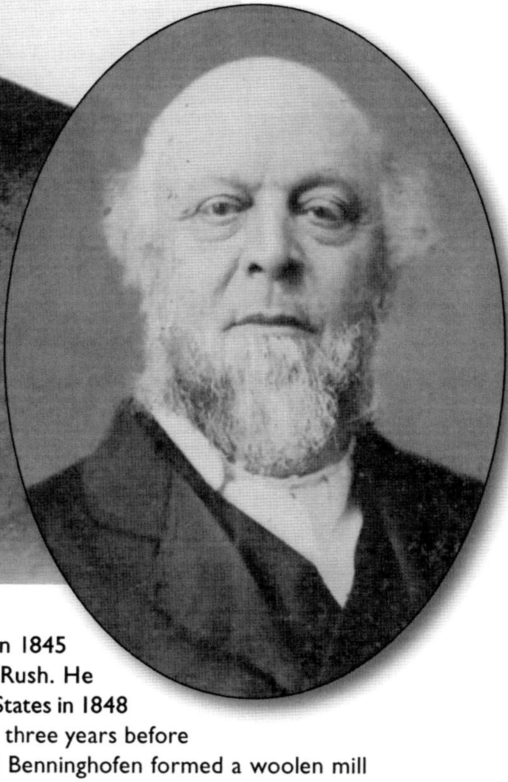

Asa W. Shuler and John W. Benninghoffen
Shuler, seen in the above photograph, came to Hamilton in 1845 and stayed four years before joining the California Gold Rush. He returned in 1852. Benninghoffen (right) came to the United States in 1848 and settled in Hamilton, where he worked as a peddler for three years before going to work at John Sohn's tannery. In 1858, Shuler and Benninghofen formed a woolen mill to manufacture blankets, yarns, clothing, and high-grade felts used in the papermaking industry. The firm moved from its first location, near Hamilton's hydraulic canal, to a new, larger mill in Lindenwald that still stands. Shuler (1823–1895) served on the board of education for four years and on the city's waterworks board for 11 years. He was a director of the First National Bank from 1879 to 1895. Benninghoffen (1812–1881) was on the school board for two years. In 1874, he bought a home, remodeled it, and decorated it in the Victorian style of the 1880s and 1890s. Members of the Benninghofen family lived in the house until 1947, when it was given to the Butler County Historical Society.

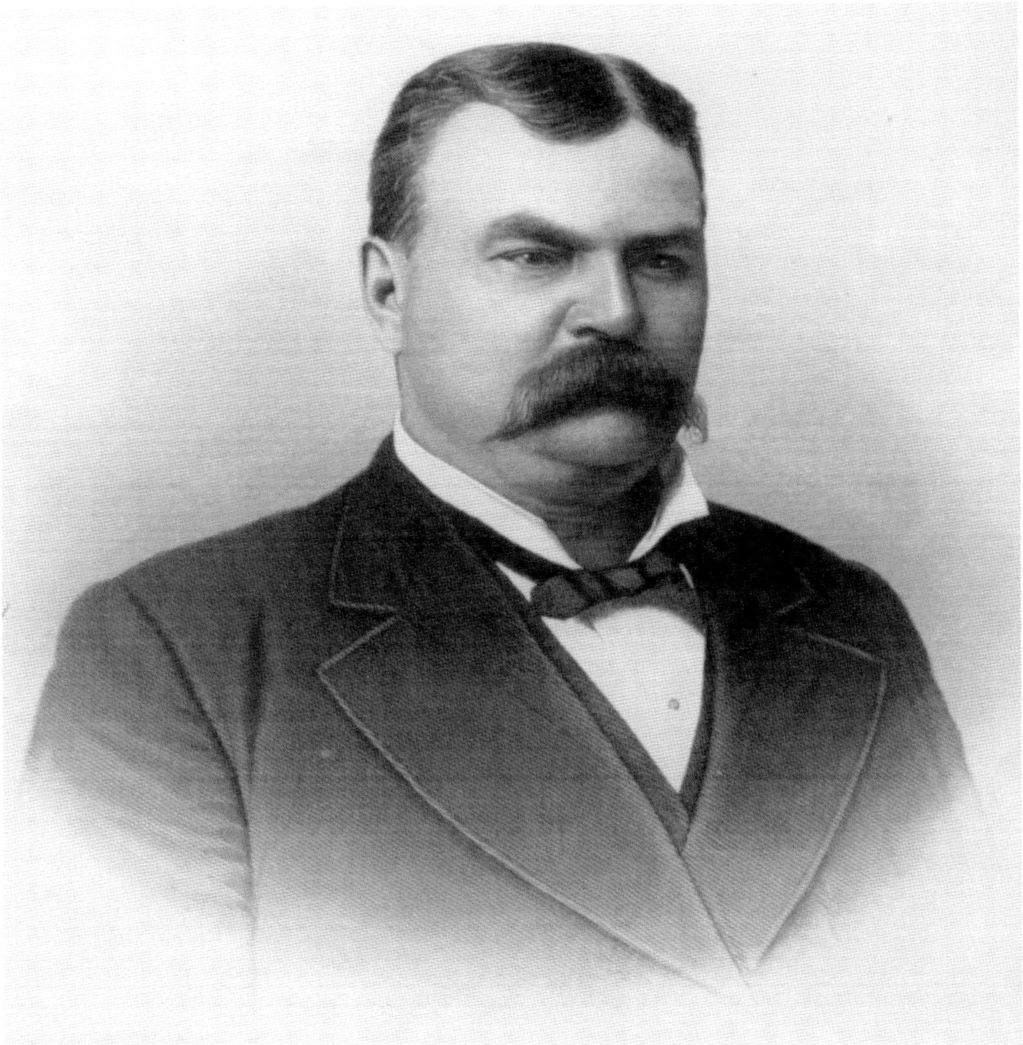

George A. Rentschler

Industrialist George Adam Rentschler (1846–1923) was one of the most significant contributors to Hamilton's reputation in the world's markets. Rentschler came to Hamilton in 1873 to manage a small ironworks. After three years, he formed the Ohio Iron Works with Henry Sohn. The firm developed a reputation for the excellence of its work. The Sohn & Rentschler Foundry made all castings the National Cash Register Company needed for their products from 1887 until the 1913 flood destroyed their shop. In 1877, Rentschler, Sohn, and two other partners organized the Phoenix Caster Company. From a small beginning in 1880, the Hooven, Owens, Rentschler Company became one of the largest manufacturers of engines. Rentschler next incorporated the Hamilton Foundry & Machine Company in 1892. It, too, became one of Hamilton's leading industries. He helped organize the Hamilton Dime Savings Bank and the Citizen's Savings Bank & Trust Company. In 1904, he built the eight-story Rentschler Building on High Street, and it was the tallest building in town until 1999. Rentschler's home on Dayton Street was acquired and restored by Sherry Corbett in 1977, work that began the formation of the Dayton Lane Historic District. During the 1880s, Rentschler bought the 350-acre Millikin farm in Fairfield Township, and the property served as the home for several family members until 1967. The farm and mansion were developed into the Walden Ponds Golf Club in 1997. (Courtesy of Lane Library.)

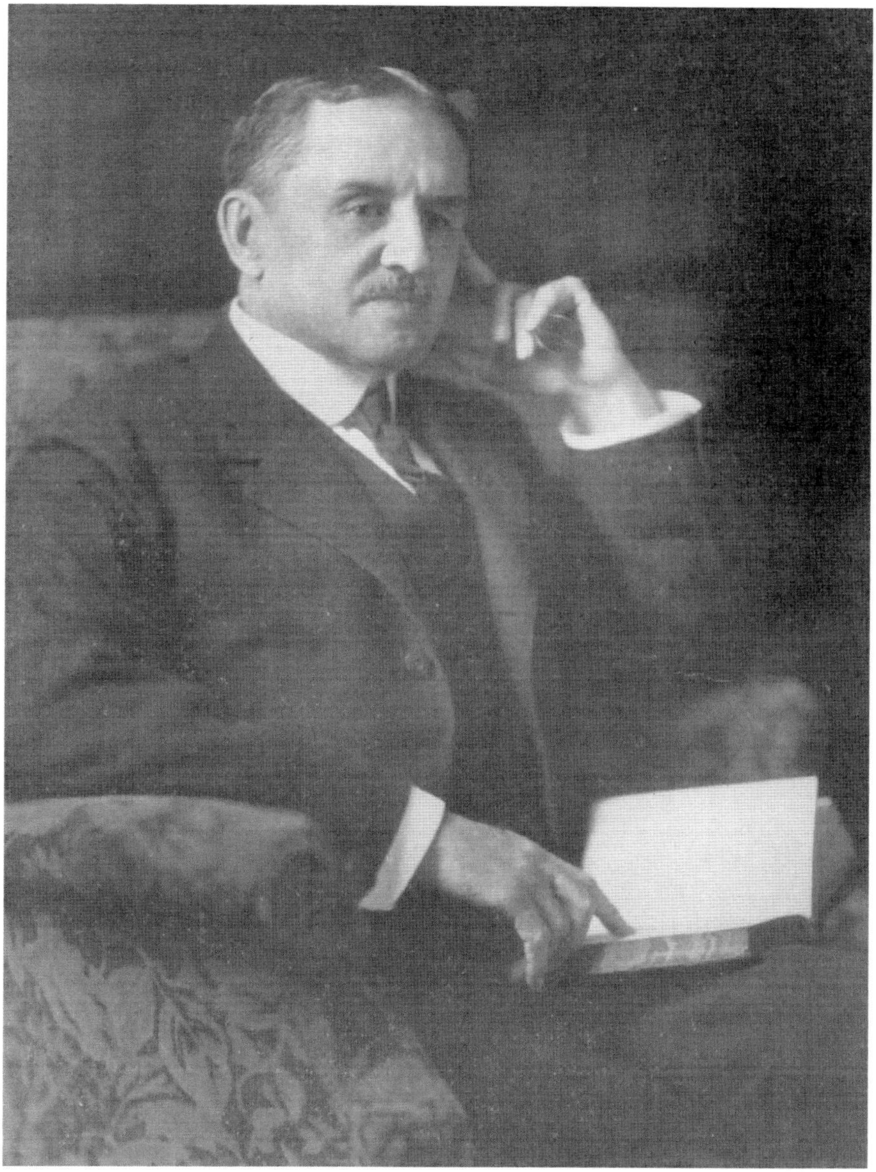

Peter G. Thomson

After starting as a shipping clerk in a Cincinnati bookstore in 1871, Thomson borrowed money to open his own bookstore and printing business in 1877. He and his wife, Laura, wrote and published many of the children's books, comic valentines, and games that made his business thrive. By 1882, the concern was so successful that Thomson sold it to a competitor for a reported $100,000. He moved his family in 1884 to the College Hill suburb, where, between 1902 and 1907, he built Laurel Court, his spectacular two-story, 36-room mansion. Thomson bought the 200-acre tract known as Prospect Hill and organized a real estate syndicate. He came up with the idea to build the Black Street Bridge to help sell homesites in his development. Thomson (1851–1931) founded Champion Coated Papers in 1893 and served as president from the firm's incorporation in 1894 until 1931. The plant was destroyed by fire in 1901, rebuilt in six months, heavily damaged by the 1913 flood, and rebuilt again in less than three months. Champion expanded by adding facilities in North Carolina in 1908 and in Texas in 1937.

Samuel D. Fitton

Fitton (1846–1920) became assistant cashier of the First National Bank & Trust Company in 1867, was promoted to cashier in 1894, and became president in 1895 after Asa Shuler died. During the 1880s, he advocated building municipal water, gas, and light plants and, when voters approved of the plan, had his bank purchase many of the bonds. He was one of the organizers of the Hamilton Chamber of Commerce in 1910. Fitton also served on the Hamilton Park Board and was a member of the city beautification campaign. (Courtesy of Lane Library.)

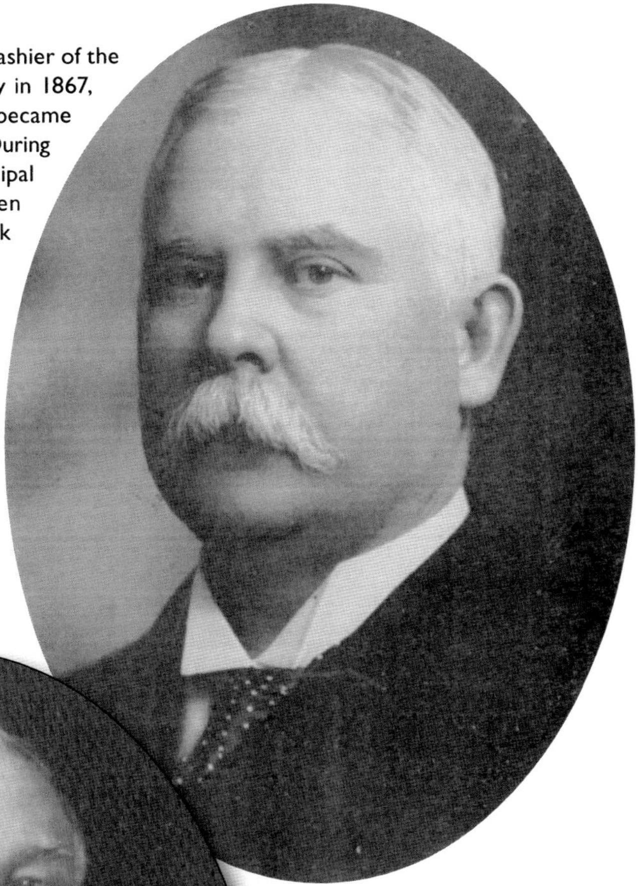

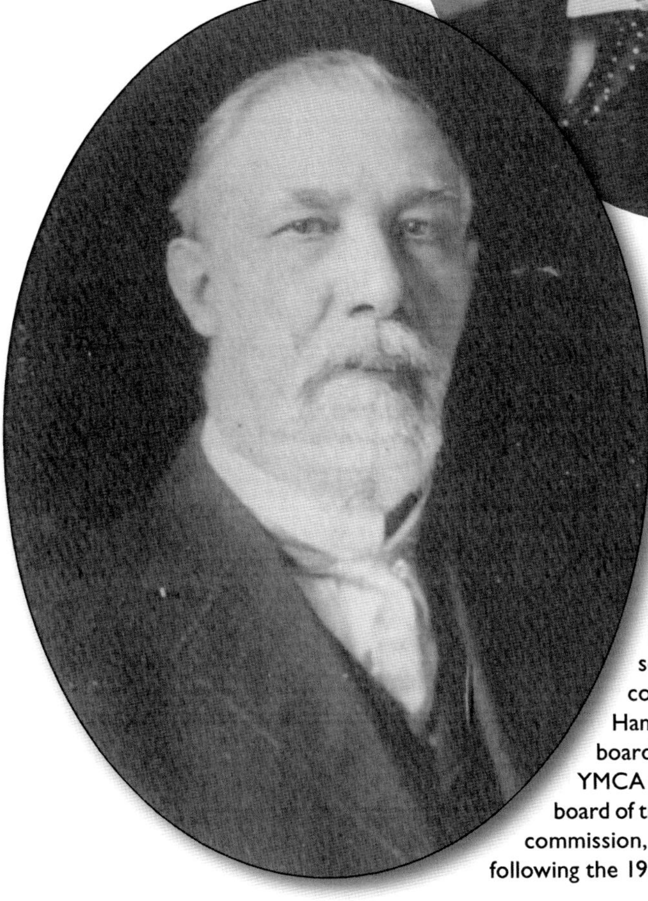

George T. Reiss

Reiss (1849–1915) became head of engineering of Niles Tool Works in 1878 and eventually became vice president of the company. He was a prolific inventor and held many patents for machine tools and machinery. Reiss served six years as president of the city council and was the first president of the Hamilton Chamber of Commerce. He was a board member for more than 20 years of the YMCA and a president of the Mercy Hospital board of trustees. As a member of the emergency commission, he administered Butler County affairs following the 1913 flood.

Lazard Kahn

Brothers Lazard (pictured) and Felix Kahn moved their stove foundry to Hamilton in 1884. The firm, renamed the Estate Stove Company in 1906, manufactured a comprehensive line of heating and cooking appliances, including, beginning in 1910, electric stoves. It also made thousands of small field kitchens that were used by American soldiers during World War I. The company's letterhead is shown in the below photograph. In 1890, Lazard (1850–1928) helped organize the Hamilton Improvement Syndicate for the purpose of attracting other industries to the city. The group purchased land on the east side of Hamilton and persuaded several businesses, including Mosler Safe & Lock Company, Fred J. Myers Manufacturing Company, Hamilton Foundry & Machine Company, and the Albert Bess Company, to locate in the area. During 1899 and 1900, Kahn acted as a member of the international jury at the World Exposition in Paris. For his service, the French government awarded him the Cross of the Legion of Honor. Kahn also worked to develop the Lindenwald area and served on the city sewer commission. In 1910, Kahn was one of the founders of the Hamilton Chamber of Commerce. The house in which he and his family lived from 1885 to 1897 was given for public use in 1943 and became the office headquarters of the Butler County United Way. (Below, courtesy of Rob Wile.)

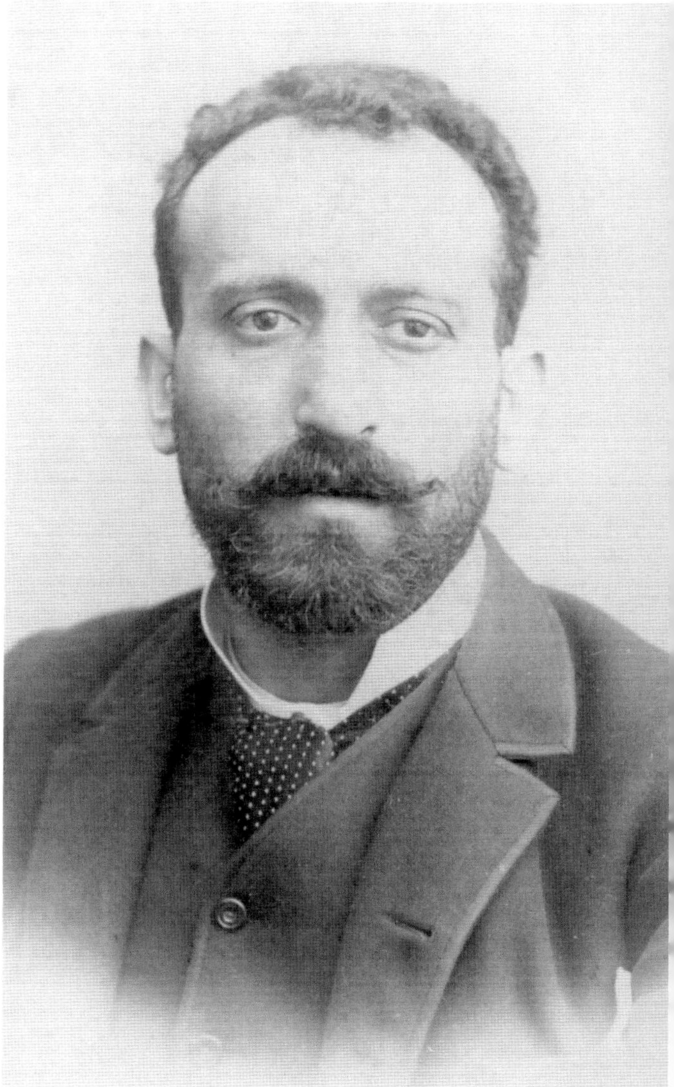

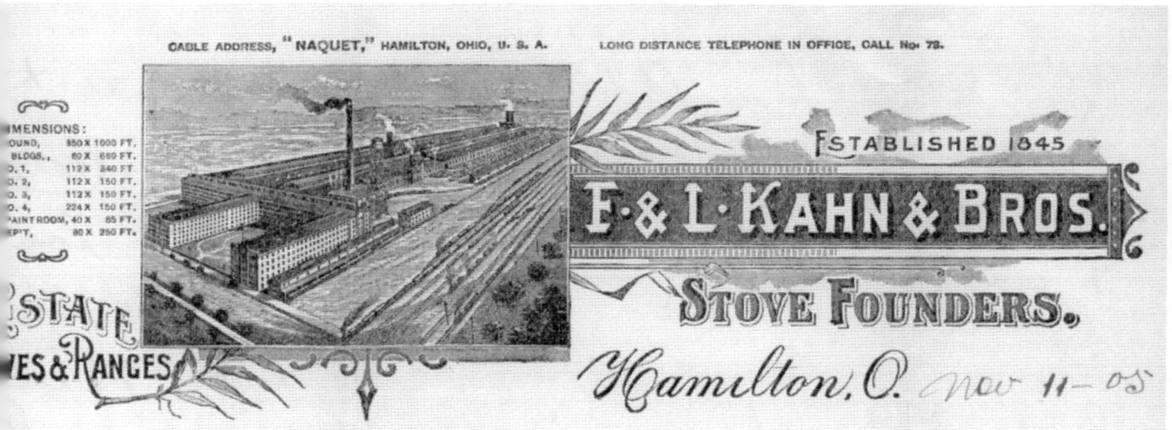

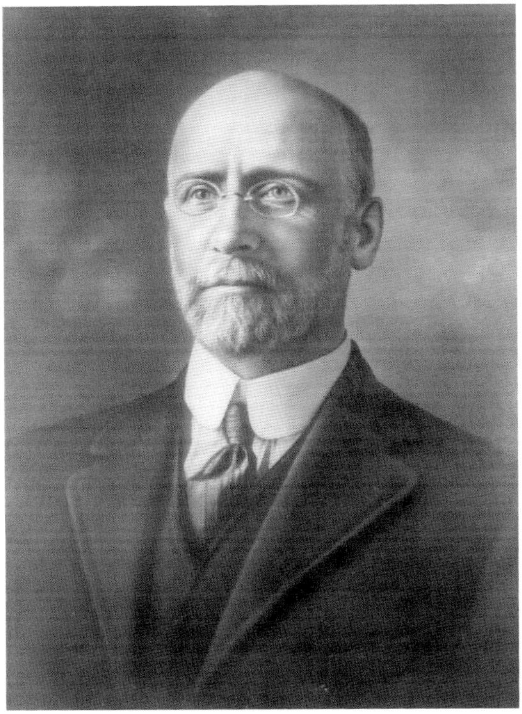

Thomas Beckett

Beckett (1860–1923) began working in the family's paper mill after graduating from Hamilton High in 1876 and took over management of the firm in 1885. Beckett developed the Buckeye Cover line of colored paper, which had superior strength and appearance and became the company's dominant product. Beckett, who married Mary Millikin, daughter of Dr. Dan Millikin, was a member of the school board from 1909 to 1913, a trustee of Lane Library for several years, and president of the Hamilton Chamber of Commerce from 1920 to 1922.

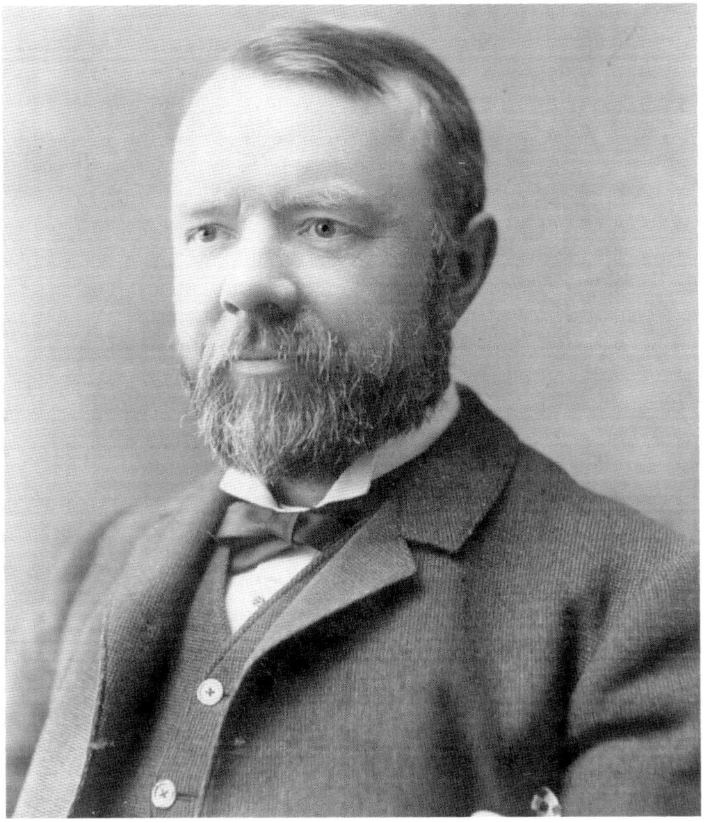

William Ritchie

Ritchie came to Hamilton in 1856 and learned to be a machinist and engineer at Owens, Lane, Dyer & Company. He served in the Civil War and took part in General Sherman's march to the sea in 1865. Ritchie (1839–1906) formed the Advance Manufacturing Company in 1887 and made high-grade gasoline engines for more than 25 years. He was a member of Hamilton's board of education for four years and worked to add manual training/industrial arts and domestic science/ home economics to the high school curriculum.

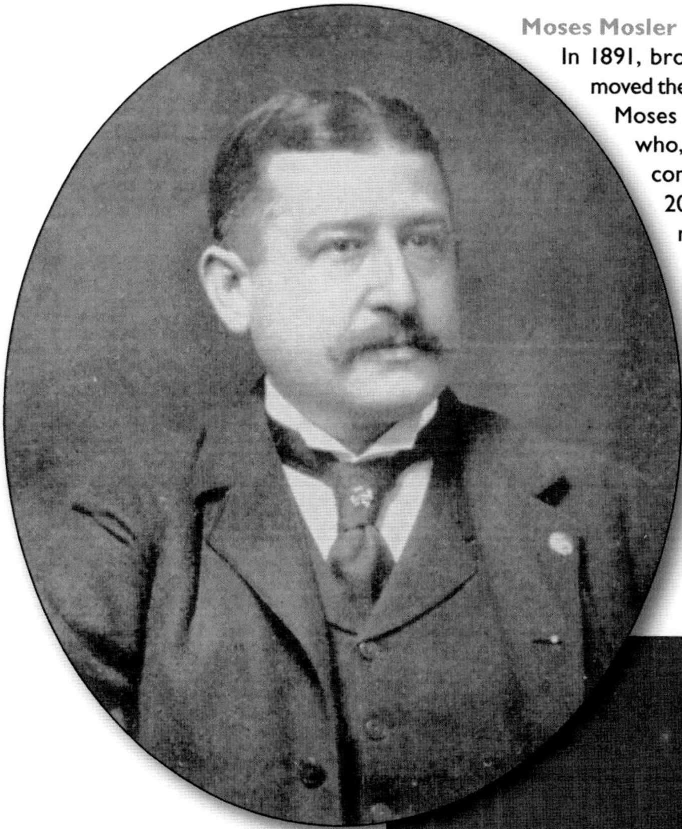

Moses Mosler

In 1891, brothers Moses and William Mosler moved their safe and lock business to Hamilton. Moses (pictured) was a mechanical genius who, through his study of intricate and complex systems, secured more than 200 patents. The company introduced major improvements in safes, vault doors, and fireproof storage products. Mosler (1851–1922) created a mutual aid society for his employees, founded a volunteer fire department, and built an electric power plant for the manufacturing site, nearby private homes, and streetlights.

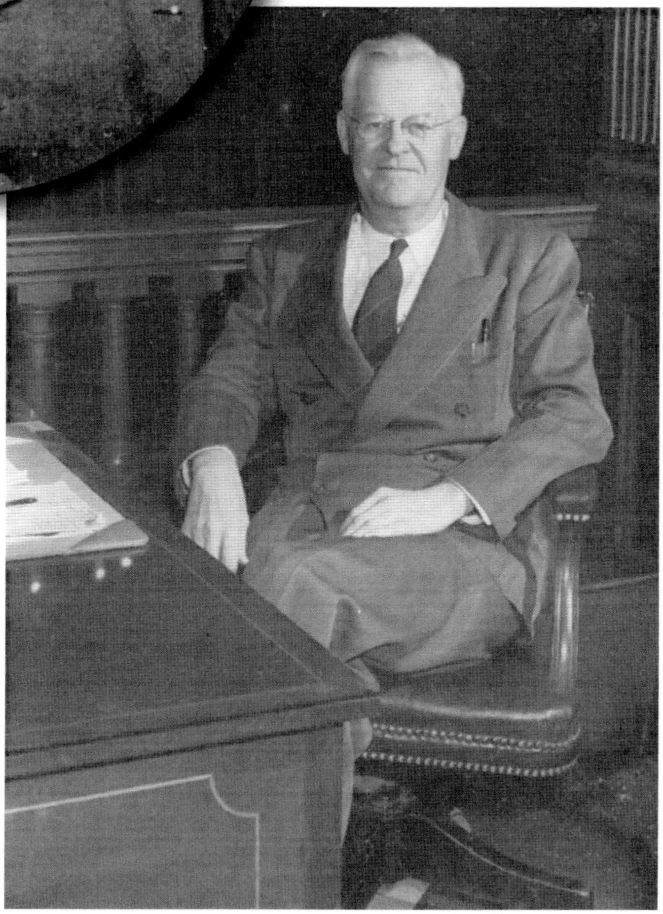

Donald Webb Fitton

In 1912, Donald Fitton began his business career as an assistant cashier at the First National Bank & Trust Company and became president in 1946. He was named the bank's chairman of the board in 1961. Fitton (1890–1972), a president of the Hamilton Chamber of Commerce, was also a director of several businesses, including the Journal Publishing Company, Beckett Paper Company, and Ohio Casualty Insurance Company. An excellent tennis player, he won the city singles championship four times and, with his brother Cyrus, the doubles championship six times.

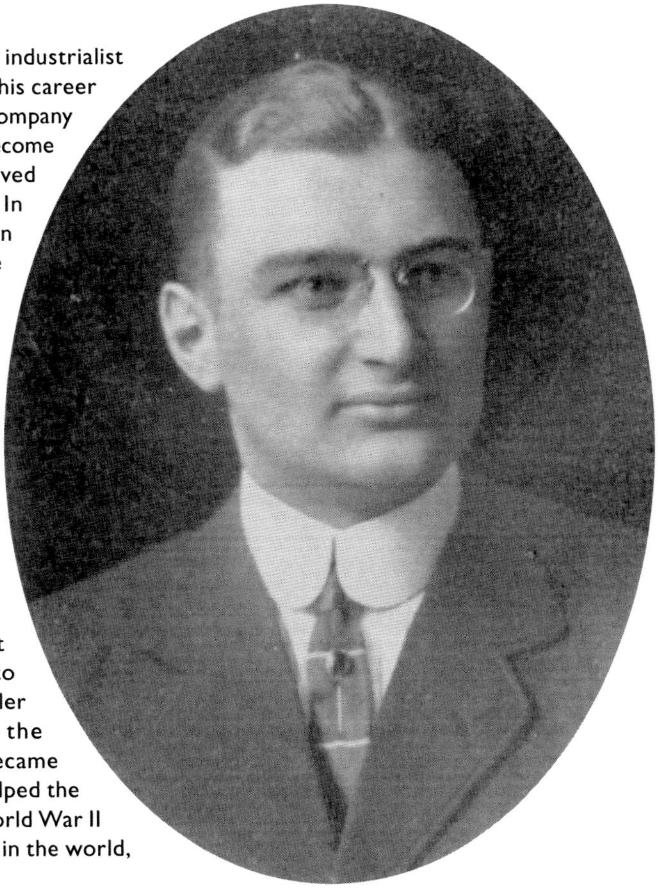

Gordon Sohn Rentschler

In 1907, Gordon Rentschler, one of industrialist George A. Rentschler's sons, began his career at the Hooven, Owens, Rentschler Company plant as a machinist. He advanced to become president of the firm and was involved in other family business ventures. In 1910, he helped organize the Hamilton Chamber of Commerce. After the March 1913 flood, Rentschler headed the Hamilton Citizens Relief Committee and the effort to secure aid and relief for the community. He advocated the formation of the Miami Conservancy District and was named one of the district's first three directors in 1915, a position he held until 1932. Rentschler went to New York in 1917 to secure funds for the flood prevention project. The National City Bank was one of the major buyers of the bonds that enabled the conservancy district to finish the project in 1923. Rentschler (1885–1948) began working at the National City Bank in 1921 and became president in 1929. His leadership helped the bank survive the Depression and World War II to become one of the largest banks in the world, known today as Citibank.

Frederick Brant Rentschler (OPPOSITE PAGE)

Frederick Rentschler (1887–1956), another son of George Rentschler, learned to appreciate engines while working during school breaks at the Hooven, Owens & Rentschler plant, which manufactured gas, oil, and steam turbines. After graduating from Princeton University in 1909, he worked as a molder and mechanic in the family-owned Republic Motor Car Company and, after that business closed in 1914, in the shops at the Niles Tool Works until 1917. Following World War I, Rentschler formed the Wright Aeronautical Corporation, which produced air-cooled engines for US Army and Navy craft. He left that company to form the Pratt & Whitney Aircraft Company, where he and his engineers developed the firm's first Wasp engine. By 1926, Rentschler's company signed a contract for 200 engines with the Navy, and Boeing purchased 28 engines for its mail planes. In 1928, Rentschler, with his partners Chance Vought and William Boeing, formed United Aircraft & Transport Corporation. The company became United Airlines and offered the country's first transcontinental passenger service in 1929. Pratt & Whitney's Wasp engine became famous for powering historic flights made by Charles Lindbergh, Amelia Earhart, and Wiley Post, and as a major asset in the Allied victory in World War II. Rentschler and his company helped manufacture the first helicopters that had been designed by his associate, Igor Sikorsky, and Chance Vought Corsair fighters. In 1982, Rentschler was named to the National Aviation Hall of Fame for his work in developing aircraft engines, establishing the first coast-to-coast airline, and helping manufacture the first practical helicopter.

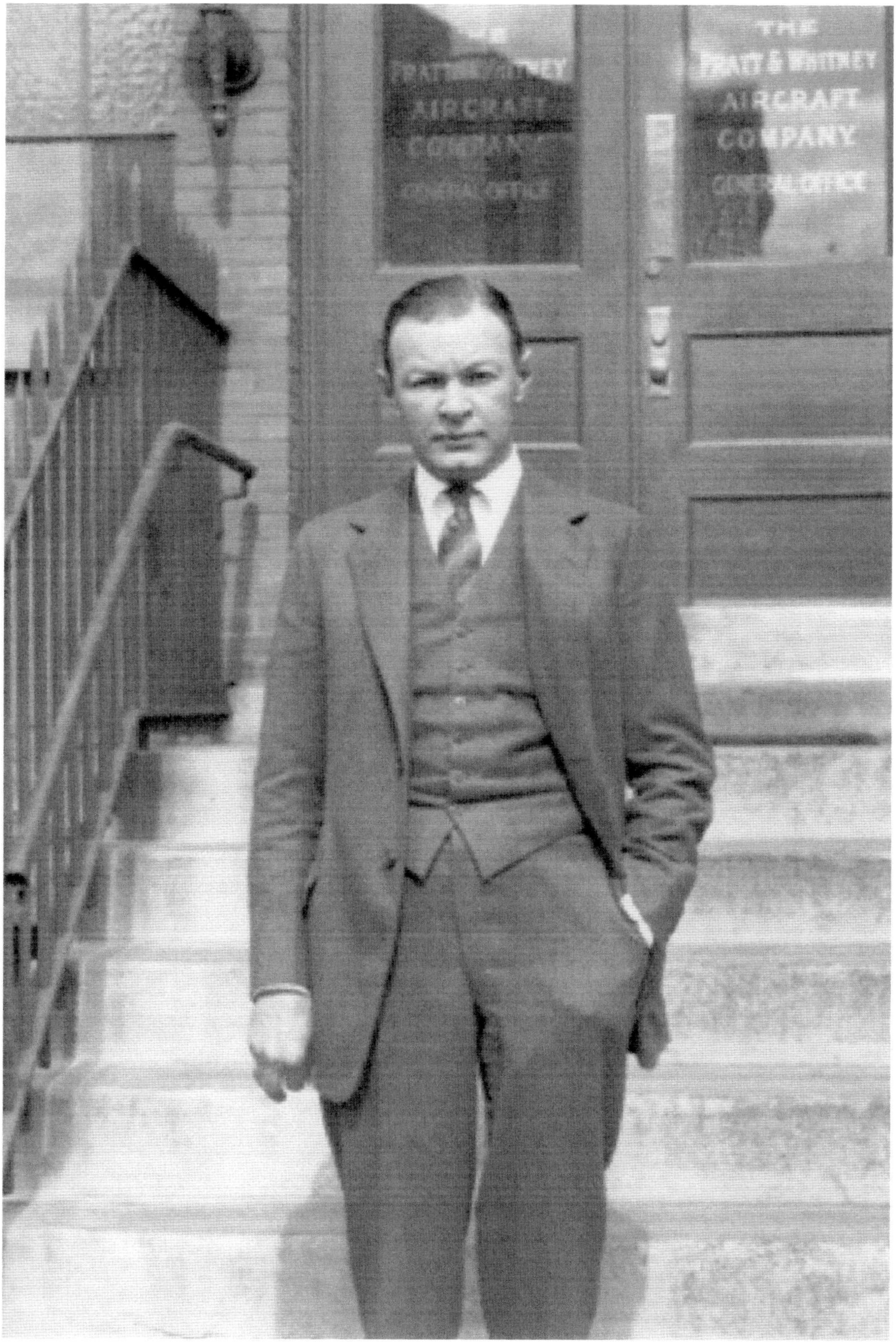
THE
PRATT & WHITNEY
AIRCRAFT
COMPANY
GENERAL OFFICE

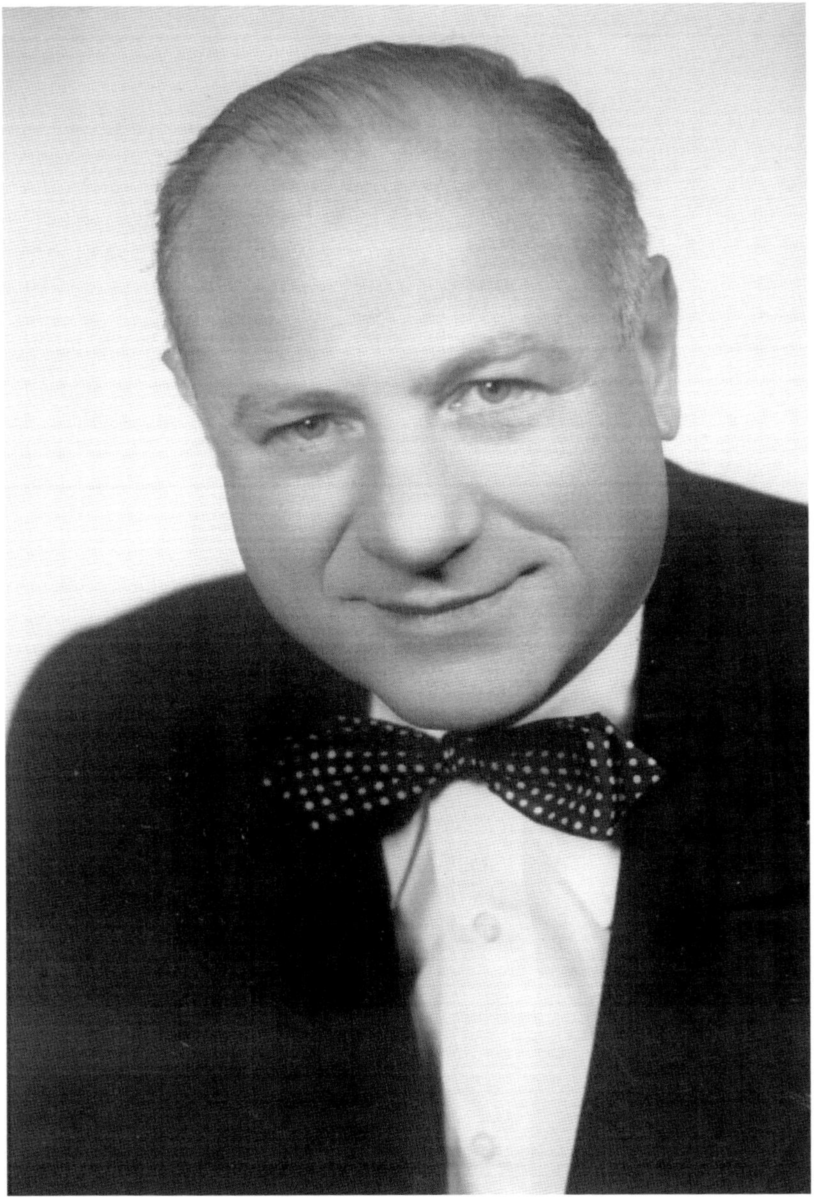

William Murstein

Murstein owned and operated the popular Wilmur's Department Store in downtown Hamilton for 32 years, from 1935 to 1967. The store, generally considered the finest in town, provided top-quality merchandise while offering customers bargains and value for their money. Murstein was a generous philanthropist who supported many charitable organizations. He was a founder of the Hamilton Community Foundation and contributed his time and money to a wide variety of organizations, including the United Appeals, Boy Scouts, Cancer Society, Booker T. Washington Center, and the Salvation Army. Murstein (1897–1967) contributed money to establish a senior citizens' center in the former Adams School. He funded three scholarships at Miami University and donated half of the needed funds to build the Murstein Alumni Center. Murstein also organized the Hamilton Jewish Welfare Fund and funded the William Murstein Synagogue at the Hebrew Union College Biblical and Archeological School in Jerusalem.

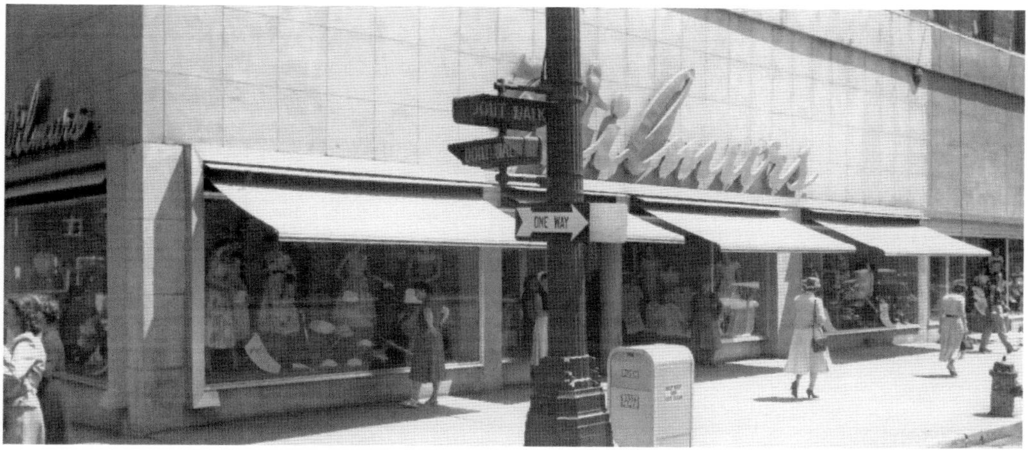

Wilmur's Department Store

Murstein always sought to improve his store and its services. He offered a very popular layaway plan, in which customers paid a small deposit to have the store hold an item until its purchase price was paid. The store was remodeled and enlarged twice, and each department's inventory was greatly increased. Escalators and elevators were added. Wilmur's added a free parking lot for customers in 1956. Attractive street-level windows, such as those in the above photograph, lured shoppers into the store. Murstein revolutionized retailing in Hamilton with targeted advertising and effective promotions. Free evening bus rides were offered to customers who shopped downtown stores, which stayed open until 9:00 p.m. The below photograph shows another Wilmur's promotion, a free showing of the movie *Davy Crockett* to Hamilton youth, sponsored by the store that was Hamilton's "Davy Crockett Headquarters."

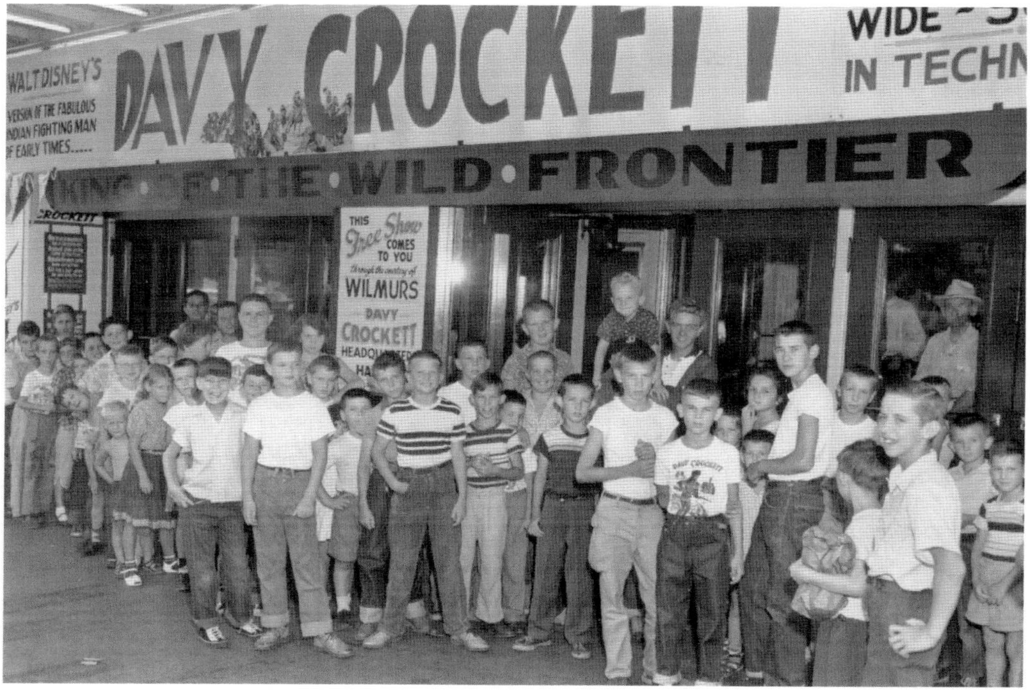

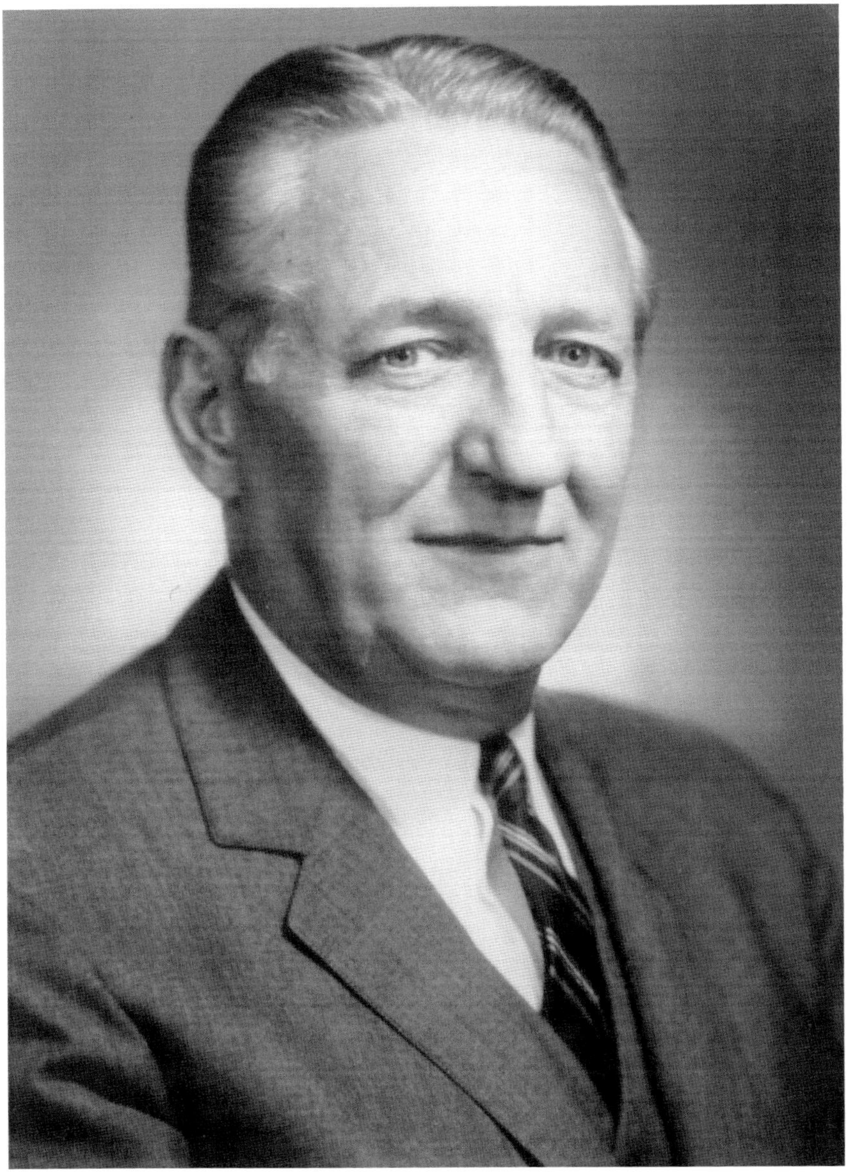

Walter A. Rentschler

Rentschler (1902–1988), grandson of George Rentschler, began his 50-year business career at the Hamilton Foundry & Machine Company in 1925 and joined the Hooven, Owens, Rentschler Company in 1928, where he advanced to become president. He also became head of the Niles Tool Works & General Machinery Company. Rentschler's companies manufactured heavy machine tools, steam engines, and diesel engines for Liberty ships and submarines during World War II. He joined the Citizens Savings Bank & Trust Company as its president in 1958 and was elected chairman of the board, serving from 1967 until 1975, when he was chosen as an advisory director. In 1950, he was elected to the Miami Conservancy District and became president in 1968, retiring in 1975. Rentschler was a major benefactor of the Butler County Park District and donated much of the land that formed the Rentschler Forest Preserve. Rentschler was a trustee of the Hughes Memorial Hospital and a board member of Mercy Hospital, the Hamilton Chamber of Commerce, and the Hamilton Junior Achievement.

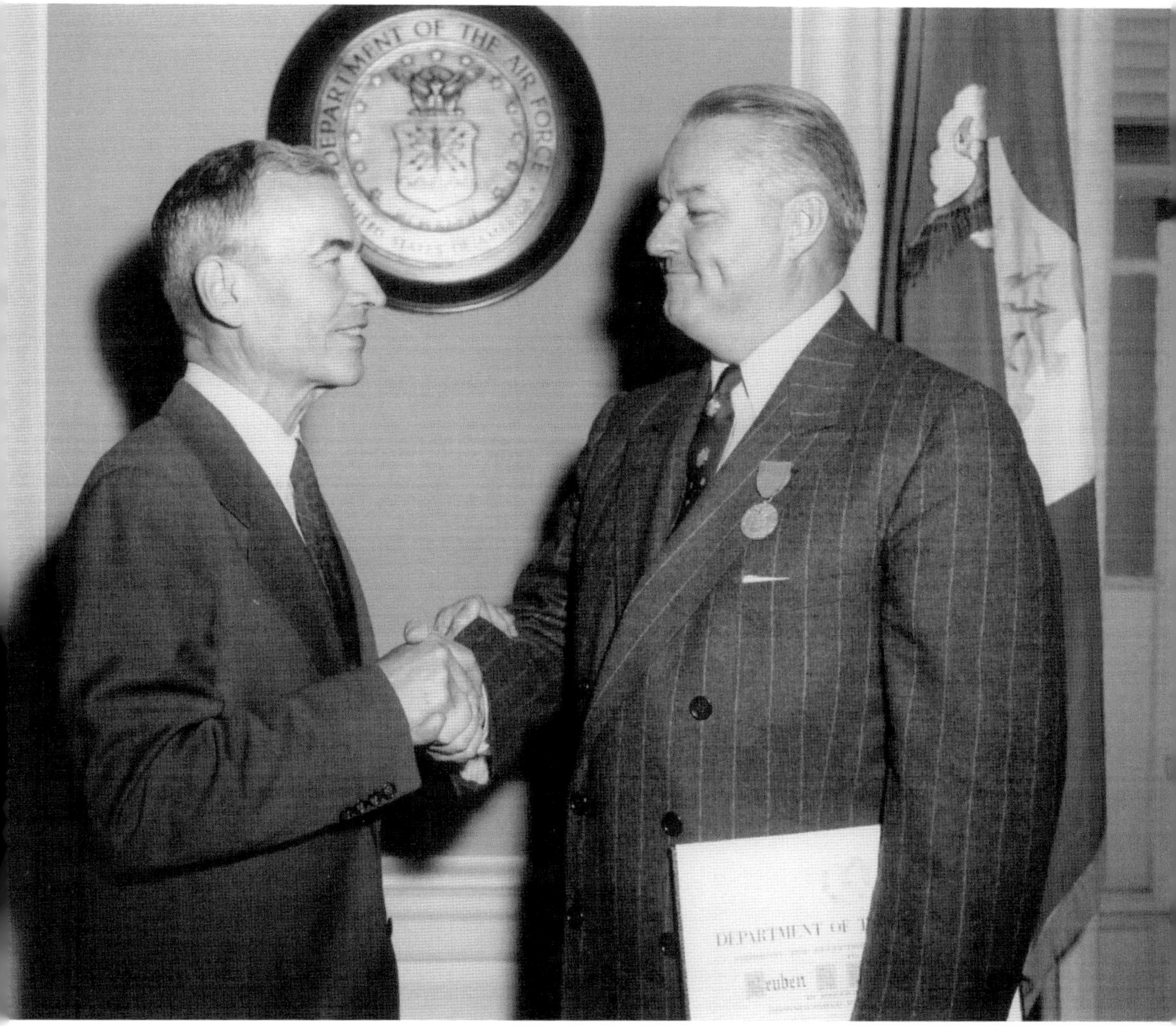

Reuben B. Robertson Jr.

Robertson, grandson of Champion Coated Paper Company founder Peter G. Thomson, began working in the company's North Carolina mill in 1930 and advanced to become production manager of the Carolina division four years later. He was named vice president in 1938, the year he moved to Hamilton, and in 1941, assumed the duties of general production manager for all of the company's plants. Robertson (1908–1960) served on the War Production Board in World War II. In 1950, he became president of the Champion Paper & Fibre Company and was named by Pres. Harry S. Truman to serve on the Wage Stabilization Board for two years. Robertson was voted the Man of the Year in 1953 by the National Association of Manufacturers, the year he appeared on the cover of *BusinessWeek* magazine. He was a member of the Hamilton Chamber of Commerce and local Industrial Council and worked to create the Hamilton Safety Council. Robertson, during a 1955–1957 leave of absence, worked for the federal government in Washington, DC. Here, Robertson (right) receives the Meritorious Civilian Service Award from Secretary of the Air Force Donald A. Quarles for his work as deputy secretary of defense in a ceremony at the Pentagon in 1957. Robertson returned to Hamilton and resumed his work at Champion Paper. On March 13, 1960, Reuben and his wife, Peggy, were driving home from a social engagement in Cincinnati when Robertson hit a stalled car. As he was walking toward the struck vehicle, Robertson was hit by another car and died at the scene.

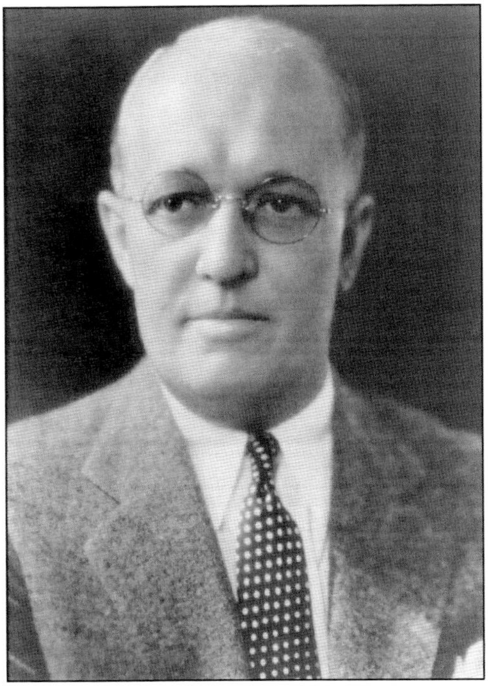

Howard Sloneker

Sloneker began his insurance career as a local agent in 1910. He and four partners formed the Ohio Casualty Insurance Company in 1919 to write automobile insurance policies. Sloneker became president of the company in 1940 and served in the position until 1953, when he was named chairman of the board. The firm sold only automobile insurance until it diversified in 1923 by offering glass insurance and writing out-of-state policies. Sloneker (1890–1963), president of the Hamilton Chamber of Commerce in 1940, was proud that his company laid off no employees during the Depression.

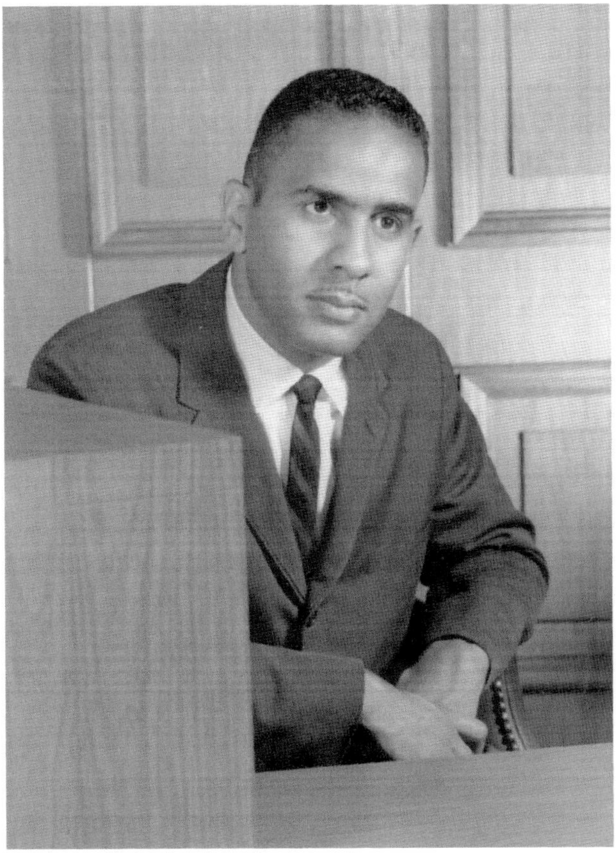

Donald H. Jordan

Reverend Jordan opened his first funeral home in 1953 in Middletown before expanding to Hamilton in 1959. He acquired several funeral homes throughout the area and built the largest funeral home operation in Ohio. During the 1960s, Jordan (1932–) helped organize the local NAACP and was a president of the Booker T. Washington Community Center. He has been a pastor at several area African Methodist Episcopal churches, beginning in 1977. The Swifton Commons Mall in Cincinnati was renamed Jordan Crossing in his honor.

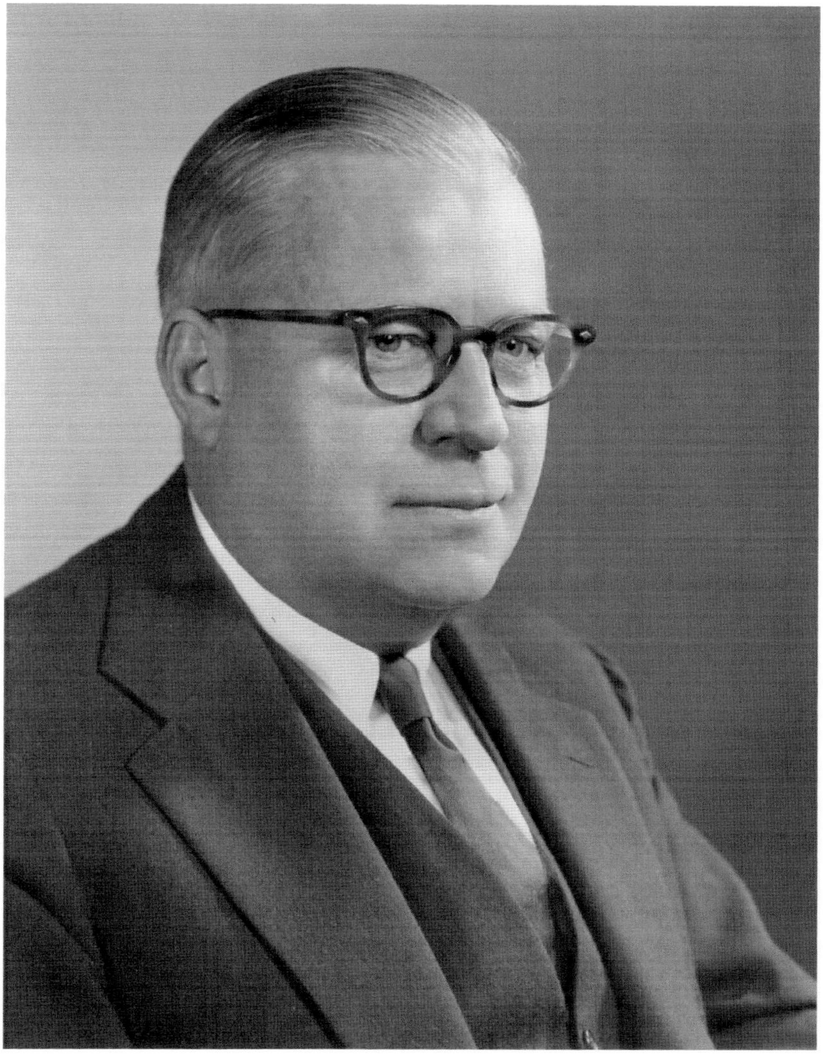

Peter E. Rentschler

Rentschler, another grandson of George Rentschler, made significant contributions to Hamilton and its business community. He joined the Hamilton Foundry & Machine Company in 1920, became vice president in 1923, and then president in 1927, serving in that office until his death in 1976. Rentschler (1897–1976) was a prominent member and officer of several national foundry and gray metal casting organizations and advised the US Munitions Board and the Department of Labor on foundry-related issues. His service to the industry was honored with a number of awards and medals. Rentschler was active in the Hamilton Chamber of Commerce and served as a director for eight years, from 1927 to 1930 and from 1933 to 1937. For several years, he chaired the chamber's Christmas in Every Home program. In 1942, Rentschler worked with Reuben Robertson to establish the Hamilton Safety Council. He had a strong interest in education. Rentschler served two terms on the Hamilton Board of Education, from 1940 to 1947, and was president for three years. He was the chairman of the 1965 fundraising committee that was charged with soliciting at least $600,000 to win matching funds totaling $1.8 million from the Ohio General Assembly to establish the Hamilton campus of Miami University. Rentschler's committee raised over $1.5 million for the school. The Hamilton campus library building, one of the first two structures erected on the campus, was named in his honor.

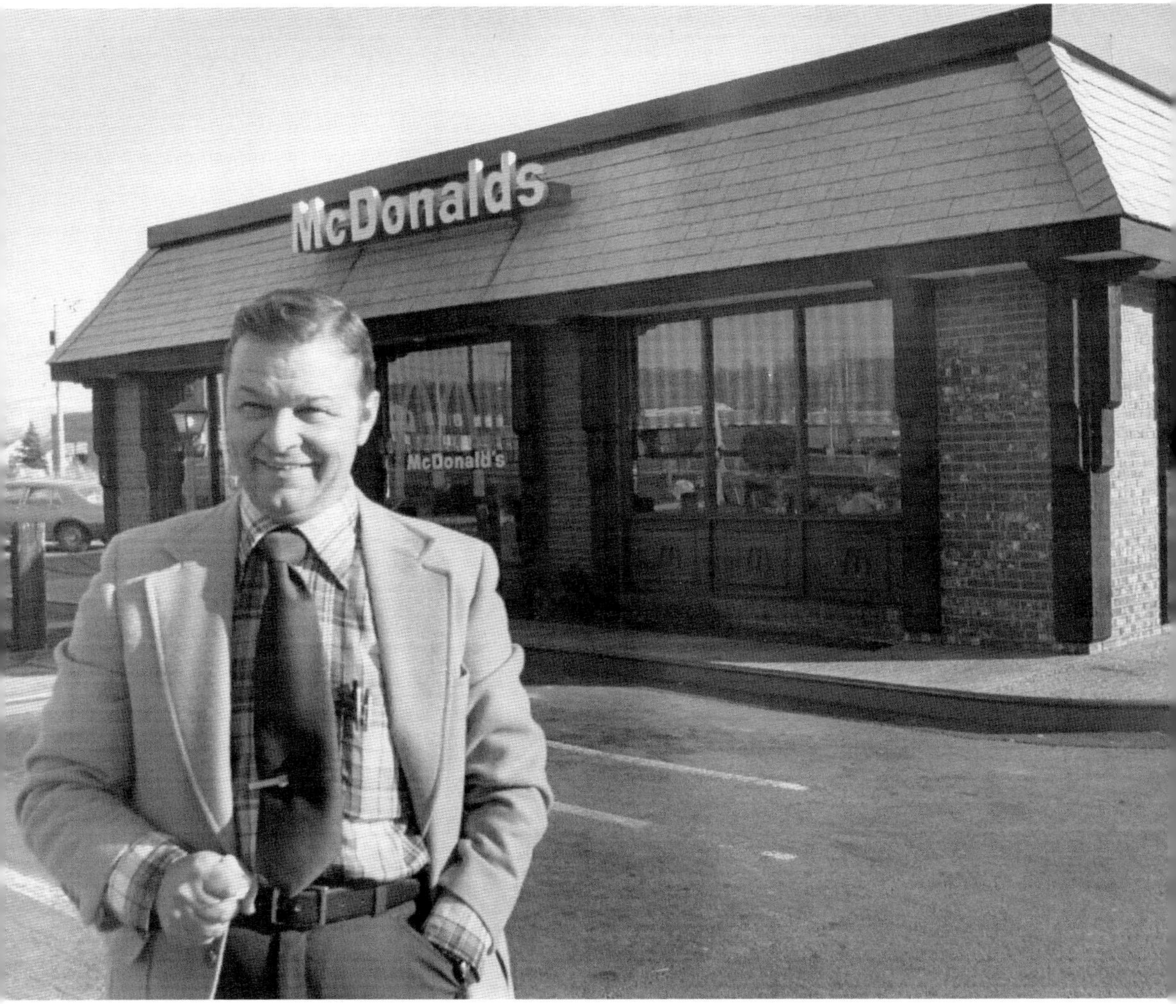

Joel Schmidt

In 1969, Schmidt (1926–) formed a partnership with Chuck Posey, who had opened Hamilton's first McDonald's restaurant on Erie Boulevard in 1959. Schmidt became the only owner of the franchise in 1969, the year a second store on Northwest Washington Boulevard opened. Schmidt built four other locations in Fairfield, Oxford, and downtown Hamilton between 1976 and 1988. The McDonald's Corporation named him as one of its top operators in the world. Schmidt, who was honored as the Fairfield Chamber of Commerce's Business Person of the Year in 1990, has actively supported the Hamilton Chamber of Commerce, Hamilton Community Foundation, Boys and Girls Club, Fitton Center for Creative Arts, Fort Hamilton–Hughes Memorial Hospital, and, especially, Special Olympics programs. In 1993, Schmidt was inducted into the Junior Achievement Hall of Fame. He has worked on a wide variety of committees and task force groups charged with solving local problems and improving life in the community. Joel and his wife, Marilyn, were given the David L. Belew Legacy Award in 2012 by the Hamilton Community Foundation in honor of their more than 50 years of philanthropic contributions to the city and surrounding area.

CHAPTER FIVE

Creative Spirits

For many years, Hamilton residents have taken part in a wide variety of artistic and creative activities. A number of writers have stimulated national and local audiences; musical performers have achieved all levels of skill; speakers have thrilled crowds; exceptionally talented actors and actresses have graced stage and screen; sculptors have created wondrous compositions; and artists using paintbrushes, cameras, and videotape have produced amazing works.

The community has been blessed with a large number of talented writers, such as Stella Weiler Taylor, a schoolteacher who wrote song lyrics, staged musicals and variety shows, and wrote the popular "Rosemary" weekly newspaper column; Alta Harvey Heiser, who detailed much of the area's history as well as the activities of local gardeners in the *Journal News*; Bill Moeller, who wrote about sports for more than 50 years; and Bill McDulin, a radio and newspaper editor. Alvin D. Smith edited and published the weekly Butler County *American*, one of the few African American papers in the area. Jim Blount, a former teacher and *Journal News* editor, has written articles and books dealing with local history.

Several writers from Hamilton have had great success on the national stage. William Dean Howells, known as the "Dean of American Letters," edited national literary magazines and wrote dozens of novels. Fannie Hurst wrote novels, short stories, screenplays, and became one of the highest-paid authors of her day. Robert McCloskey, who won awards for writing and illustrating children's books, was named one of the country's "Living Legends" by the Library of Congress. William Rentschler wrote books and newspaper columns following his career in business and politics.

Louis Jenks Beauchamp traveled around the world, speaking about temperance and advocating a positive, sunny outlook on life. Folk artist Nan Phelps created more than 1,000 paintings. George Cummins collected thousands of photographs that recorded much of the community's history. Musical talents include Bess Arlene Camacho, who has performed at Carnegie Hall and on the world's opera stages; Paul John Stanbery, the conductor of the Hamilton-Fairfield Symphony Orchestra; and Paul Thoms, a music teacher and talented performer.

Architect Frederick Mueller designed many of the most important buildings in Hamilton as well as dozens of very special homes. Rudolph Thiem crafted *Victory: Jewel of the Soul*, the bronze statue on the top of the Soldiers, Sailors and Pioneers Monument known to most residents as "Billy Yank." More recently, sculptor Edgar Tarfur worked to restore the John Cleves Symmes "Hollow Earth" monument.

Brothers Shuler and Joseph Doron pioneered early wireless radio in the United States and built Hamilton's first broadcast station. Several years later, Jack Armstrong built the city's community access television station and operated it for more than 20 years. Ray Combs, a Garfield High graduate, went on to have a bright but tragically short career in network television.

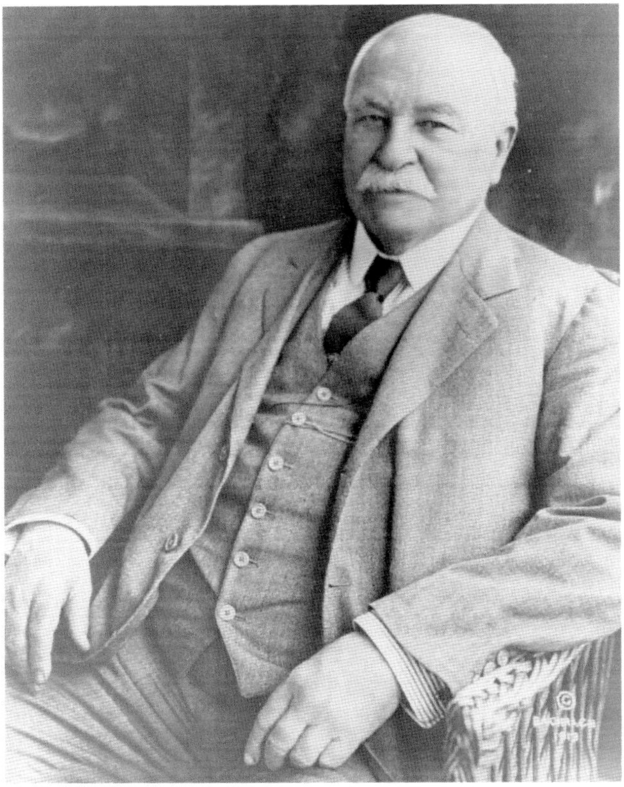

William Dean Howells

Howells (1837–1920) lived in Hamilton for only eight years, from 1840 to 1848, when his father was owner of the Hamilton *Intelligencer* newspaper. From 1866 to 1881, William Dean Howells edited the *Nation* and *Atlantic Monthly* magazines and turned to writing novels in 1871. His most famous work, *The Rise of Silas Laphan*, was published in 1885. By 1886, he began a regular literary review column in *Harper's* that consistently recognized the best in contemporary literature. Howells fondly recalled his days in Hamilton in his delightful novel *A Boy's Town*.

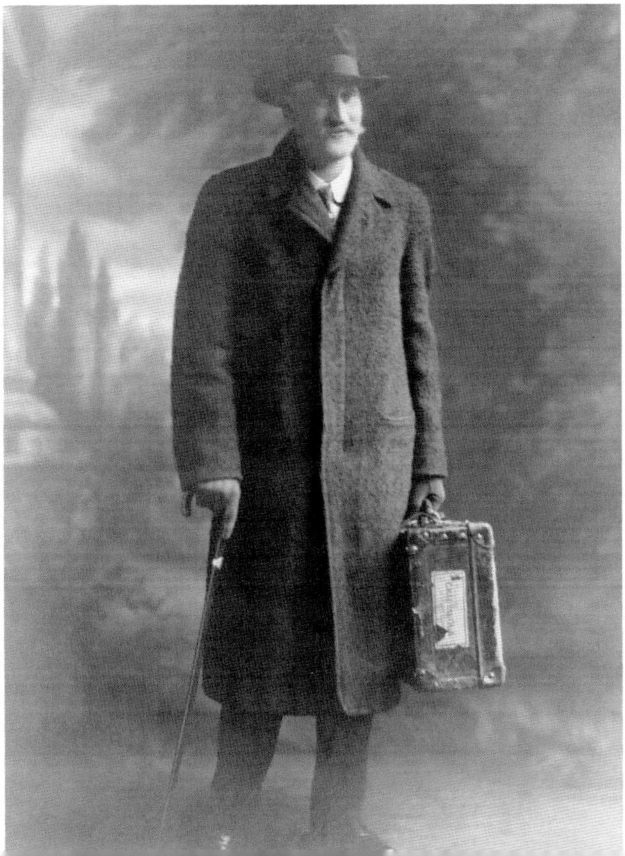

Louis Jenks Beauchamp

Beauchamp (1851–1920) reported that his wife, Millie, turned him from his abuse of liquor and helped him become a temperance lecturer and leader. He traveled 19 years and nearly two million miles in the United States and Europe, presenting his message of total abstinence. Beauchamp, known as "The Humorous Philosopher," gave thousands of speeches on the Lyceum and Chautauqua circuits. His most popular inspirational speech, "Take the Sunny Side," was given more than 1,000 times, making him the "Apostle of Sunshine."

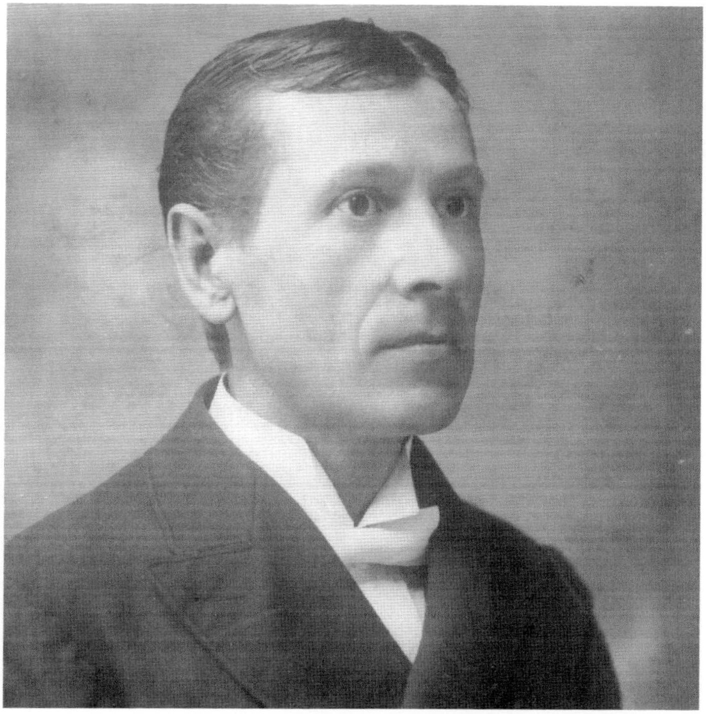

Rudolph Thiem
Thiem started his business as a model-maker and ornamental carver in 1889. He won the national competition to design the statue for the top of the Soldiers, Sailors and Pioneers Monument funded by an 1899 county-wide tax levy. Thiem (1859–1928) was paid $3,250 to build *Victory: Jewel of the Soul*, the 17-foot-tall, 3,500-pound bronze statue of a Civil War private known locally as "Billy Yank." He also carved the 79,000 letters of the names of Butler County war dead on the monument's interior marble walls. (Courtesy of Jon Thiem.)

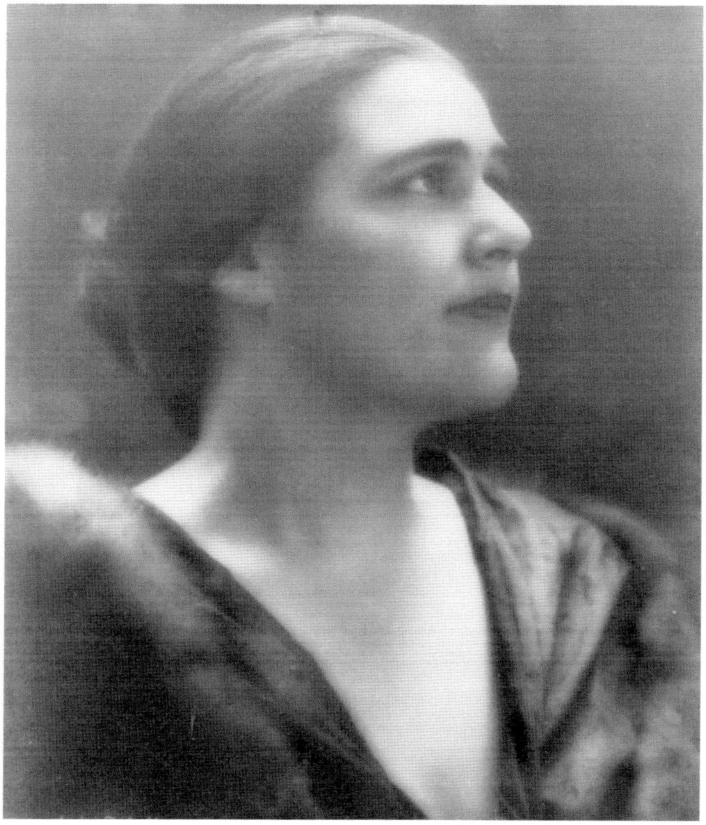

Fannie Hurst
Hurst (1889–1968) was born in Hamilton before her family moved to St. Louis. As a child, however, she spent many summer months in Hamilton and called it her "summer palace." She moved to New York, where she wrote for magazines such as the *Saturday Evening Post* and *Cosmopolitan* and became a successful novelist, dramatist, and screenwriter. Hurst wrote 18 novels, 300 short stories, 12 screenplays, an autobiography, and was one of the highest-paid writers in America. She was a social activist for the rights of women, homosexuals, and Jews.

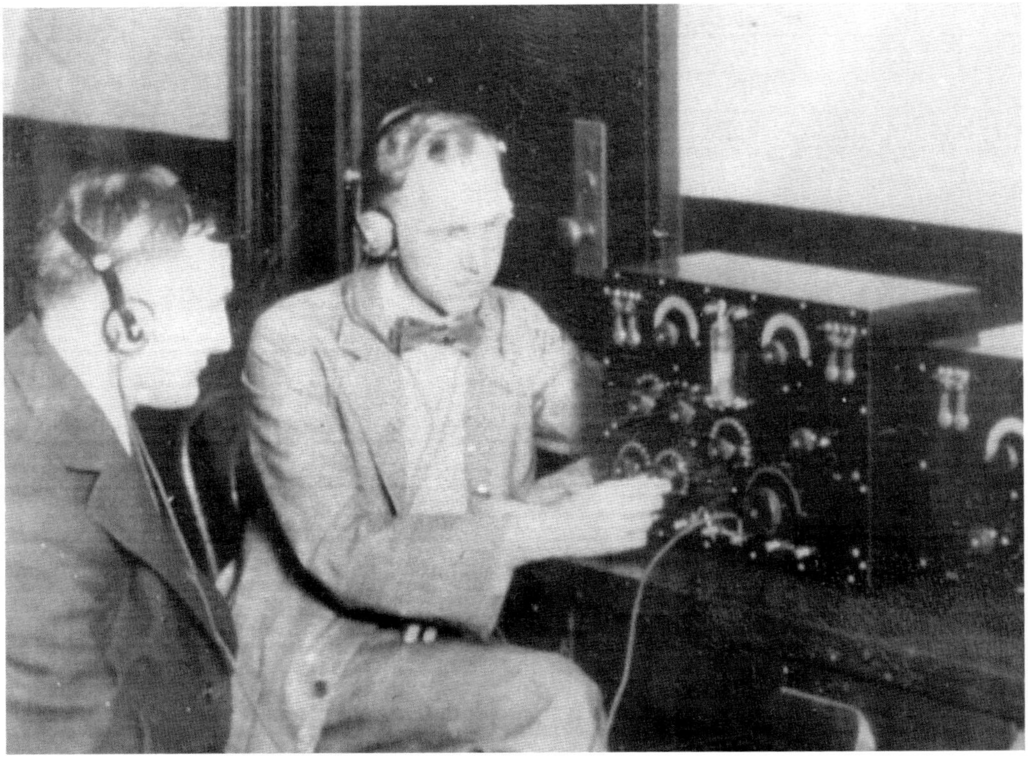

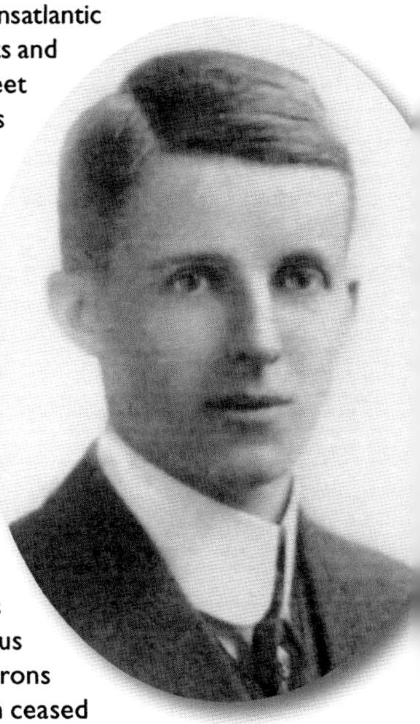

Shuler Doron and Joseph W. Doron

Brothers Shuler (1890–1955) and Joseph Doron (1895–1967) were among the early pioneers in wireless radio in the United States. Shuler began experimenting with wireless radio apparatus in 1903, two years after Guglielmo Marconi received the first transatlantic code message. By 1910, the brothers were building wireless receiving units and transmitting equipment in the basement of their home on North C Street and organizing the Radio Club of Hamilton. They built a powerful wireless station for their own use and erected two 90-foot wooden towers in their backyard. Shuler and Joseph formed the Doron Brothers Electrical Company in 1914 and sold the crystal sets, telegraph keys, and other wireless equipment they manufactured by mail order. The company was one of the first two or three radio equipment manufacturers in the country. In the above photograph, Shuler (right) shows an unidentified member of the Cincinnati Amateur Radio Club how to use a long-wave radio receiver, built by the Doron Brothers Electrical Company. The photograph to the right shows Joseph Doron in 1915, when he was a senior at Hamilton High. In 1922, after wireless voice transmissions became possible, the Doron brothers created WRK, Hamilton's first broadcast station. The station was the 57th commercial station in the United States, receiving its license one week before Powell Crosley's WLW became the country's 65th station. Signals from the Doron radio station were heard in every state in the nation, plus Alaska, Mexico, Panama, and South America. John Slade joined the Dorons in 1927 as a partner and stayed with WRK until 1930, when the station ceased broadcasting. Slade eventually started his own radio station, WMOH, in 1944. (Above, courtesy of Charles J. Stinger; right, courtesy of Hamilton City School District.)

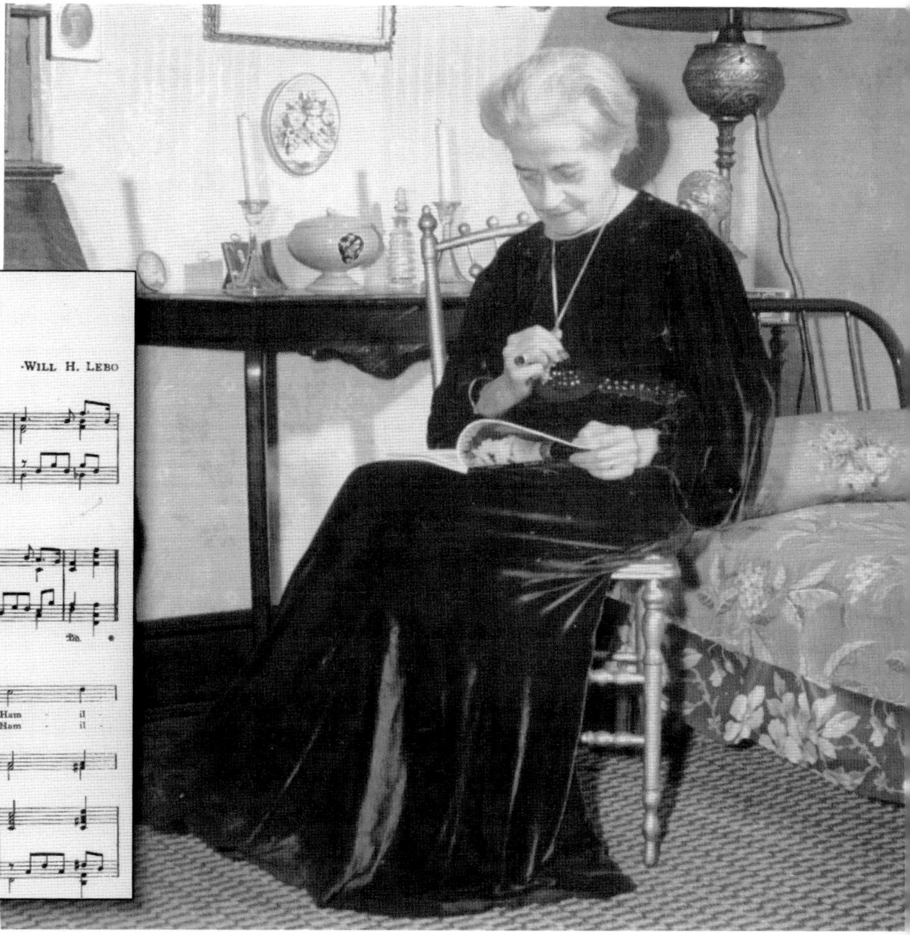

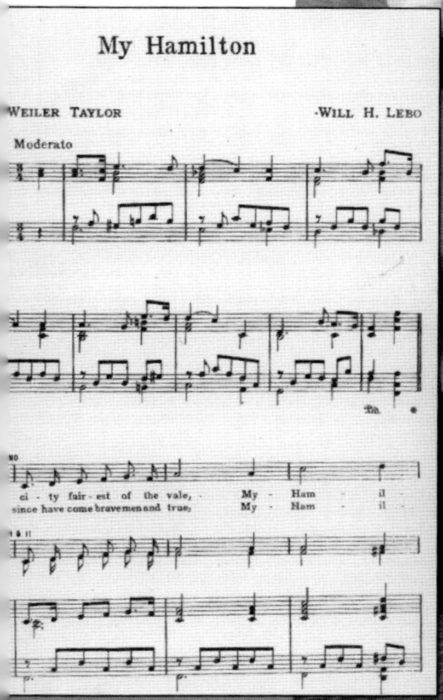

Stella Weiler Taylor

Known as Hamilton's "grand lady of letters," Stella Taylor (1869–1953) was one of the city's most beloved citizens. She was identified with the social life of the Gay Nineties and, from October 1931 to March 1948, kept the charm of the period alive through her columns in the *Journal News*. Every week, she crafted a fascinating word picture of Hamilton, its people, and its traditions in her column, "Rosemary—That's For Remembrance. A Series of Lavender Scented Memories of Other Days in Hamilton." As a little girl growing up in the Straub House, the local hotel operated by her father, she met prominent celebrities and travelers and often recalled them in her columns in later years. She collected many autographs and photographs of the famous contacts she made over the years. Taylor's love of the theater was expressed in her support, participation, and direction of amateur community productions. In 1894, she married Robert Norwood Taylor, a lawyer. He abandoned her after six months and disappeared. Her mother was a popular teacher when she died in 1898. The school board president, Miles D. Lindley, asked Stella to replace her mother, and she accepted. Stella taught first- and second-grade students at Madison School from 1899 to 1935, instilling in them high ideals and an eagerness for good and ennobling things. During her career as a teacher, Taylor continued writing her "Rosemary" column and reviewed concerts, musicales, minstrel shows, and local theatrical productions. The inset shows the sheet music for the song "My Hamilton," which Taylor wrote with Will Lebo, a longtime Hamilton schools music teacher. Taylor suffered a stroke and hip injury in a fall in her apartment in 1948 and was hospitalized for the last five years of her life. As a teacher, author, poet, and leader in the social and cultural affairs of Hamilton, Stella Weiler Taylor was truly a legendary woman.

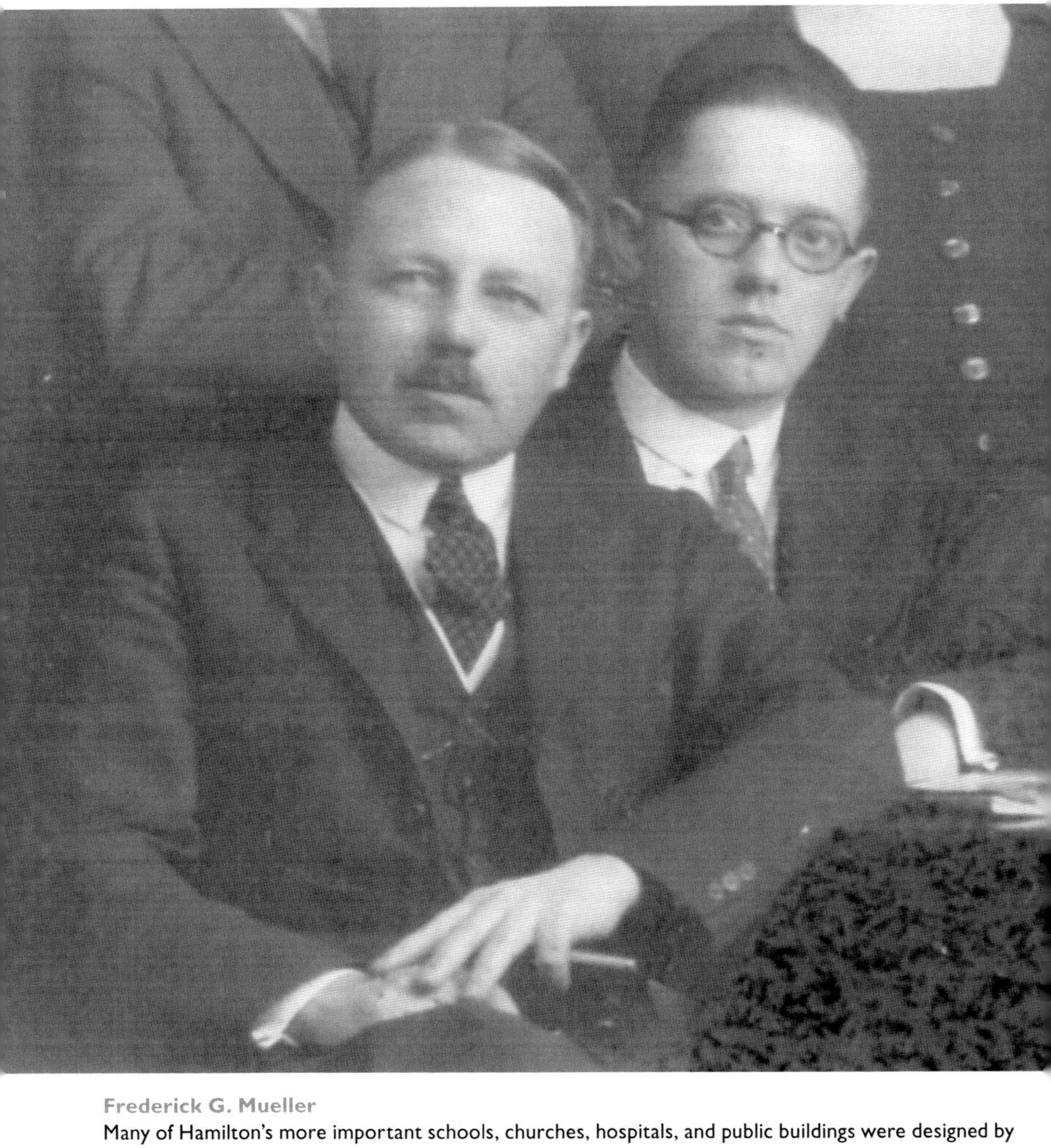

Frederick G. Mueller

Many of Hamilton's more important schools, churches, hospitals, and public buildings were designed by architect Frederick Mueller (left), seen here with associate Ralph H. Hetterich. Among the structures Mueller designed were Hamilton's Municipal Building, Fort Hamilton Hospital, YMCA, Anthony Wayne Hotel, Palace Theater, First National Bank, Ford Tractor plant, Masonic Temple, Hamilton High, Catholic High, Roosevelt and Wilson junior highs, and several public and parochial elementary schools. He also designed some of the finest homes in Hamilton. Mueller (1873–1947) was a park commissioner for 30 years and served on the city's planning commission for 27 years. In 2008, the old municipal building, erected in 1935, was named the Frederick G. Mueller Building in his honor. The design firm he started in 1901 has evolved, first into the Steed, Hammond, Paul firm and then, in 2008, becoming SHP Leading Design. (Courtesy of Mike Dingeldine.)

Robert McCloskey

John Robert McCloskey, 20, stands next to a clay model of one of the bas-relief panels he designed for Hamilton's municipal building. An unidentified woman sits to the left in this photograph taken in 1934. McCloskey (1914–2003) graduated from Hamilton High in 1932 and studied at Boston's Vesper George Art School and at the National Academy of Design in New York from 1932 to 1938. He planned to be a mural painter and commercial artist, but he achieved his greatest success as an award-winning author and illustrator of children's books. His eight books have sold more than six million copies and continue to be popular today. McCloskey won the Caldecott Medal in 1942 when *Make Way for Ducklings*, his most popular book, was named the most distinguished American picture book for children. He won a second Caldecott Medal in 1958 with *Time of Wonder* and won or shared the runner-up Caldecott Honor Book prize with three of his other books, *Blueberries for Sal* (1949), *One Morning in Maine* (1953), and *Journey Cake, Ho!* (1954). In 2000, the Library of Congress named McCloskey one of the country's "Living Legends" for his creative contributions to American life.

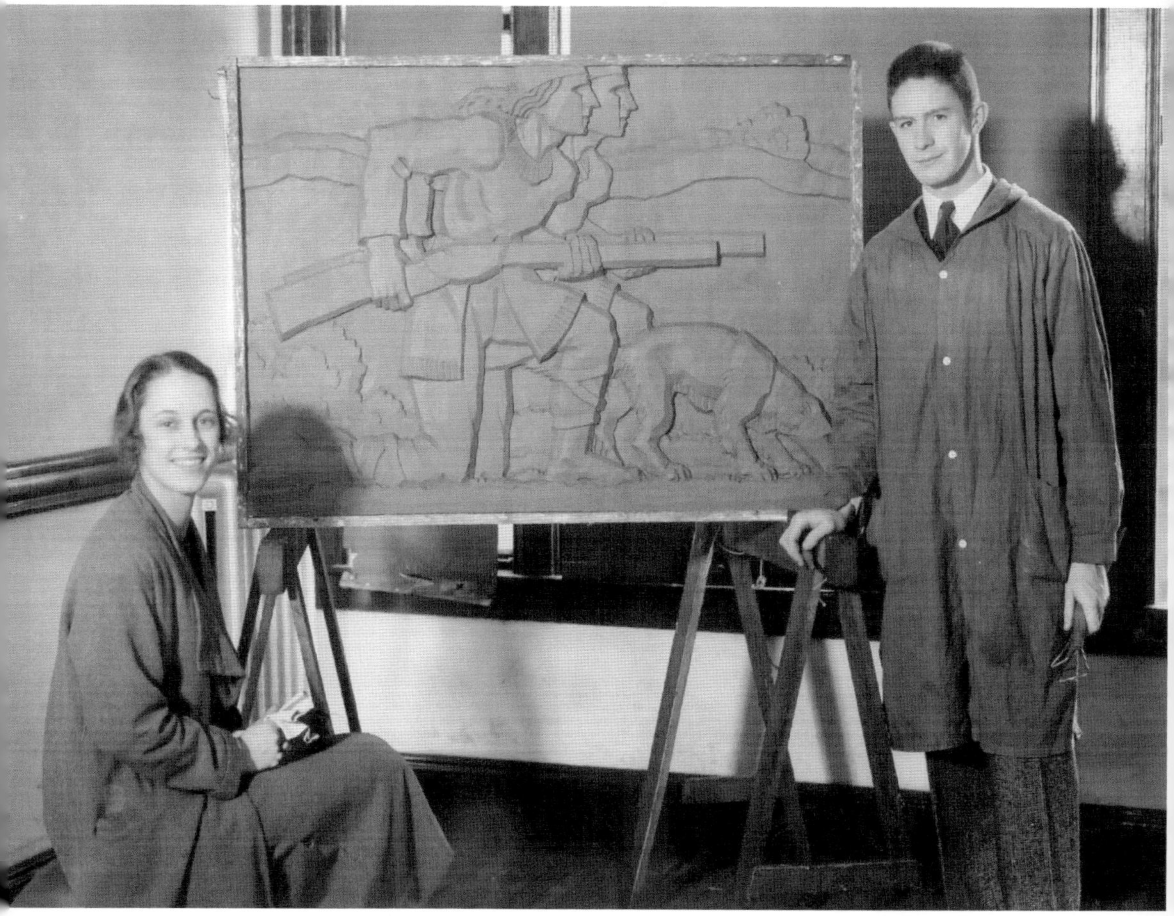

Alta Harvey Heiser

Beginning in 1934, Heiser (1877–1970), who operated Heiser's Flower Shop with her husband, Karl, wrote about gardening in her "Hamilton Garden Club" column for the *Journal News*. In 1936, she began a local history column, "Butler County History." Both ended in 1967 when she had a stroke and moved to a nursing home. Heiser wrote three valuable local history books, *Hamilton in the Making*, *Quaker Lady*, and *West to Ohio*, and coauthored the *History of the Woods Family*. She always referred to her writing as "a hobby."

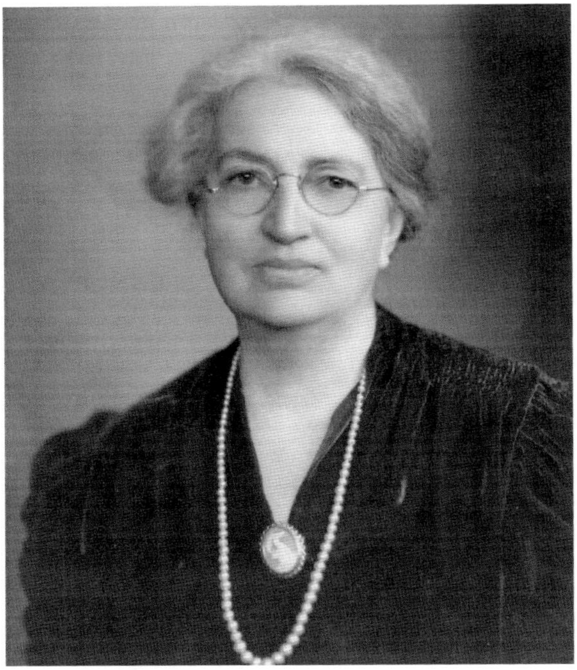

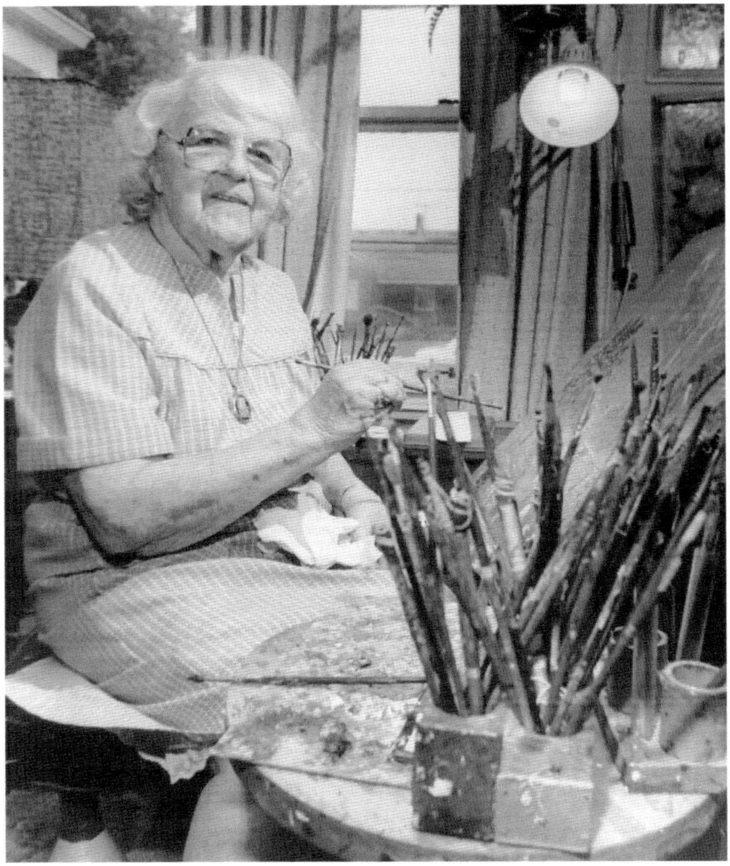

Nan Phelps

Folk artist Nan Phelps (1904–1990) was a prolific painter who worked continuously for over 60 years, producing more than 1,000 paintings. She moved to Hamilton in 1922 and continued painting through the Depression, a divorce, remarriage, and while raising five children. Phelps painted landscapes, still lifes, beach scenes, portraits, and historical figures in a style compared to Grandma Moses. Her work has been exhibited in galleries in Cincinnati, Boston, New York City, Japan, West Germany, Finland, and Denmark.

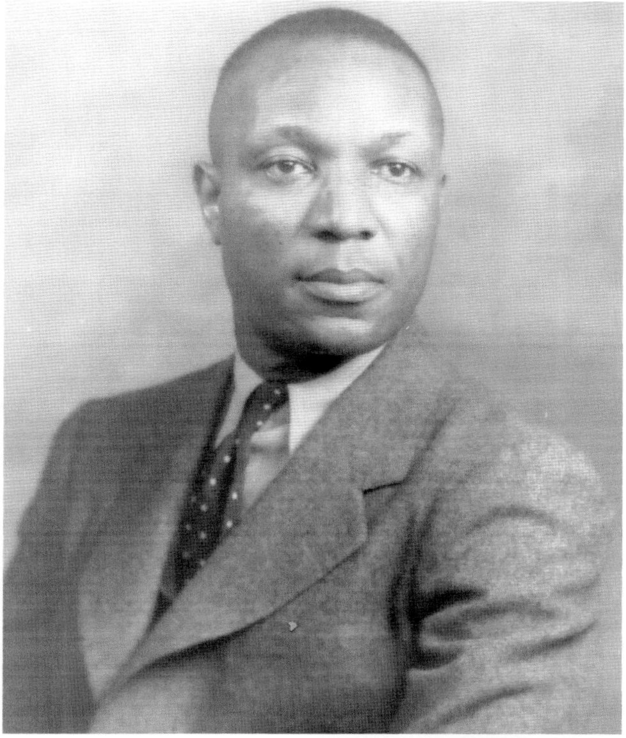

Alvin D. Smith
As editor and publisher of the weekly Butler County *American*, Smith (1899–1968) claimed to be "Fighting for Our Free Enterprise System of Government" and providing his readers with "Truth In News, In Editorials, In Advertising." He published the paper from 1940 to 1968. Smith ran for city council in 1943 and for the state senate in 1944, but did not win election. He is credited with suggesting the name for the city's Bamboo Harris housing development in 1942.

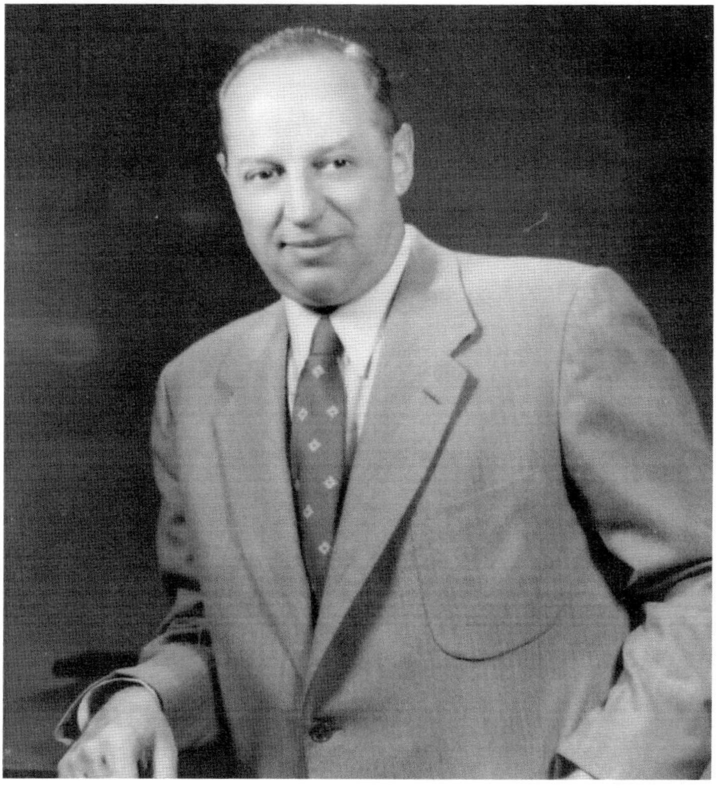

George C. Cummins
Cummins (1903–1980) accumulated an outstanding collection of Indian relics, guns, books, and more than 7,000 historic photographs concerning Hamilton and Butler County while he was a practicing attorney. In 1934, he was one of the three founders of the Butler County Historical Society. Cummins began his popular *Journal News* "Remember When" historical photograph feature in 1951. He donated much of his collection to the historical society, and the Lane Library named its local history and genealogical center in his honor.

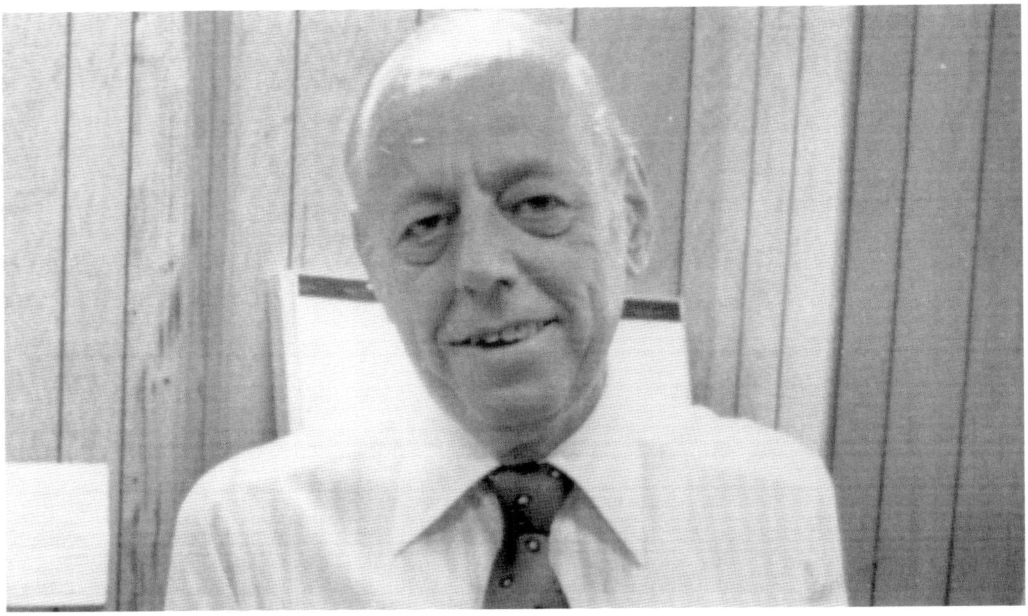

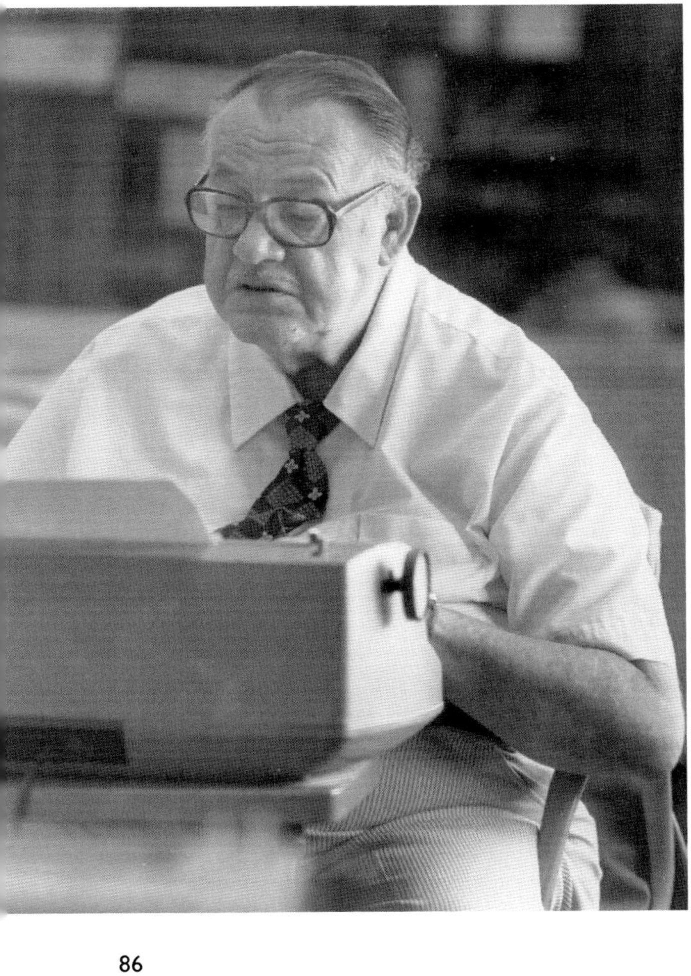

Bill Moeller
After graduating from Hamilton Catholic High in 1936, Moeller (1918–1993) began his 57-year career at the *Journal News* by covering high school sports. He worked on the paper's city desk and police beat until 1942, when he became sports editor. Moeller started writing his popular "Bill's Board" daily sports commentary column in 1945 and continued editing the *Journal News* sports pages until his death in 1993. In 1982, he cofounded the Butler County Sports Hall of Fame with *Middletown Journal* sports editor Jerry Nardiello.

Bill McDulin
Before McDulin graduated from Hamilton High in 1939, he coached the *Journal News* carriers baseball teams to the 1937 and 1938 city championship. After World War II, he covered high school sports and announced games for radio station WMOH-AM and then became a staff reporter for the *Journal News*. During the 1950s, he covered the city hall and police beats before moving to the newspaper's editorial staff. McDulin wrote the paper's popular "Got a Minute?" and "Sunday Sketchbook" features.

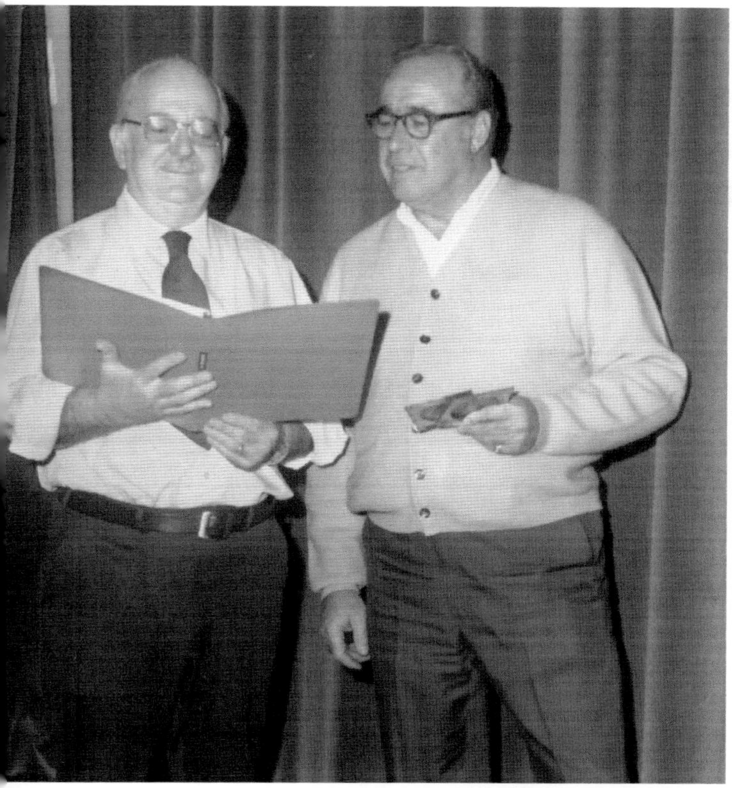

Rotary Revels
The 1973 staging of the musical *1776* was the 20th anniversary Rotary Revels production, staged by the Hamilton Rotary Club. Begun in 1953 as an activity to help raise funds for the charitable work of the club, each production involves up to 200 people. Seen here are lighting director Harold B. Frye (left) and coproducer Jack Smith. Both men had been involved in all 20 previous Rotary Revels productions.

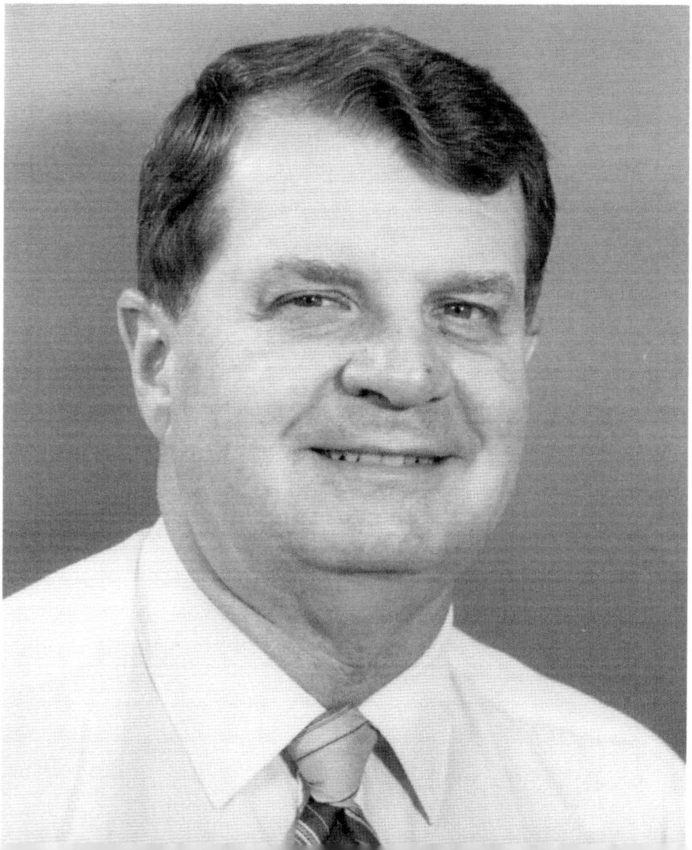

Jim Blount
After college, Blount (1936–) returned to Hamilton as a counselor, history teacher, scout, and head track coach for the city schools. He was the press box announcer for the Cincinnati Bengals from 1968 to 2009 and a member of the *Journal News* staff for 23 years, editing the paper from 1971 to 1986. He returned to teaching and was named Teacher of the Year in 1992 and Citizen of the Year in 2005. Blount has written several local history books. The Hamilton Community Foundation named its Jim Blount History Educator Award in his honor.

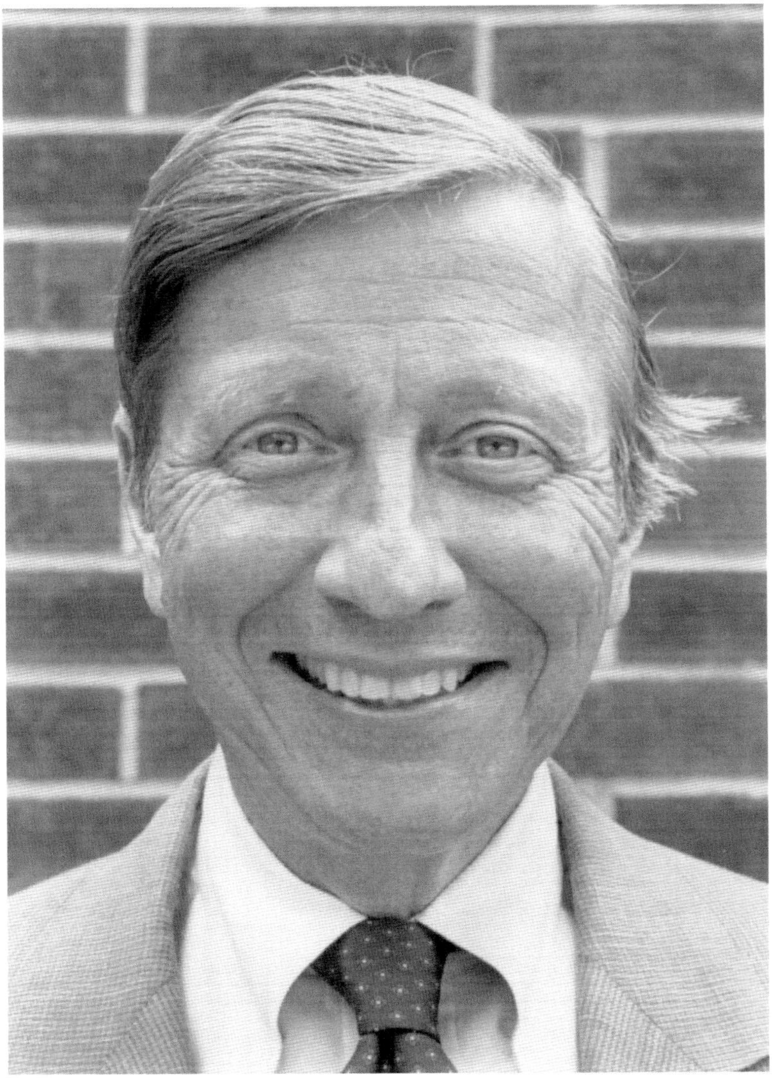

William H. Rentschler

Rentschler (1925–2009) was a widely published columnist, author, politician, and entrepreneur who moved away from Hamilton in 1949 and lived most of his adult life near Chicago. Among his early business ventures was serving as chairman of Stevens Candy Kitchens and Martha Washington Candy Kitchens and founding Candy Gram, Inc., a nationwide candy telegram service. He wrote freelance articles, op-ed pieces, sports essays, and contributed columns for a variety of newspapers, including the *Chicago Sun-Times*, *Minneapolis Star and Tribune*, *Cincinnati Times-Star*, *San Francisco Progress*, and the *Hamilton Journal News*. Rentschler wrote three books and published two collections of his newspaper columns. He was nominated for several Pulitzer Prizes but did not win. He was, however, named the "Top U.S. Columnist" in 1996 by the National Society of Newspaper Columnists. Rentschler was a Republican US Senate candidate in 1960 and 1970 and headed the re-election campaign in Illinois for Richard Nixon. After serving as a special advisor to Nixon's National Program for Voluntary Action, he abandoned his Republican roots to support the Democratic Party. In 2000, Rentschler returned to Hamilton, the town where he said he had an "ideal boyhood," and became actively involved in community activities and contributed frequent columns to the *Journal News*.

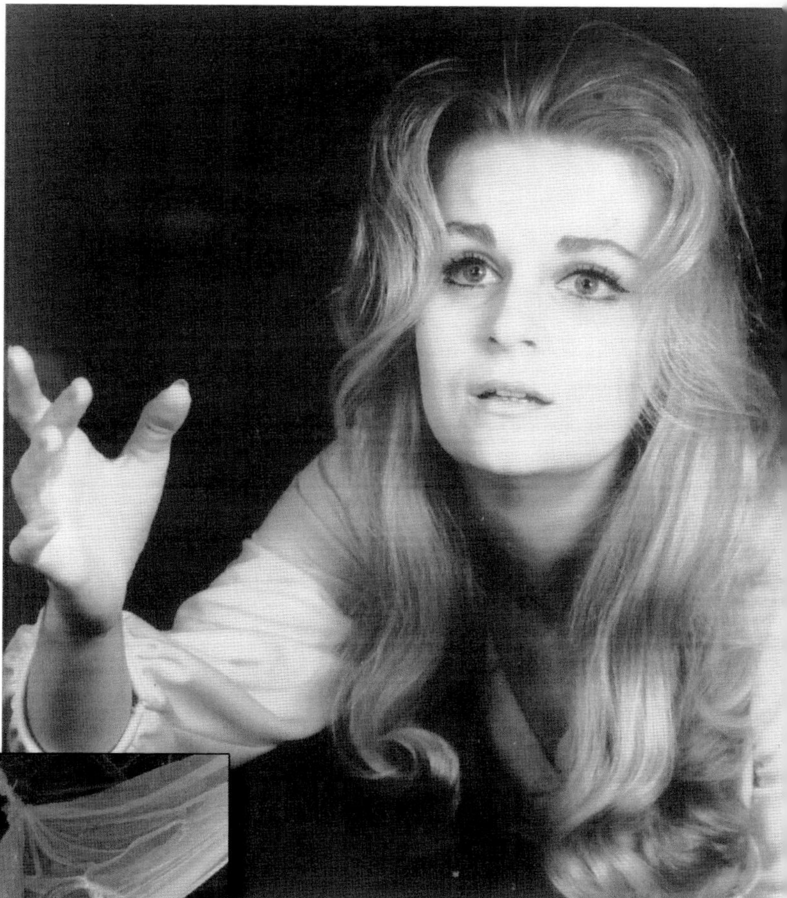

Bess Arlene Camacho
Camacho, a frequent and popular performer and soloist in Hamilton-Fairfield Symphony concerts, won the 1971 American Opera auditions. The renowned soprano has appeared at New York's Carnegie Hall and the Metropolitan Opera. She has performed in operas staged in Germany, France, Italy, Denmark, Austria, Canada, and several other countries. Camacho (1941–) has won awards for her performances in local musical comedy productions and is a respected music teacher at Miami University–Hamilton.

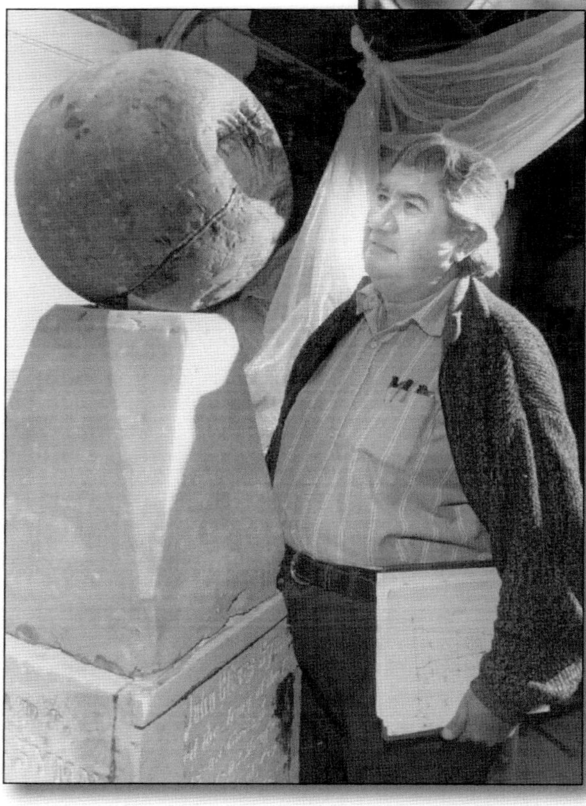

Edgar Tarfur
Hamiltonian Tarfur (1929–) created his soaring *Space Tower* sculpture for the Cincinnati Playhouse in the Park in 1970. The piece was later moved from Eden Park to Hamilton's Peter R. Rentschler Park. Historic Hamilton, Inc., commissioned Tarfur to restore the John Cleves Symmes monument, as a bicentennial gift to the City of Hamilton in 1991. Other works created by this talented sculptor include the Ondulation Column at the Oklahoma City Museum of Art.

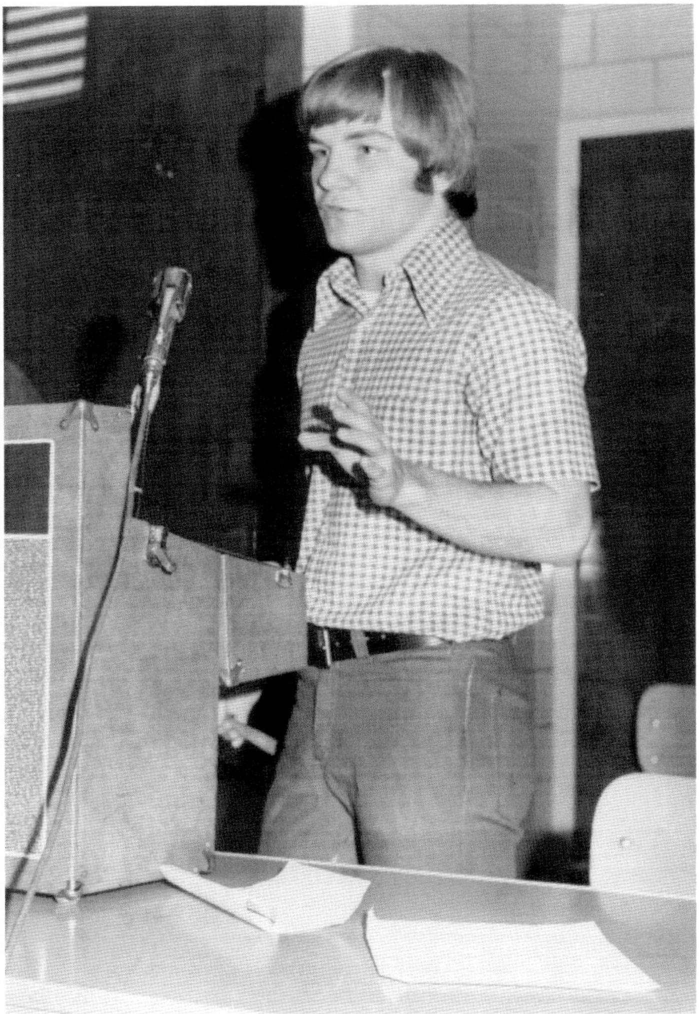

Ray Combs

Hamilton-born Raymond Neil Combs (1956–1996), seen here chairing a high school assembly meeting, was president of Garfield High School's 1973–1974 senior class. Combs was a popular member of the Hamilton Boys and Girls Club and was the group's Boy of the Year in 1974. After graduating from Garfield, Combs turned down a nomination to the US Military Academy at West Point to serve a two-year Mormon mission in Arizona. He married Debra Jo Mink, his childhood sweetheart, in 1977, and together the couple had six children. Ray wanted to pursue a career as a professional comedian, and moved his family to Los Angeles in 1982. He became the warm-up performer for studio audiences of several TV shows and made appearances in *The Golden Girls*, *Hollywood Squares*, *The Facts of Life*, and on *The Tonight Show Starring Johnny Carson*. In 1988, he began a six-year run as the host of *The New Family Feud* game show and was nominated for a 1993 Daytime Emmy award for Outstanding Game Show Host. Ray's luck changed in 1994 when he was seriously injured in a car accident and lost his TV contract. Combs and his wife separated in 1995, reconciled, and then refilled for divorce. He threatened suicide and police were called to his home on June 1, 1996. Combs was admitted to a psychiatric ward at a Glendale, California, medical center for observation. On June 2, he hung himself in his room after fashioning a noose from bedsheets. Ray's six children ranged in age from five to eighteen when he died. He was buried in Hamilton's Greenwood Cemetery. The city renamed Alsace Avenue, Ray Combs Avenue in 2010. (Courtesy of Hamilton City School District.)

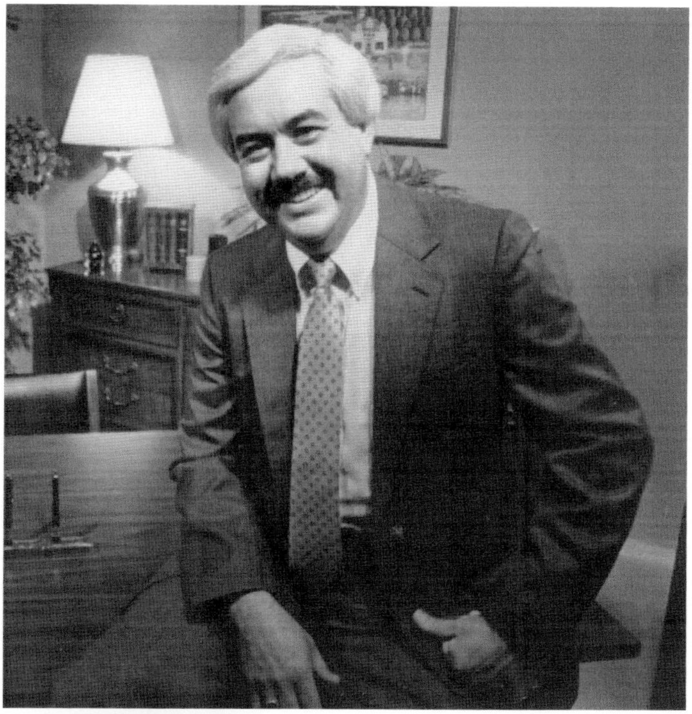

Jack Armstrong
In 1988, Armstrong was named to create a new Hamilton community television channel to help the city government better communicate with residents. As director and creative head of TvHamilton for 21 years, Armstrong (1944–) produced more than 900 programs, each one focused on some aspect of life in Hamilton. He did so with antiquated equipment, a low budget, and a few volunteers. After he retired in 2009, he became president of the Hamilton Visitor's Bureau. Armstrong was named to the school district's Fine Arts Hall of Fame in 2004.

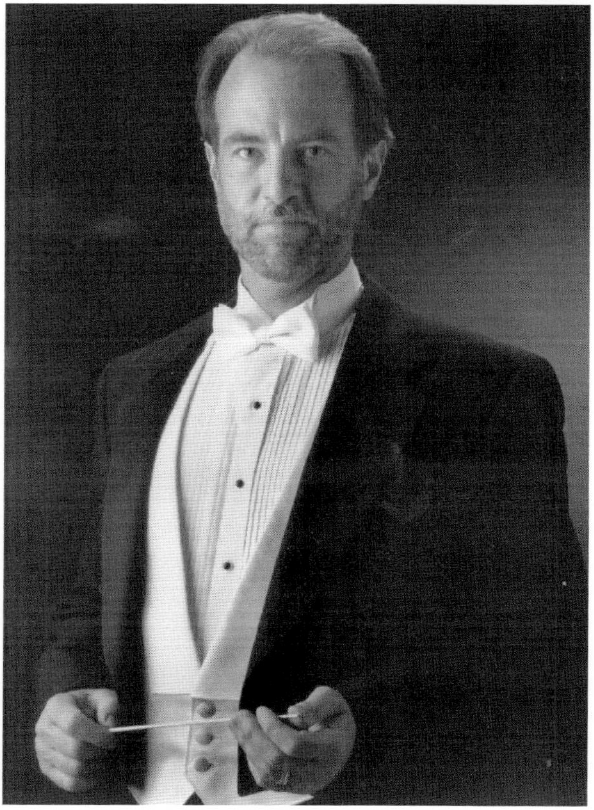

Paul John Stanbery
When Stanbery (1954–) became music director of the Hamilton-Fairfield Symphony in 1995, it was giving only one performance a year. He founded the Ohio Mozart Festival, which has given several hundred presentations of Mozart music. In addition, he increased the 75-member symphony's number of performances to as many as 10 or 12 annually and formed the 90-voice Symphony Chorale in 1997. Stanbery also founded the Blue Ash–Montgomery Symphony in 1986 and the Clermont Philharmonic Orchestra in 1997. He won the Post-Corbett Award for Performing Arts in 2005.

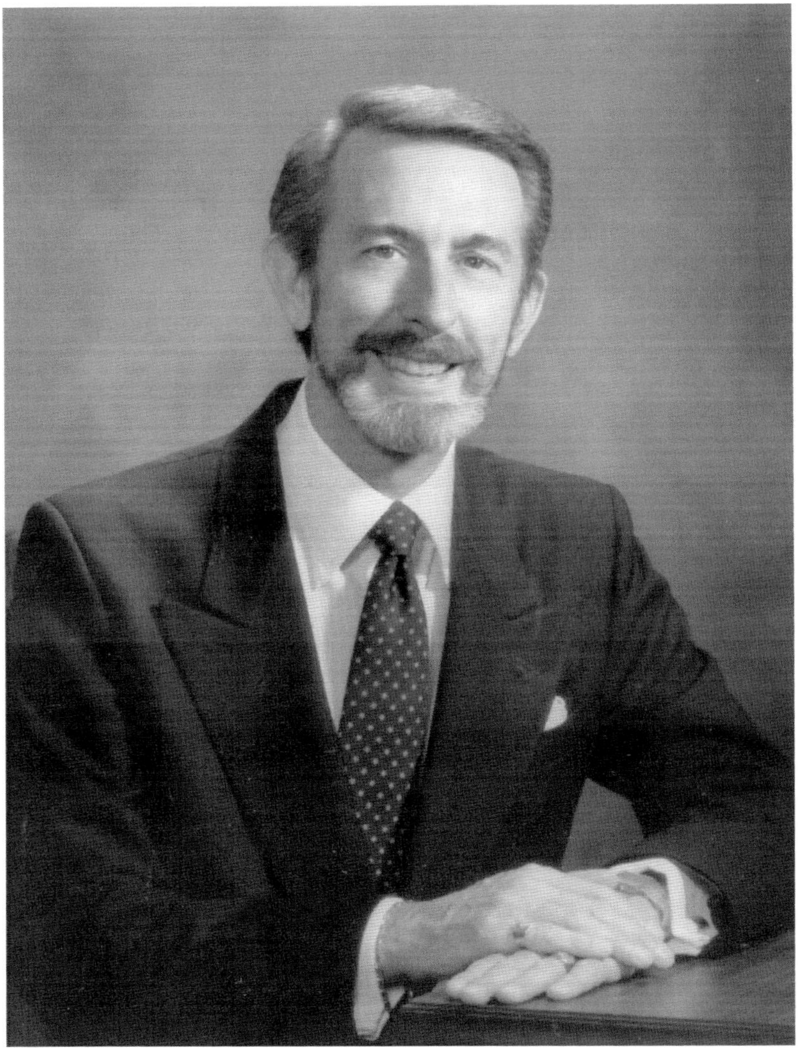

Paul Thoms

Thoms was one of the founders and a former president of the Rossville Historic Preservation Association, which worked to get the Rossville Historic District listed in the National Register of Historic Places in 1975. He has been actively involved in several community organizations and has been a board member of the Fitton Center for Creative Arts, Hamilton Fine Arts Council, Hamilton-Fairfield Symphony Orchestra, Hamilton Civic Music Association, Historic Hamilton!, and Sister Cities of Hamilton, Inc. Thoms (1936–) served in the Fairfield School District for 32 years: as district music coordinator and choral conductor for 22 of those years and as curriculum coordinator and community relations director for 10 years. In 1966, he founded the nationally acclaimed Fairfield Choraliers show choir, which gave as many as 100 performances each year. Thoms has written more than 100 articles (printed in over 30 publications) on the topic of education. He has won several regional, national, and international service awards and honors, including being named one of the "Ten Most Outstanding School Music Directors in the United States and Canada" by *School Musician* magazine. After he retired from public education, he served as director of public relations for the Fitton Center for Creative Arts from 1996 to 2006. Thoms, a multitalented musician, has performed in operas, musical comedies, oratorios, choral masterworks, and plays, and has been a longtime member of the Hamilton-Fairfield Symphony Orchestra Chorale.

CHAPTER SIX

Champion Athletes

Hamilton has taken great pride in the accomplishment of its sports teams, especially the city's high school basketball and football teams. During the decades when manufacturing companies dominated the local economy, nearly every plant and several merchants sponsored athletic teams. In recent years, residents have enjoyed the success of the town's Little League squads. Several athletes participated at the level required by professional sports franchises. Among the stars in the sports arena, many of them inducted into local halls of fame, are coaches, players, and state championship teams.

Starting in 1885, Jacob Milders coached and managed several amateur and quasi-professional baseball teams, including the team sponsored by George Krebs and his clothing store. Much more recently, Ray Nichting coached Hamilton's youth and Little League teams for more than 45 years.

There have been several legendary football and basketball coaches in the city's schools. Dana King coached Hamilton High football, basketball, and track teams for more than 15 years and led college and professional teams for several years. Lewis Hirt directed the high school basketball team to the 1937 state championship. Ray Tilton was a Big Blue football coach before becoming Butler County auditor. John Pont had coached at several universities before coaching the Big Blue.

Among the high school coaches with especially long careers are the following: Chuck Thackara, who led Hamilton High football teams for 28 years; Lou Florio, who coached at Garfield High for 18 years and Taft High for two years; Marvin McCallum, the highly admired coach at Taft for 20 years; and Warren Scholler, for 10 years the basketball coach at Hamilton High before becoming coach at Bowling Green State University. Perhaps most astonishing were the accomplishments of Terry Malone, who coached teams at Hamilton Catholic High and Badin High for a combined 45 years.

Frank Clair left the United States and made his career coaching 19 seasons in the Canadian Football League, winning several professional championships.

Hamilton's legendary athletes include Paul Sarringhaus, the best high school football player in the state in 1937, who had a short career in the National Football League; Joe Nuxhall, a Cincinnati Reds pitcher and broadcaster; Bill Wilks, leader of the Hamilton High 1949 state championship basketball team; Boo Ellis, one of the stars of the 1954 state champion basketball team; and architect Derek Howard, who played in two Rose Bowl games while attending the University of Michigan.

Two legendary local athletes participated in less popular sports. Mary Bowermaster held a large number of national and world track-and-field records for athletes aged older than 65. Darrell Pace won Olympic gold medals, several national championships, and world titles in archery.

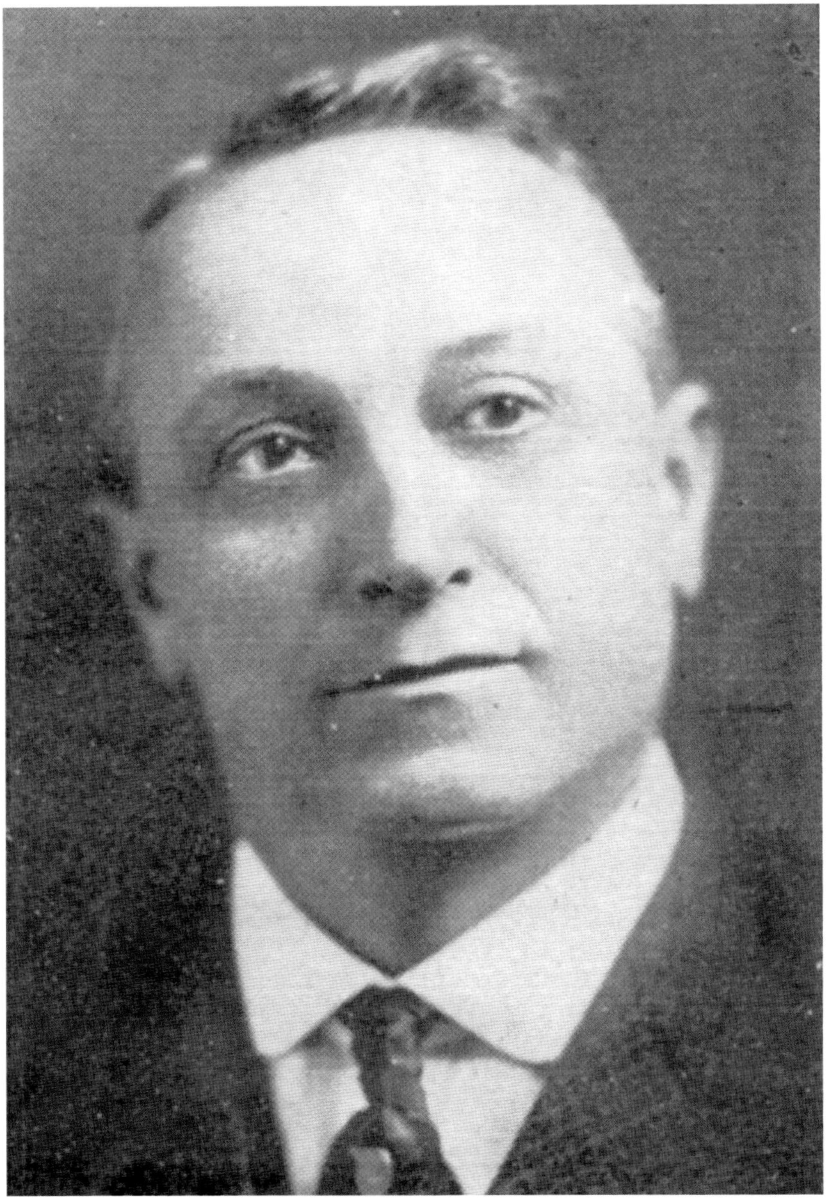

Jacob Milders

Milders was a pioneering advocate of baseball in Hamilton. He organized and coached teams named the Hamilton Kids, Hamilton Clippers, and Hamilton Browns from 1884 to 1897. He started the Krebs baseball team in 1898. Milders built the Krebs Ball Park, a stadium with a grandstand seating 1,200 with bleachers for 800, at the end of High Street on the east side of town. In 1906, Milders (1869–1935), a member of the Hamilton school board for five years and circulation manager of the *Journal News* for 17 years, also built the Coliseum sports center in Rossville. The Coliseum was used for dancing, music events, roller-skating, basketball games, and polo. The building was washed away by the 1913 flood and crashed into the Columbia Bridge, causing the bridge to collapse. After the flood, Milders purchased Meyer's Village Café at Symmes Corners in 1914 and opened Milders Inn. The popular restaurant remained in business until 1942.

Dana M. King

King (1890–1952) coached the Hamilton High football team in 1917 and, after serving in World War I, returned to coach football, basketball, track, and baseball from 1919 to 1929. His undefeated 1929 football team won the state championship. During the 1920s, he served five years as Hamilton's recreation director. King was head coach at the University of Cincinnati from 1931 to 1934, compiling a 25-10-1 record, and served as athletic director until 1936. He had an 8-14-2 record as head coach and general manager of the Cincinnati Bengals of the American Football League, from 1939 to 1941, before the league disbanded. King returned to coach Big Blue teams from 1942 to 1946. Over 16 seasons at Hamilton High, his football teams won 105, lost 26, and tied eight, and his basketball teams won 148 games and lost 59. King retired in 1947. In 1984, he was elected to the Butler County Sports Hall of Fame. (Courtesy of Hamilton City School District.)

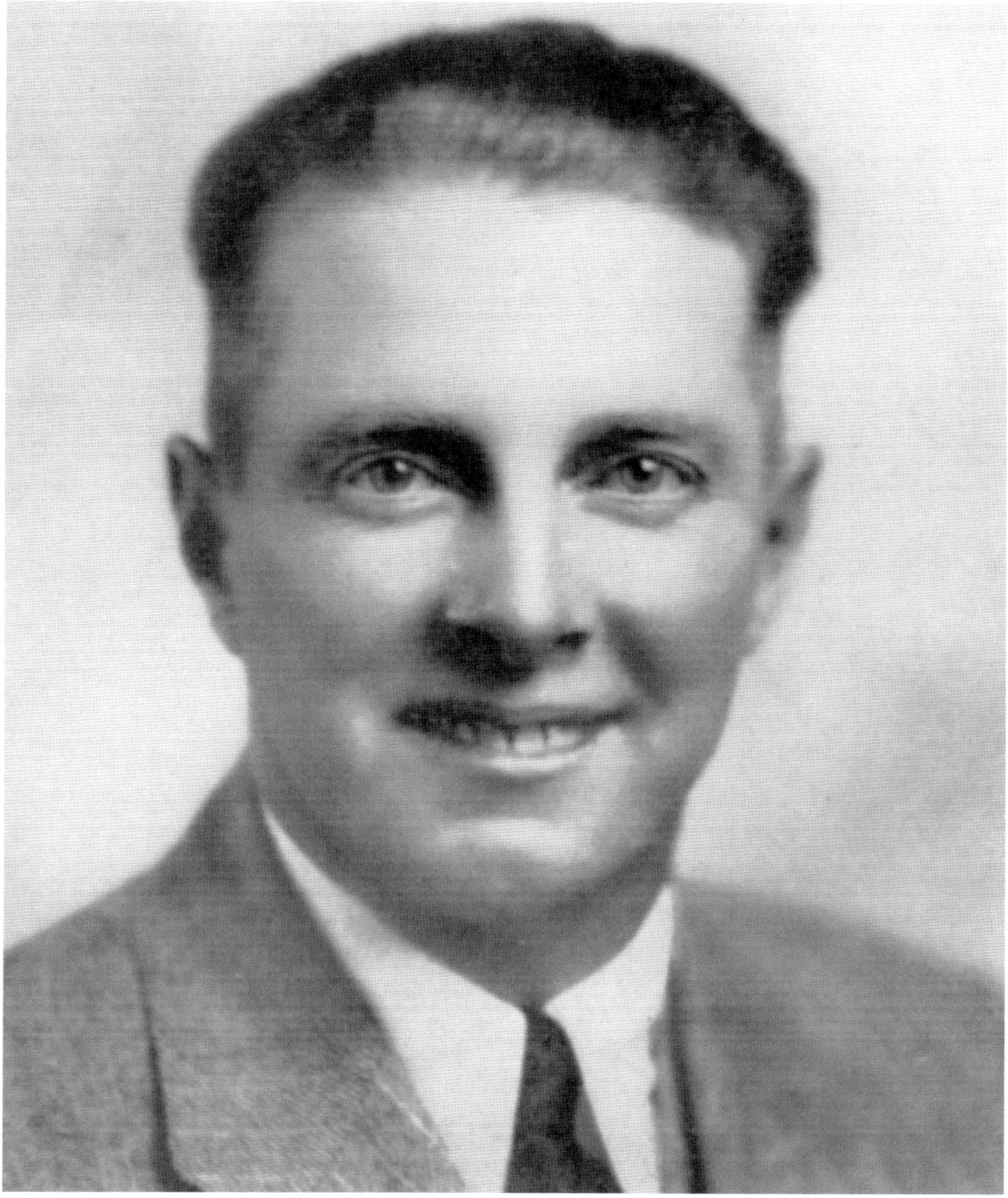

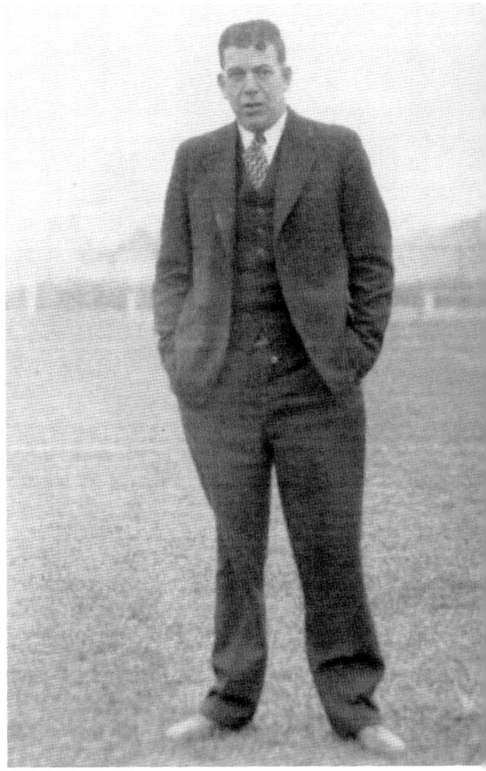

Lewis Hirt

Hirt coached Hamilton High's football teams from 1930 to 1934 and the school's basketball teams from 1930 to 1938. His football teams won 16 games, lost 17, and tied three, while his basketball squads had a 134-42 record. Hirt's 1937 basketball team was undefeated in 24 games and won the state championship. He was the first coach to allow black athletes to play on the high school's teams. Hirt (1901–1977) coached two years at Hamilton Catholic High before becoming head coach at Xavier University in 1946. (Courtesy of Hamilton City School District.)

1937 Hamilton High Basketball Team

The 1937 Hamilton High School basketball team was the first Big Blue team to win a state championship. The team capped an undefeated season with its 24th win, a 37-32 victory over the Massillon Washington High School team, coached by the legendary Paul Brown. Shown here are, from left to right, (first row) Clifton Towles, Louis Beers, Garlund Munz, Vernon Deinzer, and Carl Ott; (second row) Marvin Pettit (manager), Warren Scholler, James Frechtling, Chester Lairson, "Si" Johnson, Keith Gallacher, and Lewis Hirt (coach).

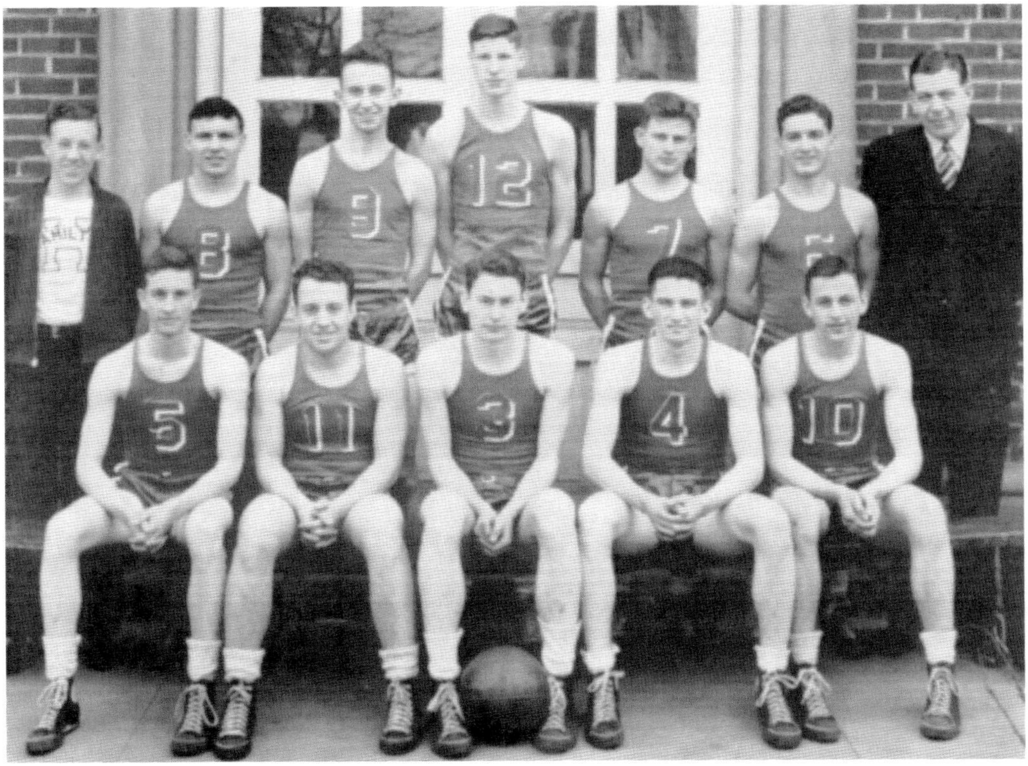

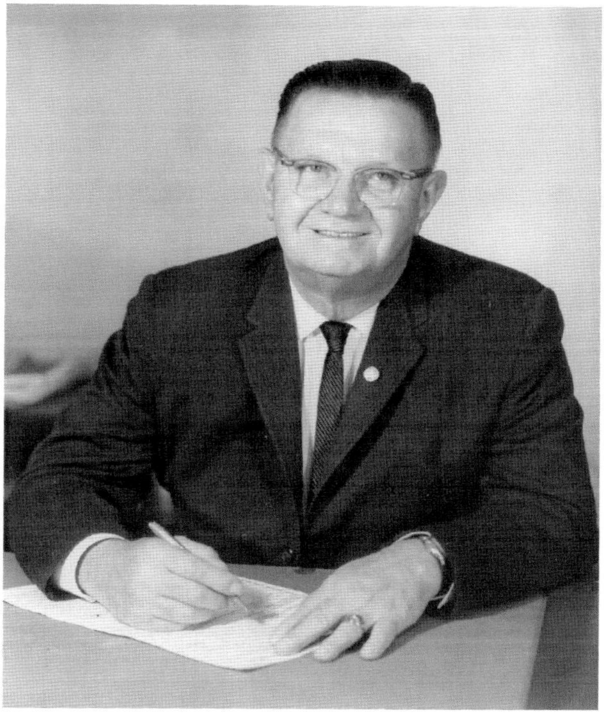

Arthur "Ray" Tilton

In 1929, Tilton joined the Hamilton High staff and served as an assistant football coach for Dana King and Lewis Hirt until 1934. He was the school's head coach from 1934 to 1942. Tilton's 1935 and 1939 teams were undefeated and won Ohio state championships. During his eight years as head football coach, his teams won 60 games, lost 10, and tied four. Tilton (1900–1978) resigned his position with the school district and became an accounting professor at Xavier University. From 1958 to 1974, he served as Butler County auditor.

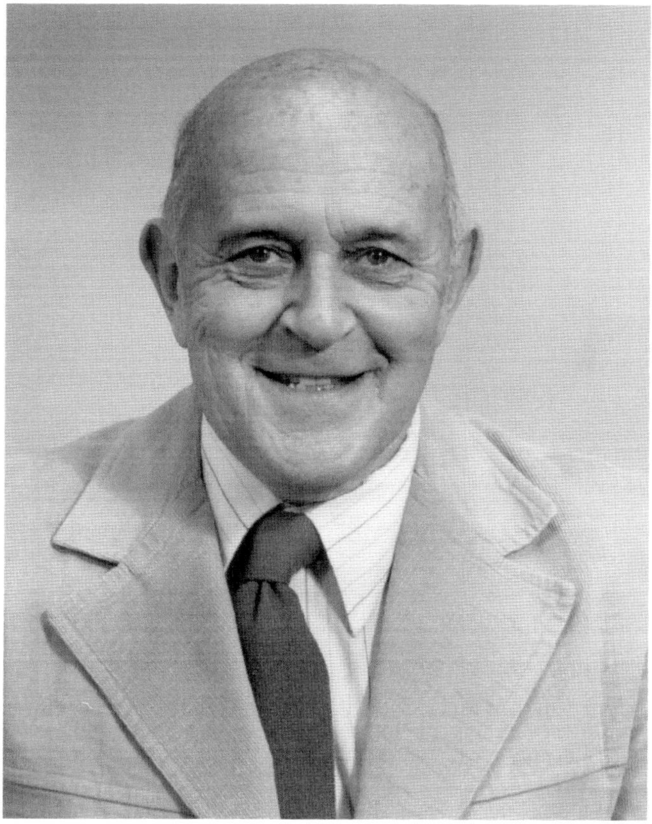

Charles "Chuck" Thackara

Thackara began his 28-year career in the Hamilton schools as coach of the 1948 football team that compiled a 10-1 record and ranked third in the state. His teams won 61 games, lost 25, and tied three over nine seasons. Thackara (1917–2008) was the first high school coach to put face masks on his players' helmets. He became athletic director, principal of Harding Junior High, and worked for 12 years as an assistant superintendent before retiring in 1976. Thackara was named Citizen of the Year by the Hamilton Chamber of Commerce in 1997.

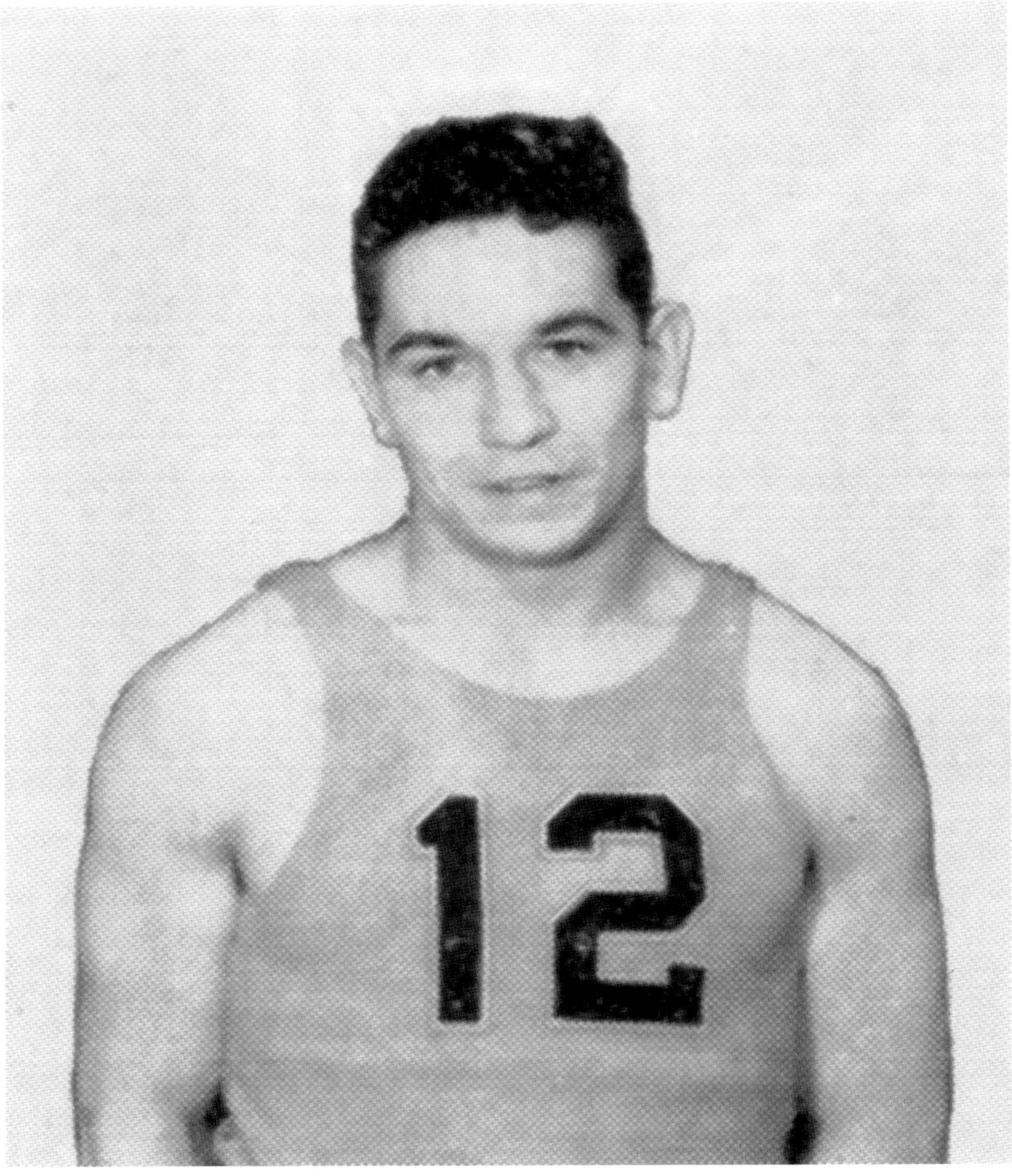

Paul Sarringhaus

Sarringhaus was captain of coach Ray Tilton's undefeated 1939 state championship football team. He was named Mr. Football, the best player in the state, that year. He also played on the 1938 Big Blue basketball team that was runner-up in the state tournament, and ran the 100- and 200-yard dashes for the track team. At Ohio State, Sarringhaus was a first-team All-American and All–Big Ten halfback on Paul Brown's 1942 national championship team. His college career was interrupted by World War II. When he returned in 1945 for his senior year, he was featured on the cover of *Life* magazine as Ohio State's star halfback. Sarringhaus (1920–1998) played professional football for two years, but injuries shortened his NFL career. He returned to Hamilton to begin a business career and served as a deputy auditor in the Butler County auditor's office.

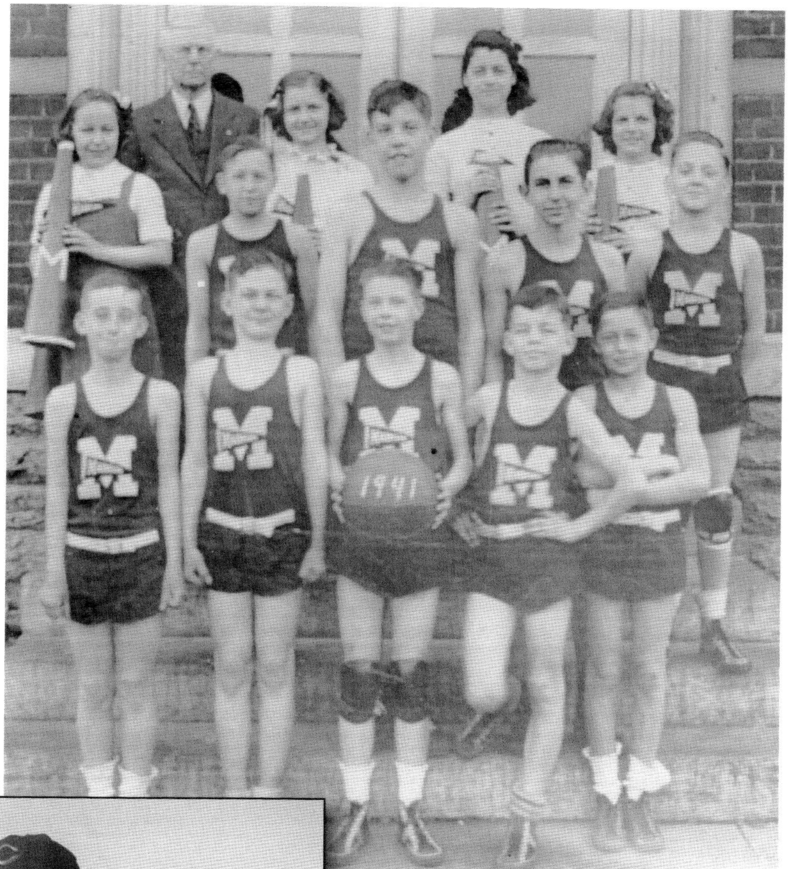

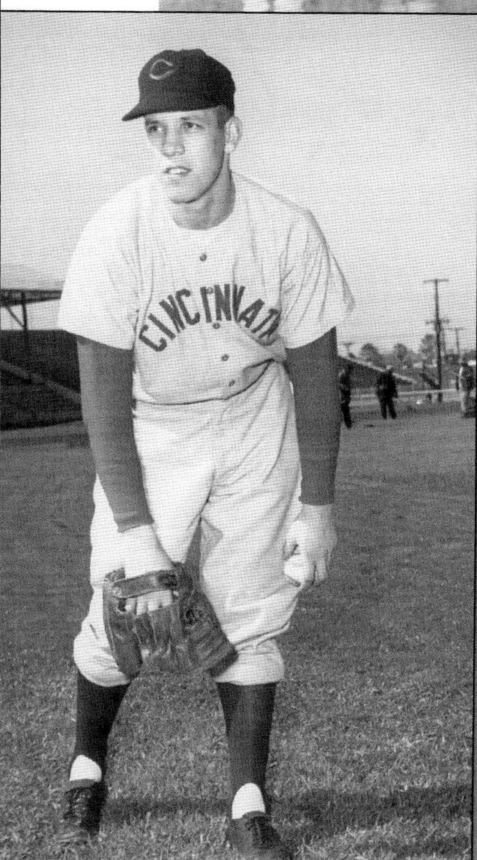

Joe Nuxhall

The athletic prowess of Joe Nuxhall (1928–2007) appeared at an early age. In 1941, he played on the grade-school championship basketball team from Madison School. Shown in the above photograph are, from left to right, (first row) Joseph Riggle, Earl Jones, John Townley, Earl Piegart, and Richard Apgar; (second row) Carolyn Jane Antenen, Harold Cook, Joseph Henry Nuxhall, Eldon Withrow, and unidentified; (third row) Principal N.B. Lamonda, Jean Withrow, Patty Newman, and Mary Jo Davidson. Three years later, in 1944, Nuxhall became the youngest player to appear in the major leagues when he pitched in a game for the Cincinnati Reds. He returned to Hamilton High, regained his amateur status in 1946, played football, basketball, and baseball, and earned all-state honors in football and basketball. In 1952, Nuxhall rejoined the Reds as a player and had a 16-year major-league career, compiling a pitching record of 135-117. He was a two-time National League all-star. In 1967, Nuxhall retired as a player and began a 40-year career as a Reds radio broadcaster.

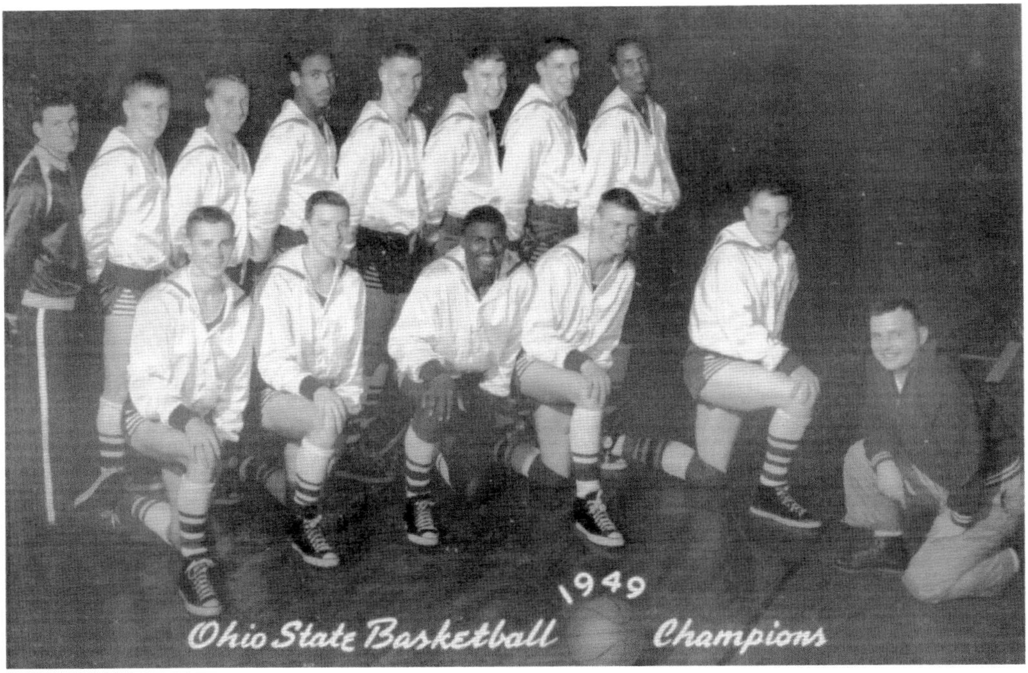

1949 Hamilton High Basketball Team
Shown here is the Hamilton High School 1949 state championship basketball team. The players and staff are, from left to right, (first row) Bernie Griesinger, Don Wieche, Jim Bailey, Bill Wilks, Eugene Baldwin, and coach Warren Scholler; (second row) manager Elgene Mainous, Joe Okruhlica, Don Knodel, Ike Wells, Lowell Kiger, Joe McGuire, George Janetos, and Bob "Pappy" Smith. The team won the championship with a 70-52 win over Toledo Central High School and finished the year with a record of 25-1.

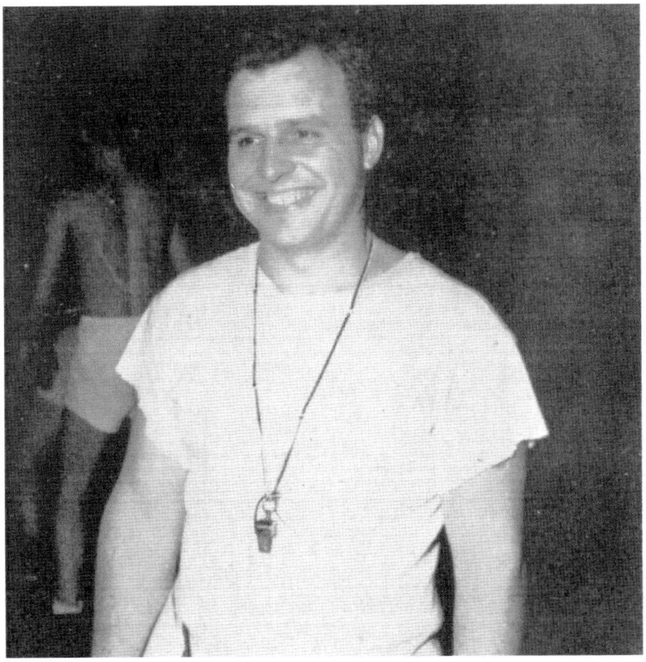

Warren Scholler
Scholler won three state championships with Hamilton High's basketball team—one as a player on coach Lewis Hirt's undefeated 1937 team, and two (1949 and 1954) as the Big Blue's head coach. During his 10 seasons as coach, his teams won six league championships and had a 195-45 win-loss record. Scholler (1920–2010) left the district in 1958 to coach for Bowling Green State University, including serving as head basketball coach during the 1963 to 1967 seasons. He retired from the university in 1984.

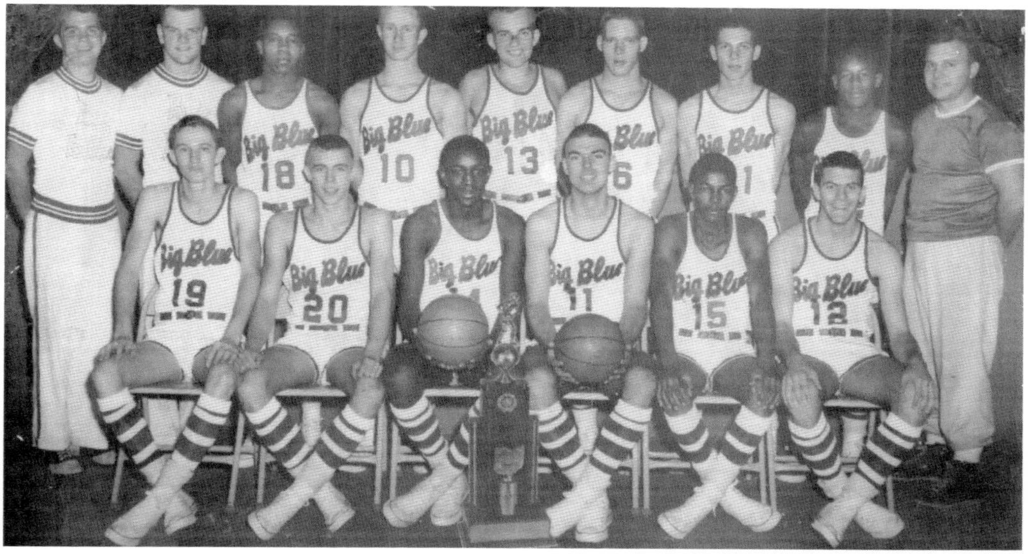

1954 Hamilton High Basketball Team
In 1954, for a third time, a Hamilton High basketball team won the state championship. The team's record during the season was 25-3. Big Blue defeated Columbus South High School in the championship game, 66-56. Team players and staff are, from left to right, (first row) Bob Sweeten, John Bercaw, Alex Ellis, Philip Phelps, Bob Henderson, and Rusty Bowermaster; (second row) manager Ronald Riley, trainer Lowell Strong, John Rogers, Dave Allen, John Holcomb, Woody Herzog, Bob Crist, Doug Rogers, and coach Warren Scholler. (Courtesy of Hamilton City School District.)

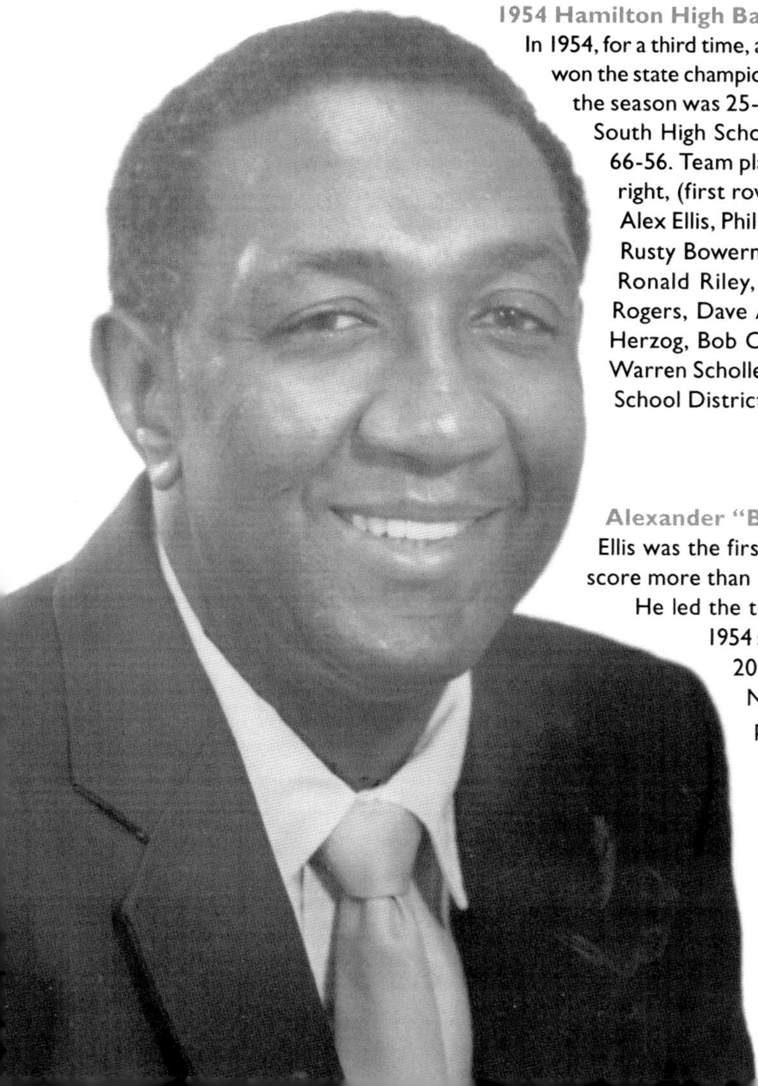

Alexander "Boo" Ellis
Ellis was the first Big Blue basketball player to score more than 1,000 points during his career. He led the team to a 25-3 record and the 1954 state championship. Ellis (1936–2010) played college basketball at Niagara University and began his professional career as a member of the Minneapolis Lakers of the NBA in 1958. He played six years in the Continental League and three seasons with the Fabulous Harlem Magicians, a traveling team that featured Marcus Haynes.

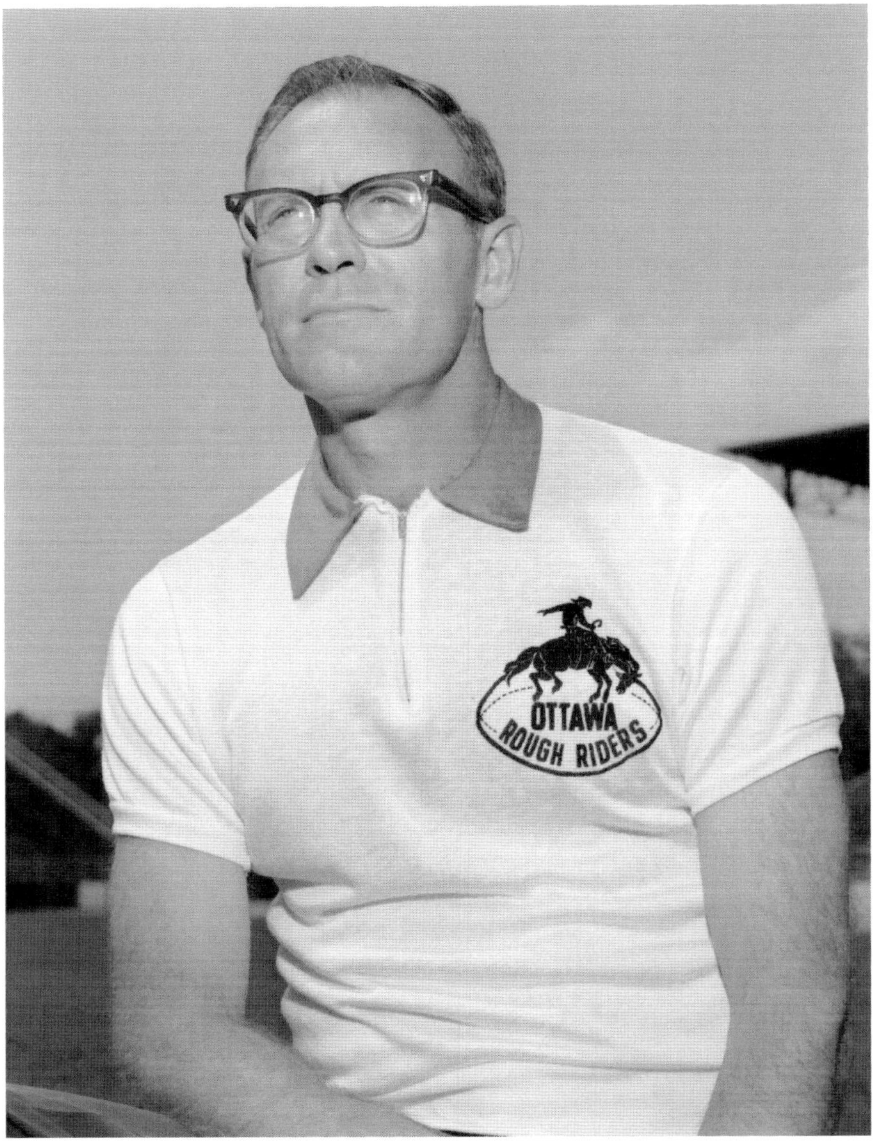

Frank Clair

Clair was captain of the Hamilton High 1935 state champion football team. After playing at Ohio State University and for the Washington Redskins of the NFL, he coached at Miami University, Purdue, and the University of Buffalo. Clair (1917–2005) became the head coach of the Toronto Argonauts in 1950 and led the team to the Grey Cup title. He coached in the Canadian Football League (CFL) for 19 seasons and led teams to the playoffs in 17 of those years. His teams won five Grey Cup championships, two by the Toronto Argonauts and three by the Ottawa Rough Riders. Clair was the general manager of the Ottawa franchise from 1970 to 1978 and saw his team win two more Grey Cups. As a coach, Clair's teams won 174 games, lost 156, and tied nine. He was the CFL's Coach of the Year twice and was named to the Canadian Football League Hall of Fame in 1981. The football stadium in Ottawa's Lansdowne Park was named the Frank Clair Stadium in his honor. Clair was elected to the Butler County Sports Hall of Fame in 1985 and the Hamilton City School District Athletic Hall of Fame in 1997. (Courtesy of Ted Grant/Image Communications.ca.)

Lou Florio

From 1957 to 1976, Florio (1926–) coached the Hamilton High football team for two seasons and Garfield High's team for 18 years. His combined record as a coach was 97-99-1. He also was principal of Harding and the reunited Hamilton High. In 1982, Florio saved two statues from the old Hamilton High during its demolition and took them to Florida when he retired in 1989. One of the rescued statues was the white carrera marble Venus de Milo purchased by the American History Club in 1928 with money earned by sponsoring a Will Rogers visit. In 2008, Florio returned the two statues to Hamilton, where they are on display in the Robert McCloskey Museum in Heritage Hall at the Frederick G. Mueller Building.

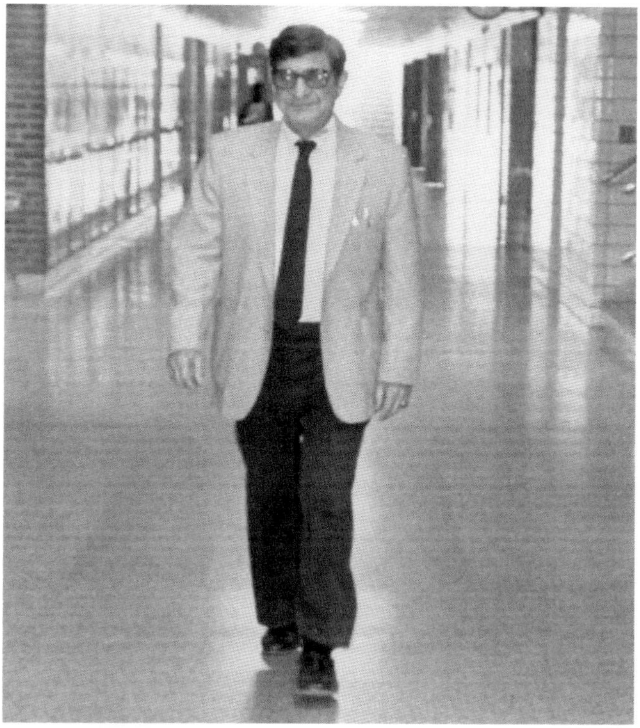

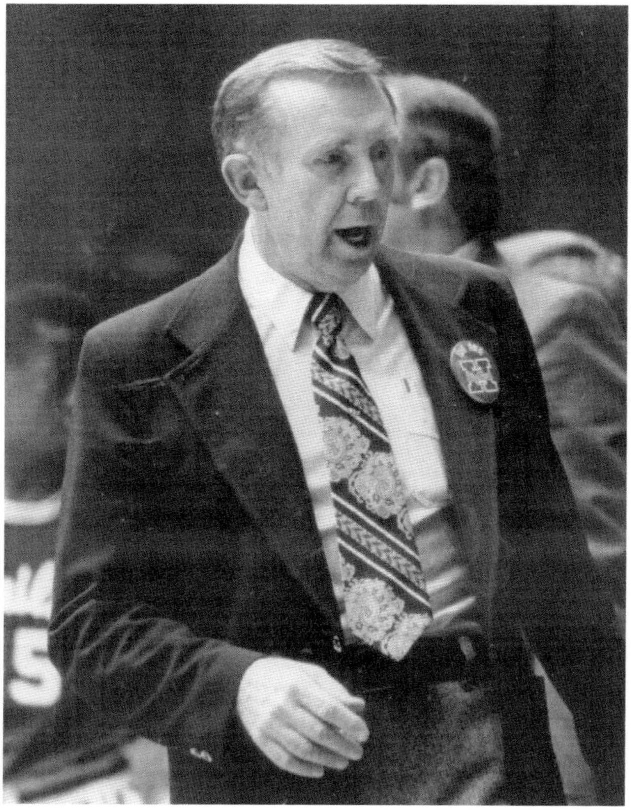

Marvin McCollum

In 1958, McCollum coached the last Hamilton High basketball team before the district went to two high schools. From 1959 to 1979, McCollum (1922–1991) coached Taft High's basketball team to 10 conference titles, 13 sectional championships, and five district crowns. The team had an undefeated season in 1962, capping it off with a state championship. He also coached Taft's football team to a 7-23 record between 1959 and 1961. McCollum, who never had a basketball team with a losing record, had a career record of 485-145.

Bill Wilks

In 1949, Bill Wilks was named Ohio's Mr. Basketball, the best player in the state, when he was the leading scorer on coach Warren Scholler's state championship team. He was the quarterback on the school's football team, including the 1948 team that was ranked as the third best in Ohio. Wilks (1931–) was a three-year starter for Ohio State's basketball team (1951–1953) and was an All–Big Ten pick during two of those seasons. He also played quarterback two years for coach Woody Hayes. After graduation and service in the US Air Force during the Korean War, Wilks opened an insurance agency in Hamilton's Rentschler Building in 1955. He moved his agency to the German Village area in 1965 and began to restore the buildings in the vicinity of his office. For several years beginning in 1973, Wilks helped lead the effort to create the German Village Historic District. Wilks, who had been a member of the Hamilton Board of Education from 1962 to 1970, opened a wine and cheese shop in 1975 and developed it as Wines-N-Such, a fine-dining restaurant. In 1991, the German Village section became the third Hamilton area to be listed in the National Register of Historic Places. The Hamilton Chamber of Commerce has honored his contributions to the community by creating the annual William C. Wilks Award for persons working to revitalize the city and by naming him Hamilton's Citizen of the Year for 2005.

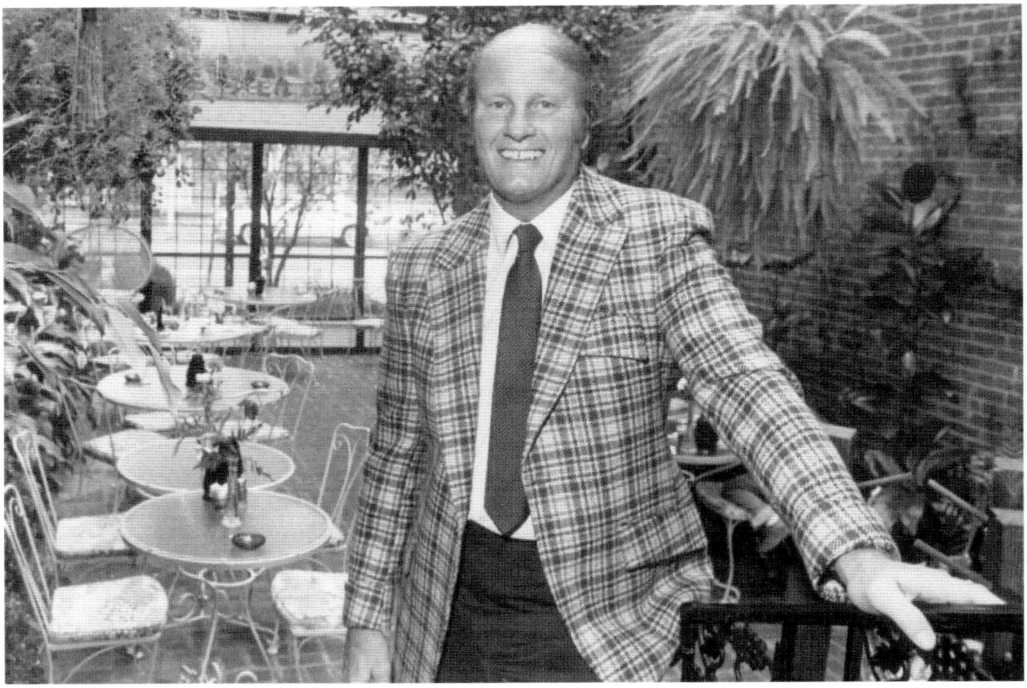

Mary Bowermaster (OPPOSITE PAGE)

Bowermaster (1917–2011), a retired nurse's aide in the Hamilton schools health department, began her athletic career at age 62 following treatment for breast cancer and undergoing a bilateral mastectomy. She participated in her first senior track-and-field event in 1980, at age 63. For more than 25 years, she competed nationally and internationally in Senior and Masters Olympics, including world championships in Melbourne, Rome, San Juan, and Portland, Oregon. Bowermaster set world records in the high jump at age 67 and at age 70; the long jump at age 70; and, at age 82, in the shot put, long jump, high jump, and 100-meter yard dash. She was a five-time US Masters Track and Field Athlete of the Year. Bowermaster was inducted into the Butler County Sports Hall of Fame, the Ohio Women's Hall of Fame, the Ohio Senior Citizens Hall of Fame, the US Masters Track and Field Hall of Fame, and the Ohio Senior Olympics Hall of Fame. In 2002, she was one of the runners who carried the Olympic torch through the Cincinnati area as it made its way to Salt Lake City.

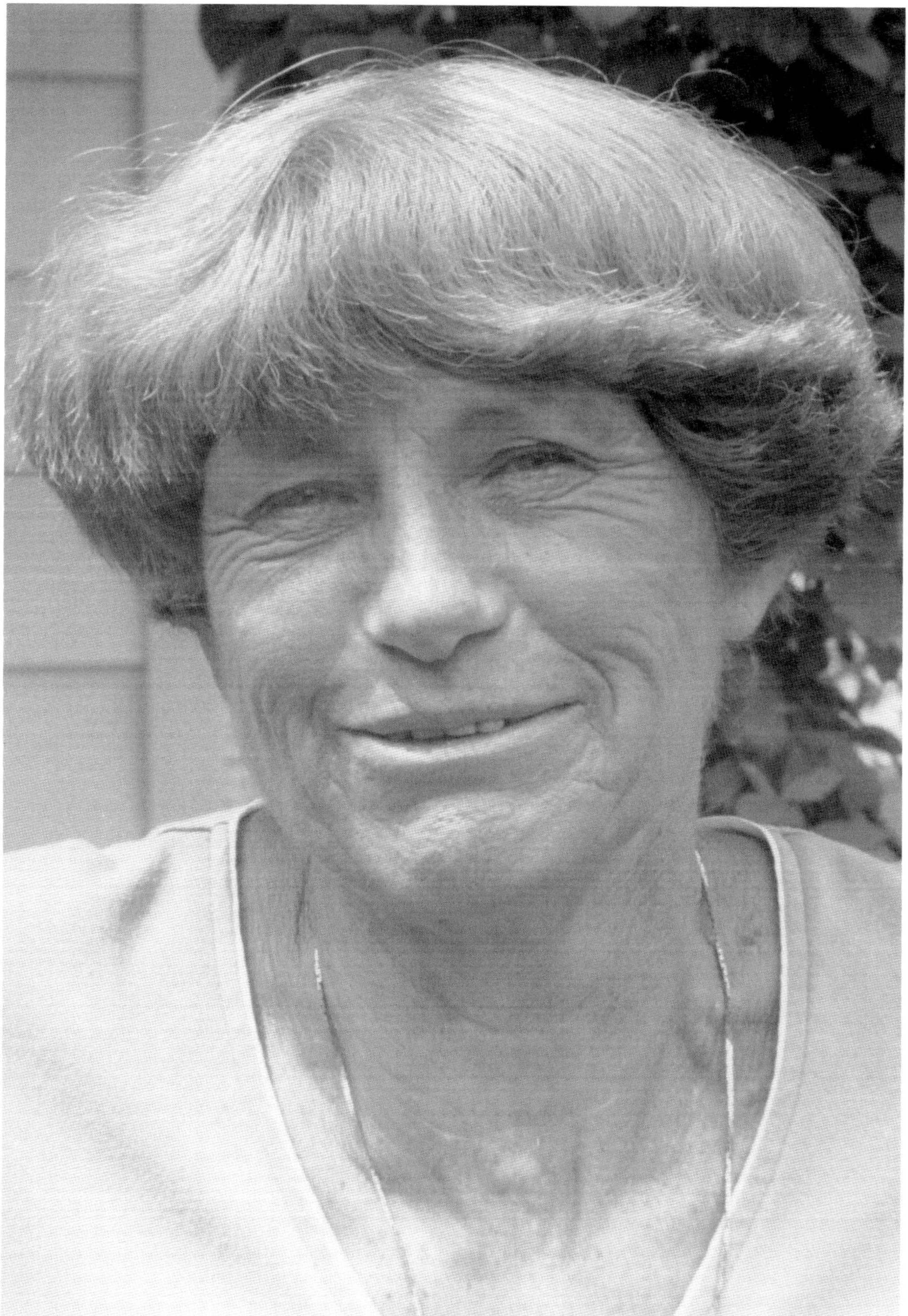

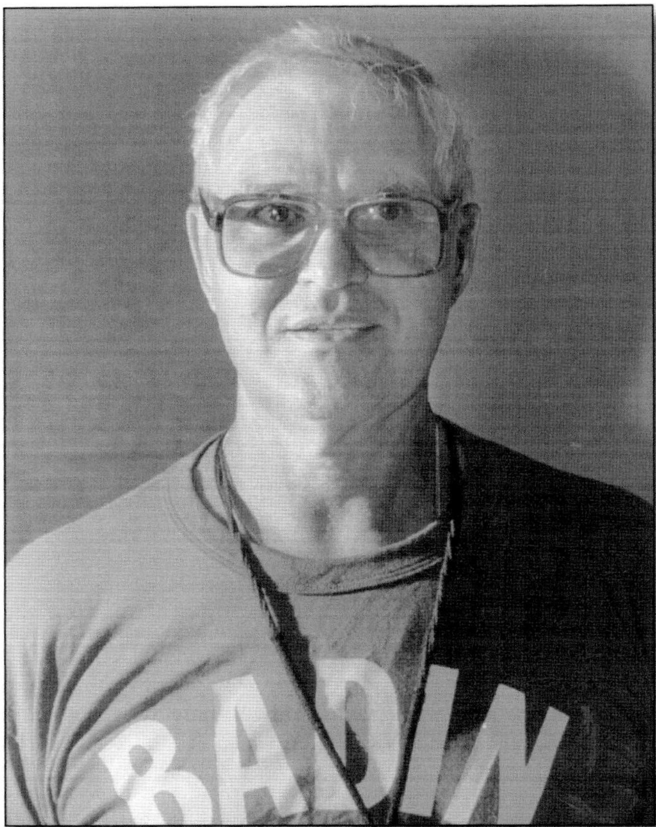

Terry Malone

When Malone ended his spectacular career as a football coach, he had the most coaching victories in Ohio high school history. Between 1958 and 2003, his teams at Hamilton Catholic and Badin high schools won 360 games, lost 117, and tied eight. He coached eight undefeated teams, 14 teams that lost only one game, and 16 that made the state playoffs. His 1990 squad won a state championship, and the 1978 and 1980 teams finished second. Malone (1935–) taught American history for 47 years.

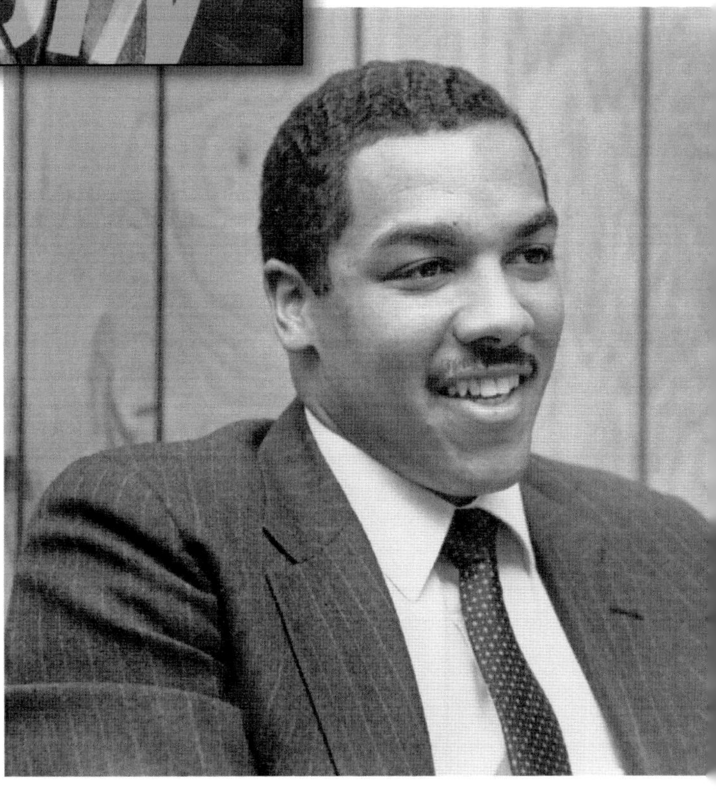

Derek Howard

Howard was a standout athlete at Garfield High School, where he participated in football, basketball, and track. He was named to the 1973 Associated Press All-Ohio team and was the captain of the 1974 Ohio All-Star team. Howard (1956–) played football at the University of Michigan and took part in one Orange Bowl and two Rose Bowl games. The university named the Derek Howard Hustler Award in his honor. In 1986, Howard started a successful full-service architectural firm. He was named Business Person of the Year in 2002 by the Fairfield Chamber of Commerce.

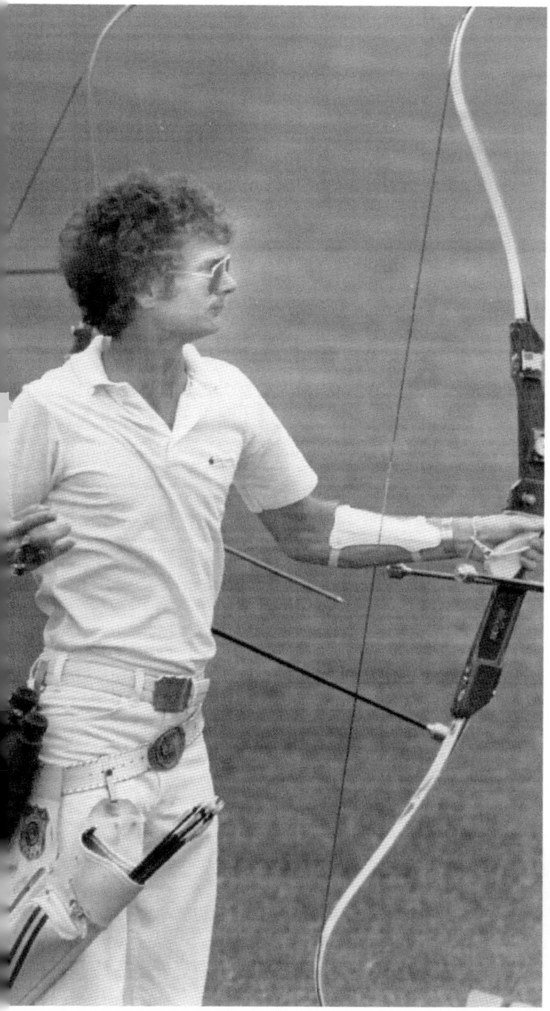

Darrell Pace

Pace (1956–), regarded as the greatest archer in Olympic history, won gold medals during the 1976 and 1984 Olympics and was a member of the team that captured the silver medal at the 1988 games. Between 1973 and 1980, he won six national championships, two world titles, and placed second in two other world competitions. Pace won other international awards, including six gold medals at the 1979, 1983, 1987, and 1991 Pan American Games. In 2011, the International Archery Federation named him the "Men's Archer of the 20th Century."

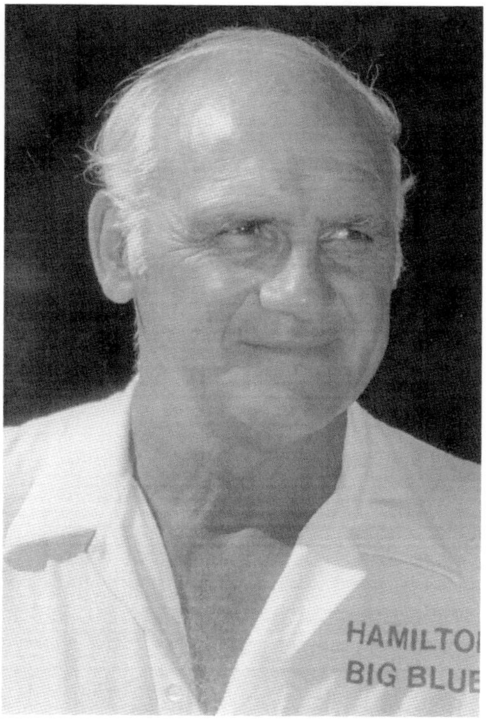

John Pont

When Pont (1927–2008) came to Hamilton High in 1985, he had 22 years of experience coaching football teams at Miami University, Yale University, Indiana University, and Northwestern University. He was named NCAA Coach of the Year in 1967, when his Indiana University team was the Big-Ten champions and played in the school's first Rose Bowl. During his three years as Big Blue coach, his teams won 12 games and lost 17. Pont left Hamilton to build a new football program for the College of Mount St. Joseph in Cincinnati.

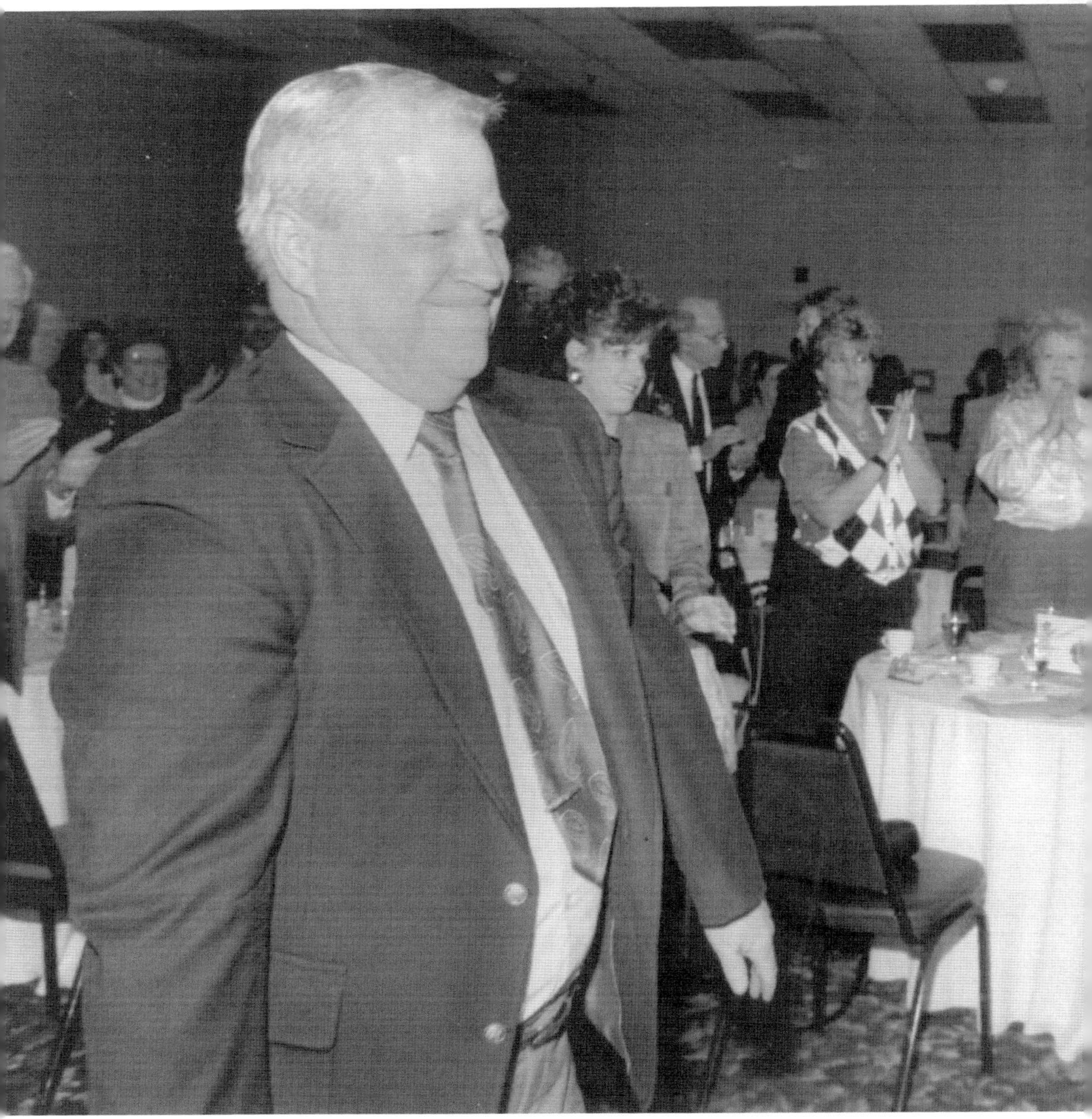

Ray Nichting

Nichting, the Hamilton Chamber of Commerce's Citizen of the Year for 1991, made his mark coaching youth baseball teams for more than 45 years. He began with an American Legion team in Price Hill that he managed to a 1954 national title. Nichting started coaching the Hamilton West Side Little League team in the 1960s. His 1991 and 1993 teams played in the Little League World Series. Nichting (1932–) played two seasons of minor-league baseball in 1951 and 1952 before serving in the Korean War. His company of 244 men was attacked by Chinese soldiers during a 1953 battle on "Pork Chop Hill." Nichting was one of six men who survived the fighting, but he was seriously injured and lost his right leg below the knee in a grenade blast. After recovering at Walter Reed Hospital, Nichting attended barber school and opened a shop in Middletown that he operated for more than 50 years. He also spent nearly as many years on the baseball field, teaching youngsters life's lessons and the value of hard work.

CHAPTER SEVEN

Improving the Quality of Life

There have been many Hamilton residents who have worked to make the community a better place in which to live. Some have worked to create organizations and facilities that enabled others to improve some aspect of their life. Others have donated personal funds to solve problems or provide facilities. Still others gave their time, energy, and did what was asked of them to achieve things for the common good. Some of these people are the notable locals featured here.

Julia Goodman began what became the city's YWCA. Gladys Sepin and Mary Pat Essman worked through the Lane Library to improve the community, especially the reading skills of children.

Among those who raised needed funds for a wide variety of activities, often assisted by the United Appeal or United Way, were W. Otis Briggs Jr. and Jim Paulus. Aiding low-income families when they were faced with emergencies was the mission for Eva Lande. Dr. Henry A. Long worked to arrange good health care for residents, especially those living in low-income households.

Lutie and Homer Gard did many things to improve the quality of life in Hamilton. Their most lasting contribution was giving the community's youth the YMCA's Camp Cambell Gard. William Shuler donated another camping facility, Camp Luella May, for use by young women and the YWCA. Ellis Potter donated land to the city for a municipal golf course.

Ann Antenen, Jay Antenen, Sherry Corbett, Jim Boerke, and Michael Dingeldein, among others, have been at the forefront of preserving the past and keeping alive the city's history. Virgil Schwarm, Harry Wilks, and Donna and Pat Carrothers donated large amounts of money to provide facilities to improve the arts, education, high school athletics, and hospital capabilities.

Finally, many volunteers have been willing to do whatever is needed to improve life in Hamilton. The people who have given much time, effort, personal skill, and talent include Dave Belew, Dick Fitton, Neil Cohen, and Nancy Wiley.

Hamilton is indeed a better place in which to live thanks to the contributions of these community-minded residents.

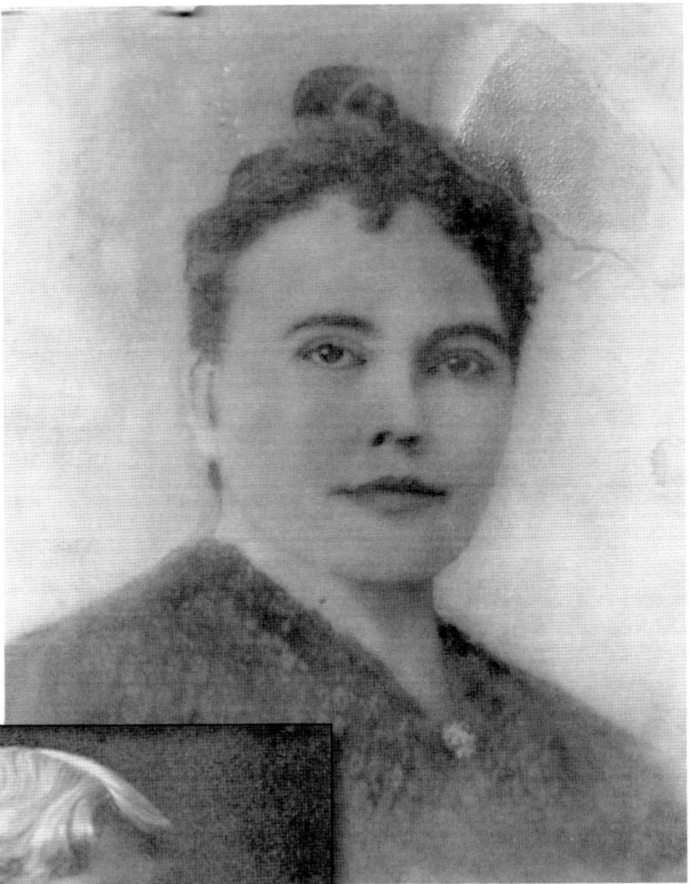

Julia Goodman
Dr. Julia Goodman was the first and, from 1890 to 1902, the only woman physician to practice in Hamilton. She worked to improve the quality of life of working women; taught girls' physiology, hygiene, and cooking classes; and, in 1900, organized what would become the local Young Women's Christian Association. Goodman (1848–1902) even rented a "home" for the group and paid the $30 monthly rent for 20 months. She died 19 days before the Hamilton YWCA was granted its charter by the state of Ohio. (Courtesy of the Hamilton Young Women's Christian Association.)

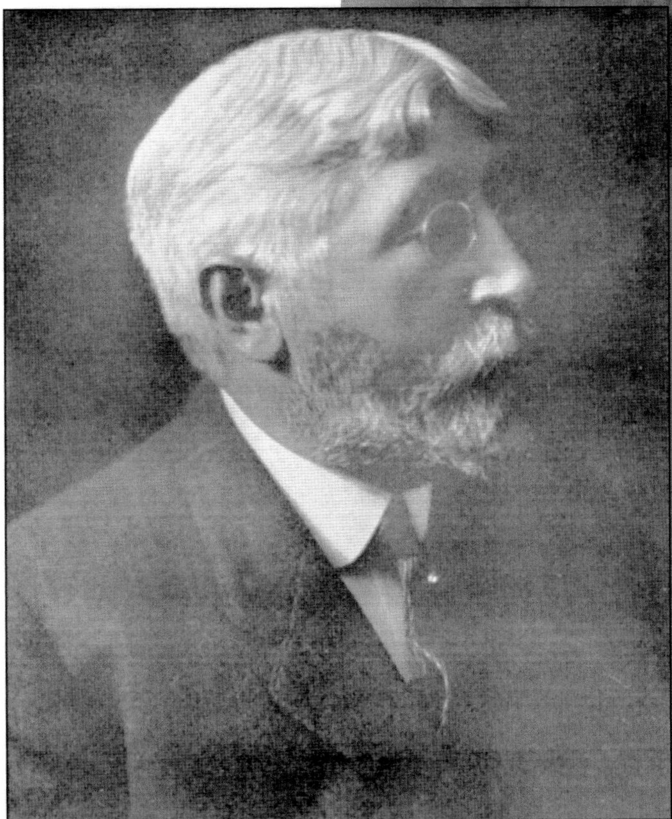

Ellis M. Potter
Potter (1849–1929), a poet and real estate developer, left Hamilton in 1892 after city officials rejected his plan to electrify a Main Street trolley line he operated. He moved to New York City, received a patent for a coffee-roasting system, and formed a very profitable combine of coffee roasters, importers, and distributors. Potter, who never lost his love for Hamilton, gave 100 acres to the city in 1925 for the municipal golf course that bears his name. A book of his poems, *Along the Road*, was published shortly before his death. (Courtesy of Diane Kuhlmann Beaty.)

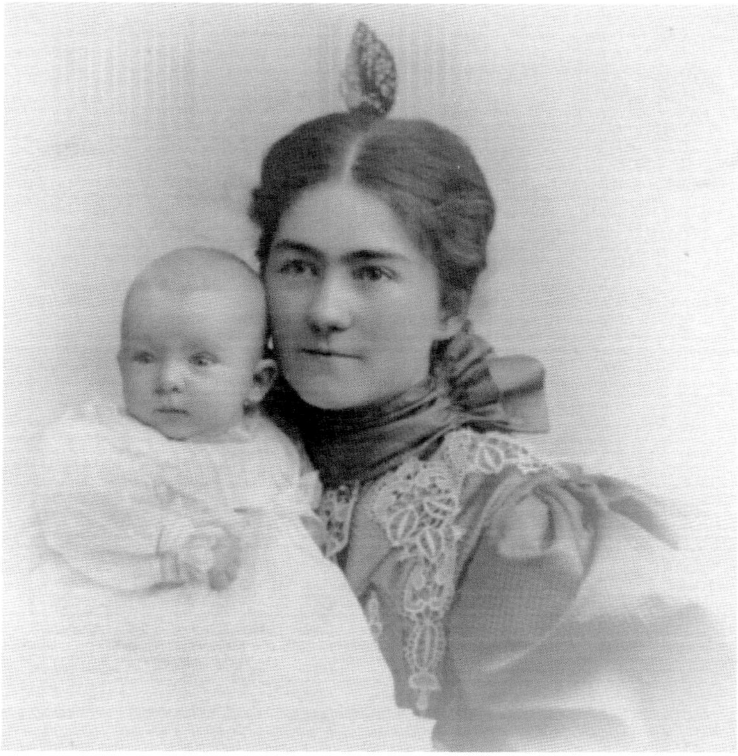

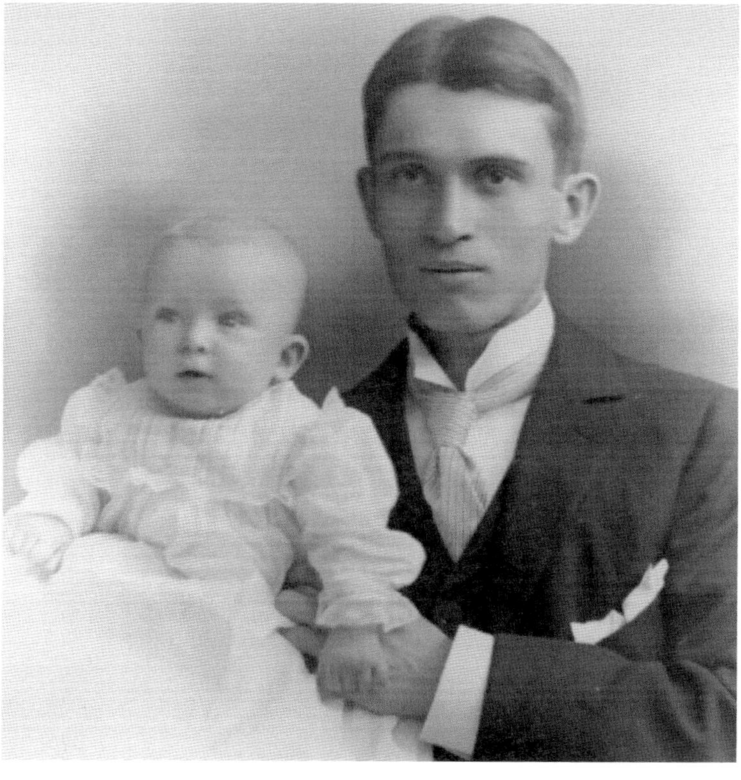

Lutie Matthias Gard and Homer Gard
Lutie Matthias and Homer Gard attended local schools together and were two of the six members of the Hamilton High class of 1884. During their graduation exercises, Lutie read an original essay titled "Proverbs," and Homer gave an oration he named "Action." After high school, Homer went to Amherst College in Massachusetts and Lutie attended Buchtel College in Akron, Ohio. Homer began his journalism career by taking a position as a society and city hall reporter with the *Hamilton Daily News* in 1887. He achieved some security when he became managing editor of the *Hamilton Daily Democrat* in January 1891. Lutie (1866–1934) and Homer (1866–1952) married in 1892. Their only child was born in 1895. The Gards were active in a wide variety of community organizations and Universalist church activities and were officers of the Children's Home Association. They were also doting parents of their son, Charles Campbell Gard, seen in these photographs at the age of three months.

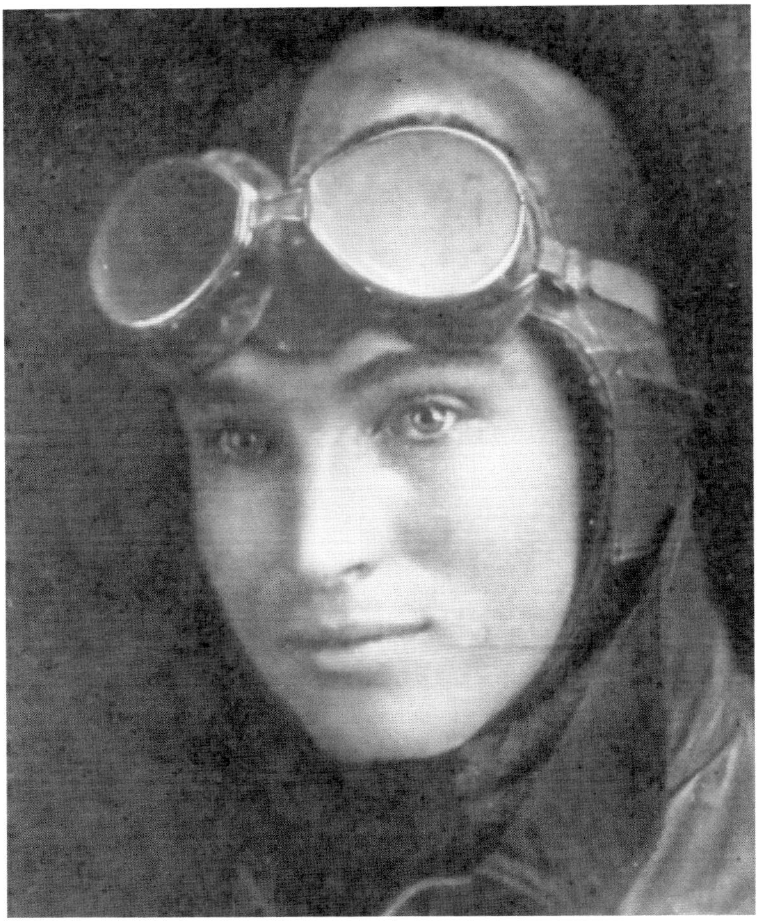

Charles Campbell Gard

After graduating from Hamilton High in 1913, Gard attended Amherst College for one year and then studied journalism at the University of Wisconsin. He returned to Hamilton in 1915 and joined his father at the *Hamilton Evening Journal*, working in several areas to learn the publishing industry. In 1917, Gard enlisted in the First Ohio Field Artillery and volunteered for the Aviation Corps. He was trained as an observer-bomber and assigned to the 186th Aerial Squadron in France during the latter part of World War I. Gard was a member of the squadron that dropped flowers on Pres. Woodrow Wilson when he arrived in France. Before his service in France ended, Gard was injured when his plane crashed. He returned to Hamilton and resumed his work as managing editor of the *Evening Journal*. On October 25, 1921, he collapsed and died at his desk in the newsroom from the injuries he had received during the war. Gard was a young man of ability and conviction, a sportsman, tennis champion, and outdoor enthusiast. Less than three months after his death, a still-grieving Homer Gard privately wrote, "The last thing that he would want would be that the *Journal* he loved should falter because on the deck the 'captain lies fallen, cold and dead.' I, who am left without my partner and pal, will go on as best I can. I must never forget that I have a compact with his memory—a trust to which I must be true. His tongue is mute, his whistle is stilled, his smile is gone—but his spirit commands me and will command thru the years—until we meet again." In 1926, the Gards revealed their plans to build and donate to the Hamilton Young Men's Christian Association a fully equipped camp as a living memorial to their son. Camp Campbell Gard, dedicated on July 1, 1927, consisted of 20 buildings on 30 acres when it opened. The camp was expanded over the years and enjoyed Homer Gard's continued support until he died in 1952. It is still in operation.

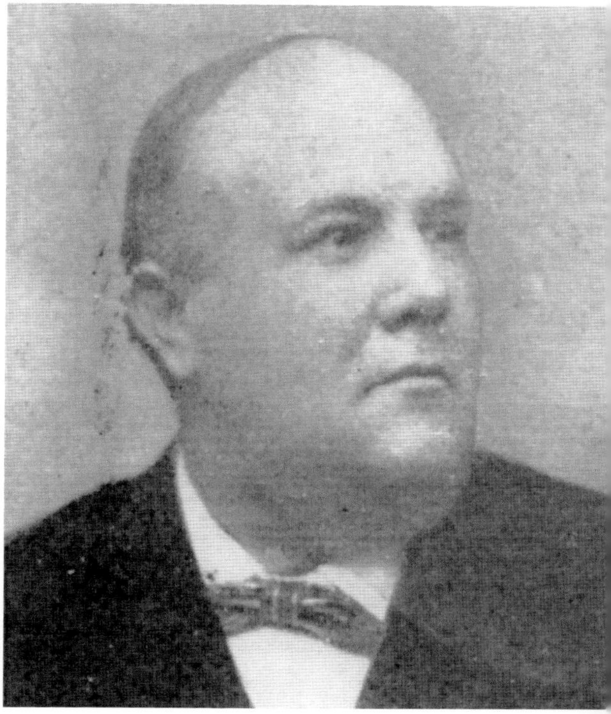

William B. Shuler

Shuler (1860–1938), a co-owner of the Shuler and Benninghoffen woolen mill, supported Fort Hamilton Hospital and made generous contributions to furnish the YWCA building, which opened in 1931. Shuler gave the YWCA a recreational park for girls aged 8 to 18 in 1936. The facility, named Camp Luella May in his wife's honor, was located in Somerville and had a lodge, cabins, swimming pool, tennis court, craft house, and more than 60 acres of campgrounds. It was used every summer from 1936 to 1973. (Courtesy of Lane Library.)

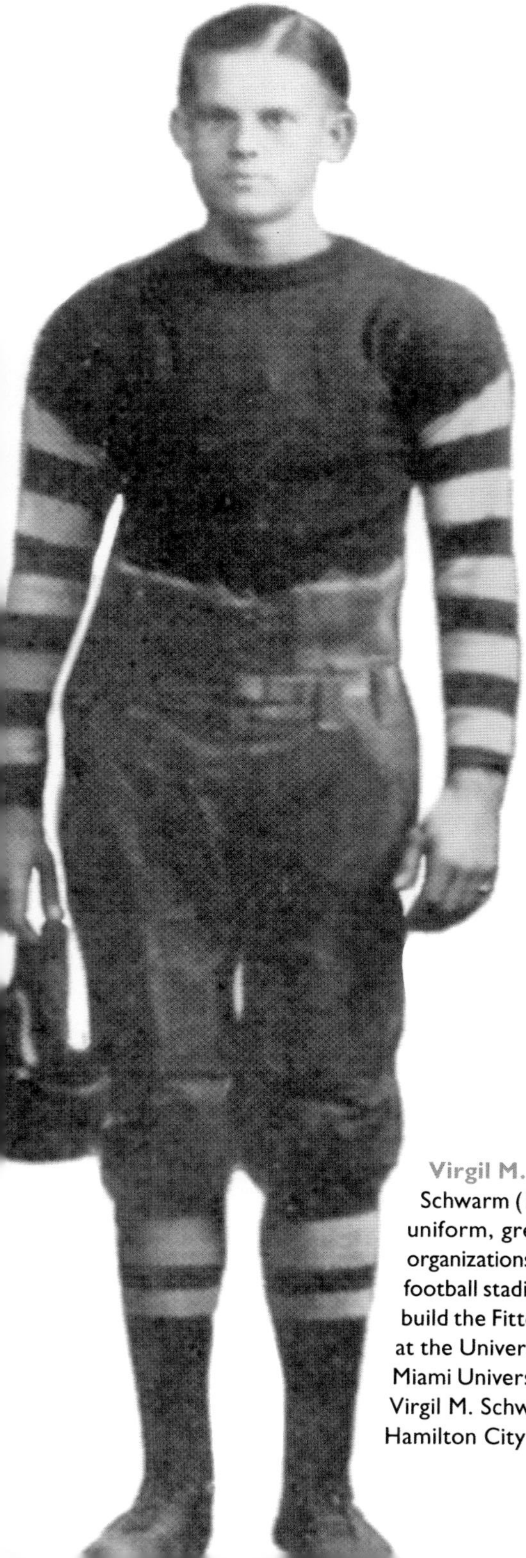

Virgil M. Schwarm

Schwarm (1904–1993), seen to the left in his 1922 Big Blue football uniform, grew up to be one of the leading benefactors of local organizations. He contributed $500,000 to renovate the high school's football stadium; funded the school's wrestling room; gave money to build the Fitton Center for Creative Arts; endowed a professorship at the University of Cincinnati; and was a major contributor to the Miami University campus in Hamilton. Miami's Schwarm Hall and the Virgil M. Schwarm Stadium were named in his honor. (Courtesy of Hamilton City School District.)

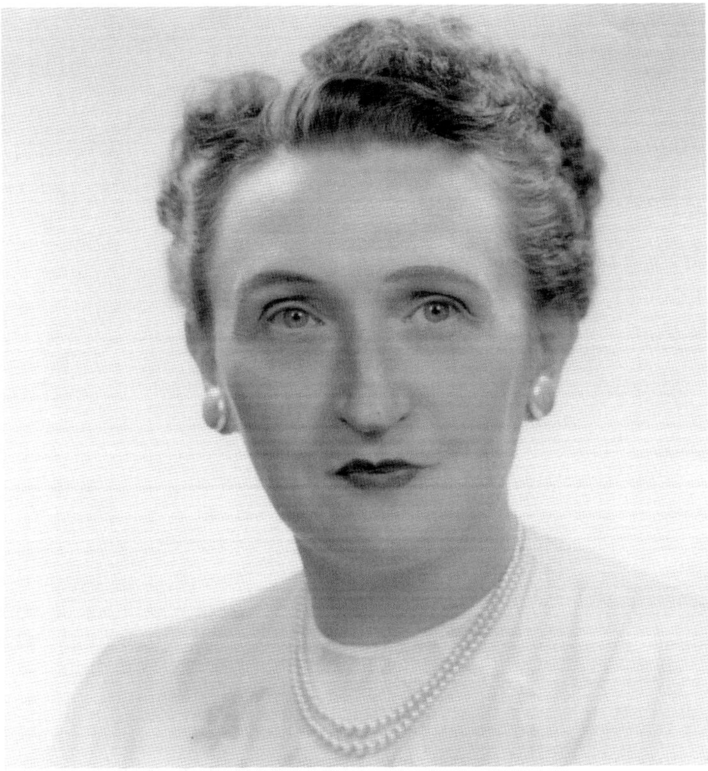

Gladys S. Sepin
Sepin became the director of Lane Library in 1940. She was very involved in developing children's reading programs and promoting adult education. During her administration, the library opened branches in Lindenwald in 1948 and in Oxford in 1958 and greatly expanded its bookmobile service. Sepin (1904–1996) was a founding member of the Greater Hamilton Civic Theatre and was involved in the Civic Music Series, which brought world-famous musicians to Hamilton. She retired from the library in 1964, after 24 years of service.

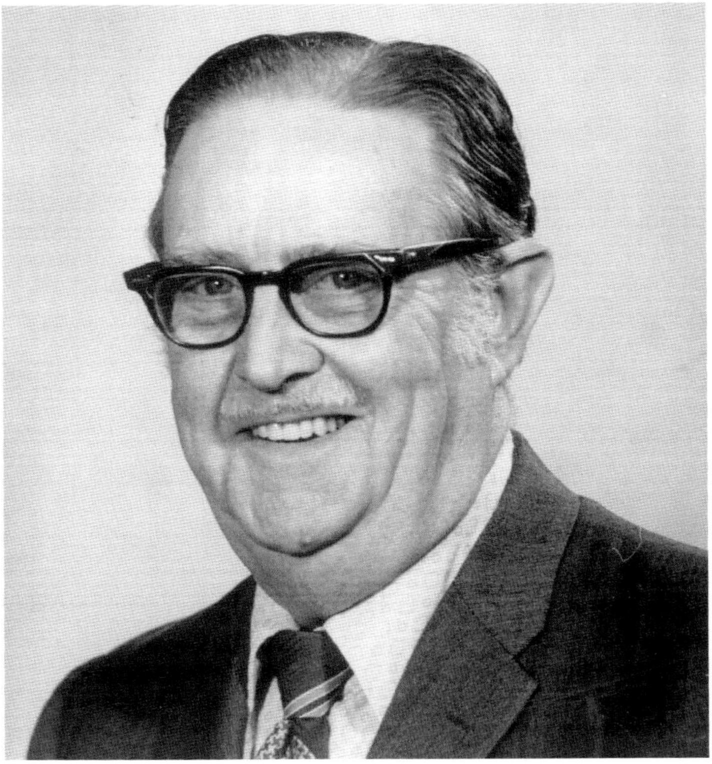

W. Otis Briggs Jr.
In 1943, Briggs was named the first full-time executive director of what became the Butler County United Way, a position he held until 1976. During his administration, he increased fundraising from $96,000 to nearly $1 million. He was one of the founders of the Hamilton Community Foundation and served as that charity's executive director from 1951 to 1980. Briggs (1914–1995) provided leadership in other philanthropic endeavors and worked to develop the Butler County Mental Health Association, Senior Citizens Center of Hamilton, and Family Services of Hamilton.

Dr. Henry A. Long
Dr. Long (1910–1996) practiced medicine in Hamilton for 36 years. He was a member of the staff at Fort Hamilton Hospital and at Mercy Hospital and was one of the few African American doctors with a local private practice. Long, who catered to low-income residents, was greatly admired for his willingness to make house calls day or night. He was a longtime member of the Butler County Metropolitan Housing Board. In 1974, the housing board named a senior citizen high-rise apartment building in his honor.

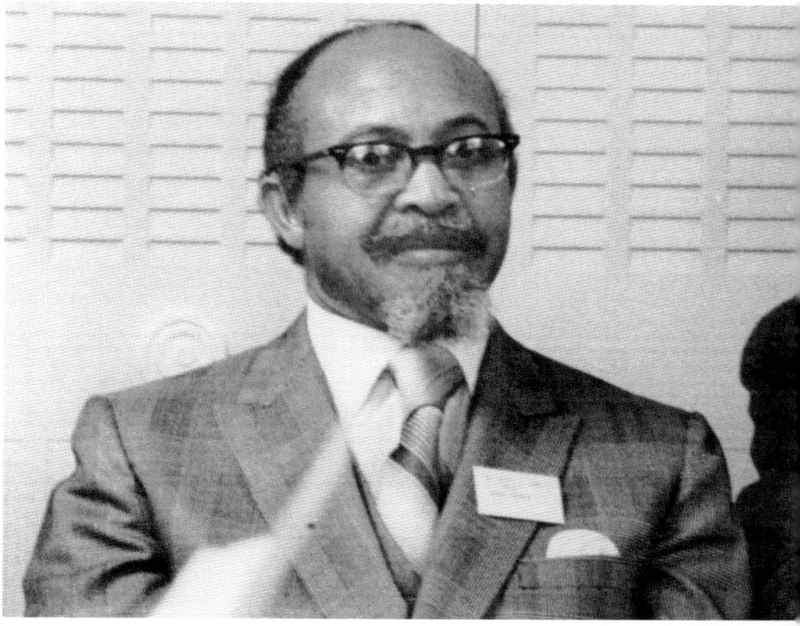

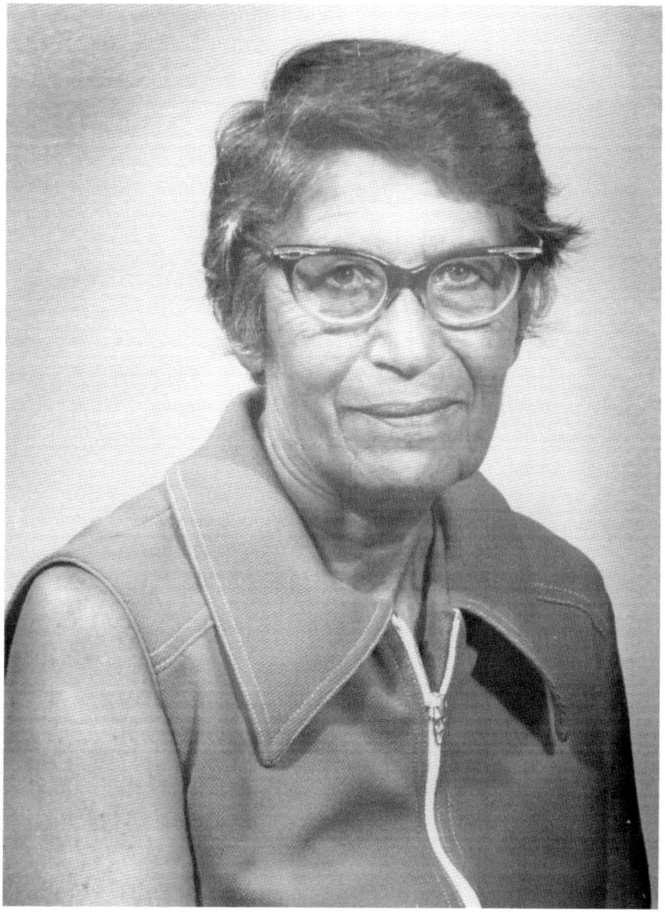

Eva M. Lande
Lande (1909–2005), a refugee of Nazi Germany and resident of Hamilton since 1944, spent much of her life working to help others. She owned and operated a nursery school from 1948 to 1970 before turning her attention to civic causes. In 1975, Lande founded the Hamilton Emergency Money Fund, which has helped thousands of people in need. She served on the fund's board for nearly 30 years and was a board member of more than two dozen other civic groups.

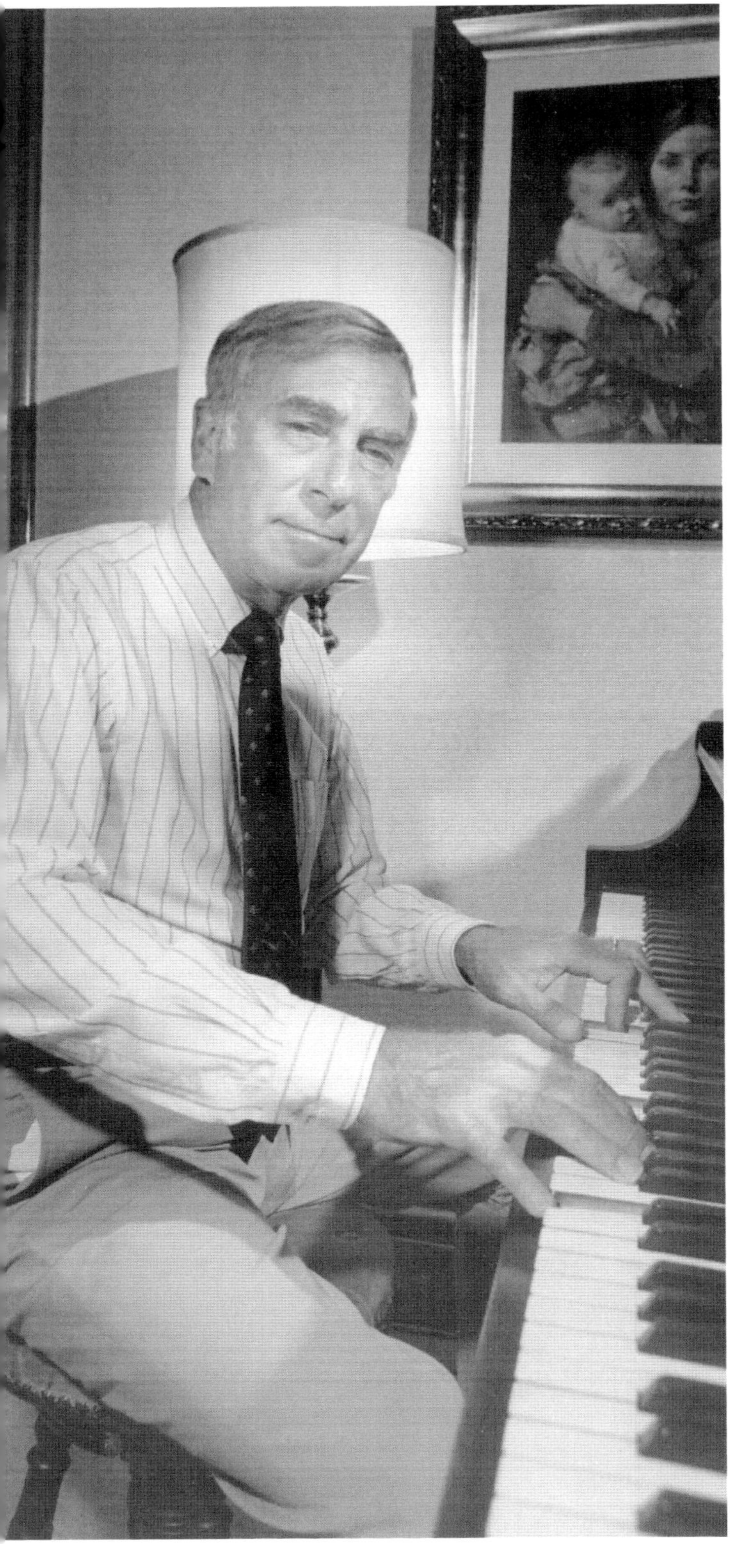

David L. Belew

For many years, Dave Belew has been one of the most respected and admired members of the community. He joined the Beckett Paper Company in 1960 and advanced from the firm's advertising department to become president, serving in that position from 1974 until his retirement in 1992. Belew (1931–) began volunteering with the Hamilton Community Foundation in 1961 and has been involved with the group for more than 50 years, including serving two terms as president. Other community organizations that have benefited from Belew's leadership and service include the United Way, Lane Library, Hamilton Boys and Girls Club, Fitton Center for Creative Arts, Hamilton Economic Development Corporation, Citizens for Historic and Preservation Services, the city's Parks and Recreation Commission, and Hillsdale College in Michigan. He has worked to raise funds for the Open Door Pantry for more than 20 years, the American Heart Association starting in 1988, and the Boys and Girls Club every year since 1975. Belew has helped with the development of Foundation Field near the Booker T. Washington Center, the Joyce Park skateboard facility, and the Lentil Park on High Street with the *Lentil and His Dog Harmony* sculpture. He is a talented pianist who has entertained at a variety of business functions and gatherings and is a lifetime board member of the Hamilton-Fairfield Symphony Orchestra. Belew, who was named to the Junior Achievement Hall of Fame in 1993, has been honored by the Hamilton Community Foundation with its creation of the David L. Belew Legacy Award to honor significant contributors of philanthropy. Without a doubt, Hamilton is a far better place in which to live as a result of Dave Belew's contributions.

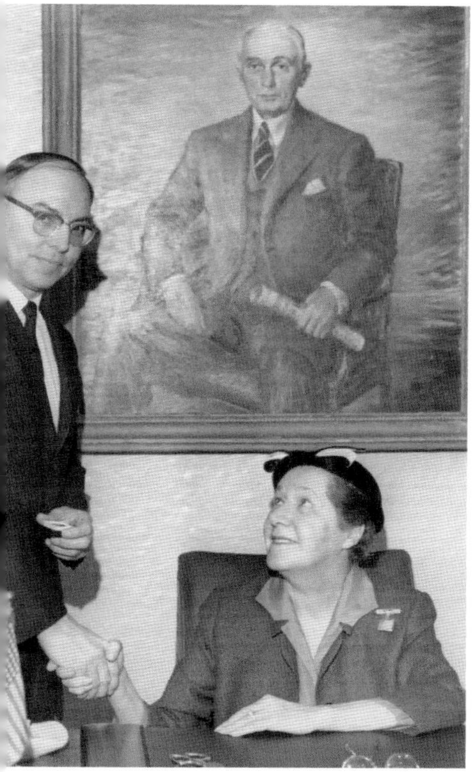

Ethelyne Grove Gard Gramm

Ethelyne Grove married Homer Gard in 1935 and served as *Journal News* publisher after his death in 1952. She married Harry Gramm in 1953 and continued Homer Gard's commitment to the Hamilton YMCA, making a bequest in 1970 to maintain and improve Camp Campbell Gard. Over the years, more than 100,000 young camp-goers have benefited from the Gard family generosity. Ethelyne (1908–1970) is seen here with Robert Cawein, a *Journal News* employee from 1940 to 1986, in front of a portrait of Homer Gard.

Mary Pat Essman

Essman (1952–) served as Lane Library administrator from 1983 to 2011. Starting in 1995, she supervised an extensive renovation of the library and the addition of many new services, including Internet access. Essman, a longtime member of several community boards, oversaw the computerization of the library's card catalog, circulation procedures, and other important library services. She was named an Outstanding Woman of Achievement in 2000 by the YWCA. Essman is seen with Michael Cupp (left), a local genealogist, and Jerry Lanich, St. Clair Township zoning administrator.

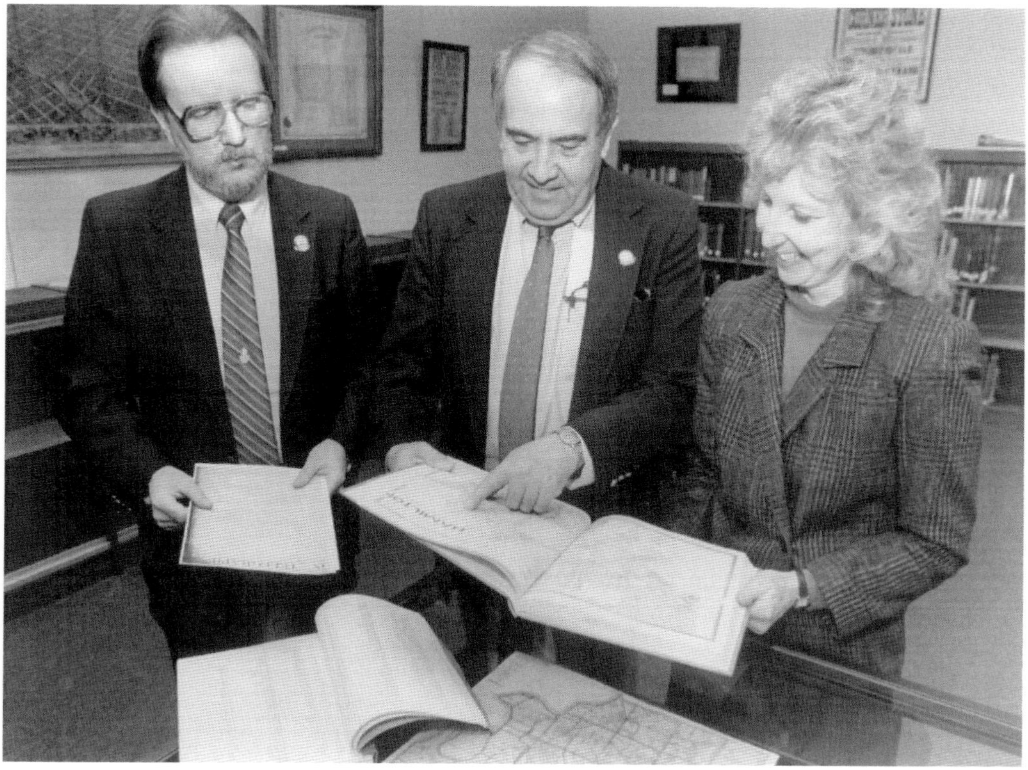

Richard J. Fitton

During Fitton's 45-year career in banking, he rose from being a branch manager at the Main Street office of the First National Bank & Trust Company to serving as president, chief executive, and chairman of the First National Bank of Southwestern Ohio and First Financial Bancorp. He was an officer of the American Banking Association and a member of the board of directors of the Federal Reserve Bank. Fitton (1927–2004) also excelled in his service to the community. He served on the Hamilton city council from 1960 to 1963. He was involved in developing and promoting many projects to improve life in Hamilton, including the low-level dam, Columbia Bridge, Hamiltonian Hotel, Jack Kirsch Underpass, and the Miami University–Hamilton campus. Over the years, he was an officer of the Hamilton Cancer Society, Rotary Club, Fort Hamilton–Hughes Memorial Hospital, Senior Citizens Board, and Greater Butler County Junior Achievement. He did committee work for the Miami University Citizens Advisory Committee, Hamilton-Fairfield Arts Council, and the Vision 2020 Committee. The *Journal News* named him one of the 25 most influential citizens of Hamilton four times between 1979 and 1984. Because of his efforts toward the city's 1991 Cultural Action Plan and Bicentennial Legacy Project to develop an arts center, and his family's establishment of the center's original endowment fund, the building was named the Fitton Center for Creative Arts. Fitton, named Hamilton's Citizen of the Year in 1990, also provided the funds to build the botanical Conservatory on the Miami University–Hamilton campus in 2004. By any standard, Dick Fitton left Hamilton an incredible legacy.

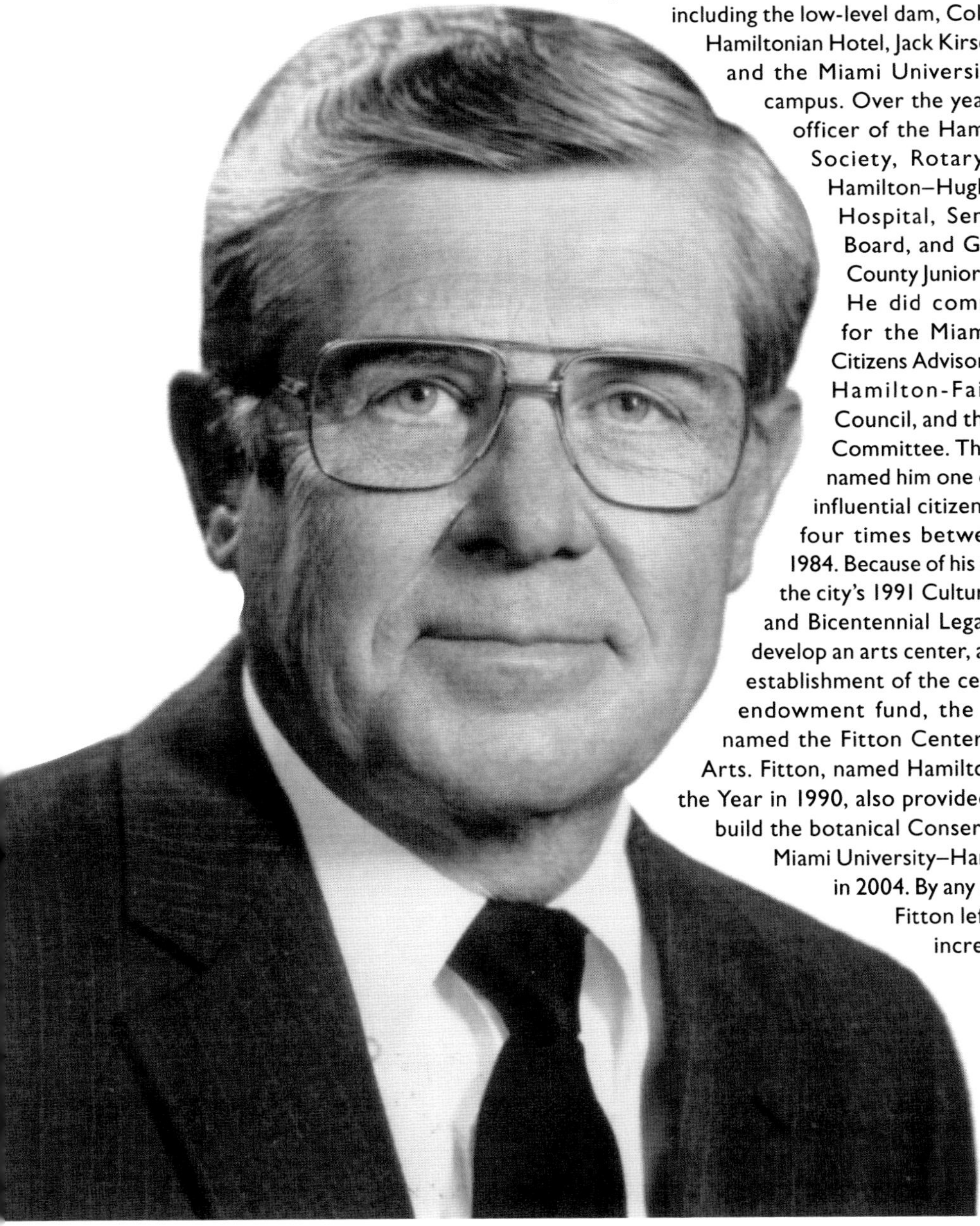

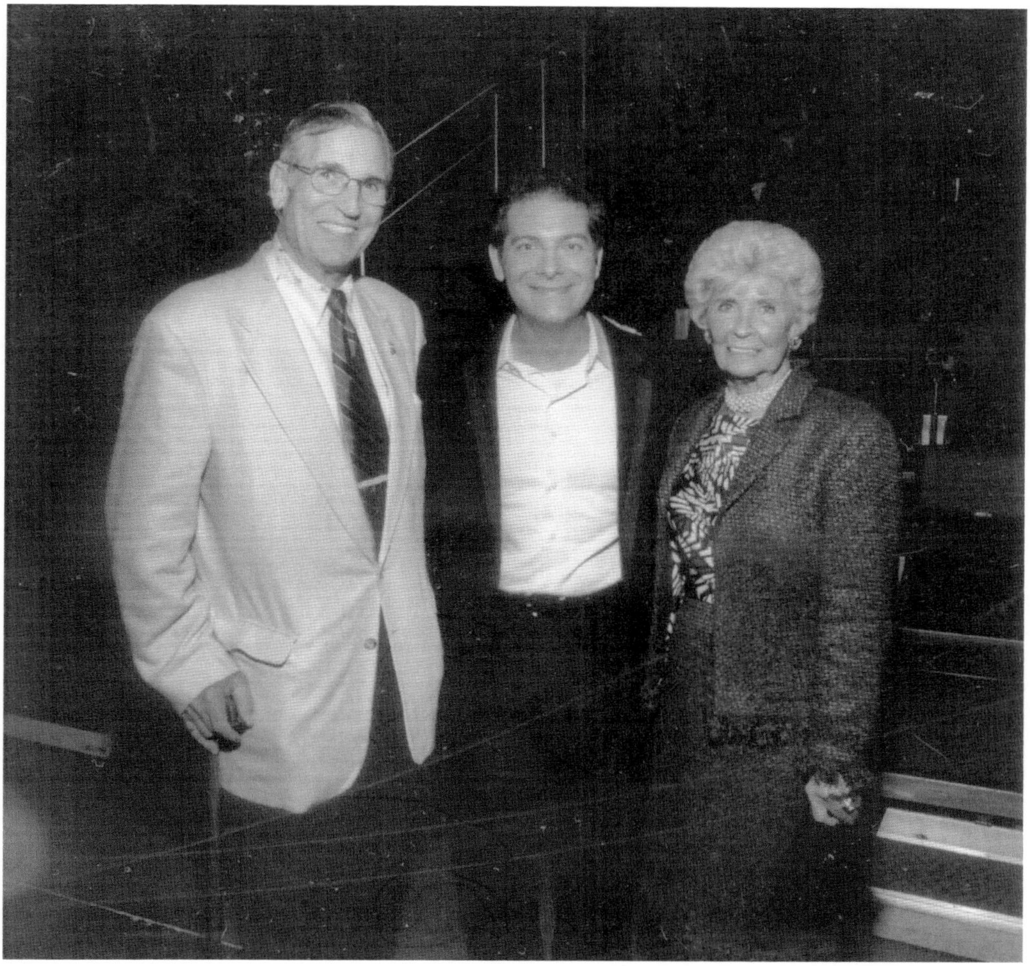

Donna Young Carruthers and Ralph Rogan "Pat" Carruthers

Donna and Pat Carruthers, seen here with entertainer Michael Feinstein (center), have been major benefactors to the Hamilton community, and their generosity has left a lasting mark on the city. They have helped to improve the quality of life of area residents in several important ways. Donna (1929–2009) and Pat (1930–) have been avid community volunteers, helping with the Westover Retirement Community, American Heart Association, and Mercy Hospital. They have supported the Fort Hamilton Hospital by providing funds for a major expansion and remodeling of the hospital's emergency room and the development of a new intensive care, outpatient, and diagnostic services unit. The Carruthers have contributed to the renovation of Hamilton High's auditorium, donated the *No Child Left Behind* sculpture, and paid for the construction of the fine arts wing at Wilson Junior High. The Fitton Center for the Creative Arts has received funds for the Carruthers Center for Arts and Technology and the Signature Ballroom. More recently, the family contributed money to build the Carruthers Manor House at Berkeley Square. For several summers, the Carruthers have contributed funds to keep the city's swimming pools open. Other organizations that have received support from the Carruthers include the Hamilton Boys and Girls Clubs, German Village Association, Junior Achievement of Butler County, YMCA, YWCA, and the Greater Hamilton Civic Theatre. They were named Hamilton's Citizens of the Year in 2001 and were honored with the Post-Corbett Award by the Corbett Foundation.

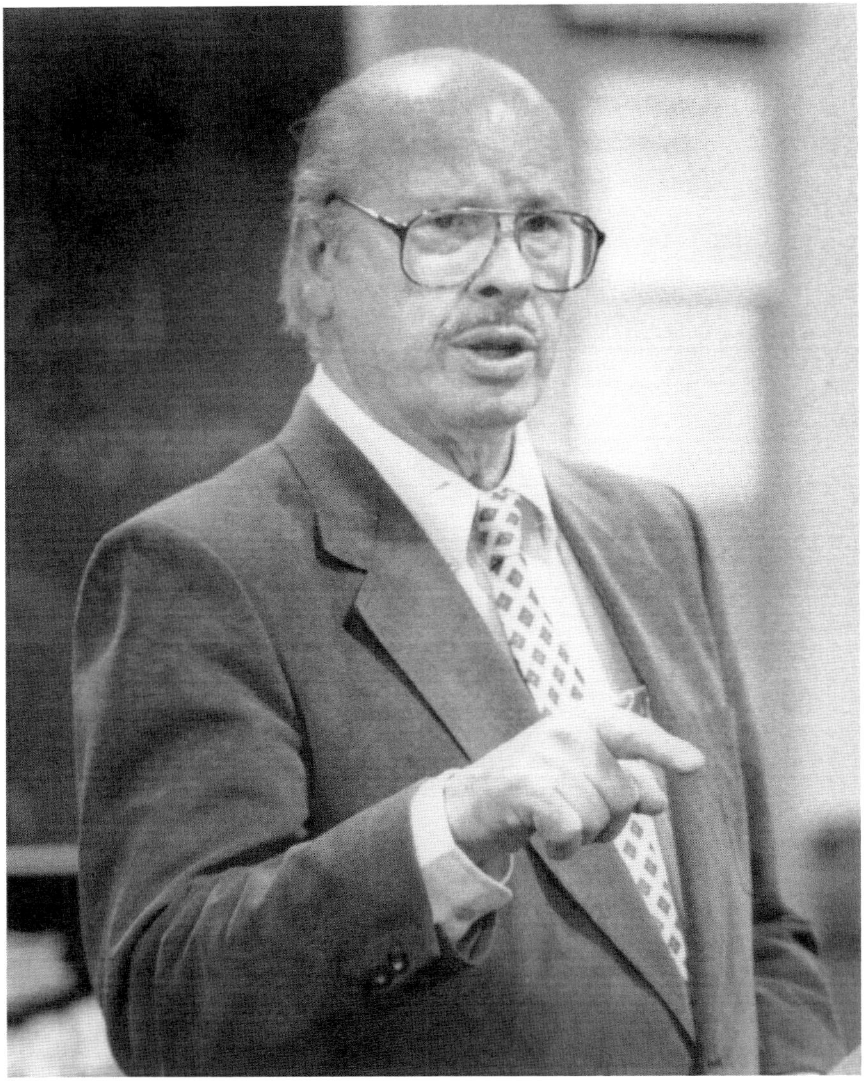

Harry T. Wilks

Wilks, a 1943 graduate of Hamilton High, began a 30-year career as a lawyer in 1950. One of his early philanthropic contributions to the community came in 1954, when he helped to found the Greater Butler County Junior Achievement. He began investing in downtown Hamilton properties in 1962 and worked to revitalize the downtown area over the next 30 years. He was appointed to serve on Hamilton's city council in 1966 and 1967. In 1980, Wilks retired from his law practice and devoted most of his time to traveling and collecting ancient Greek, Roman, Egyptian, and Etruscan art. Wilks (1925–) bought 40 acres of heavily wooded land on Hamilton's west side and began to build a unique subterranean home with a glass-pyramid roof. He acquired more land and established the 265-acre Pyramid Hill Sculpture Park with more than 60 contemporary monumental sculptures and an Ancient Sculpture Museum housing his art collection. Wilks has given generous financial support to Miami University, including funding scholarships, a lecture series, and a leadership institute—all named in his honor. He also donated the funds to build the Harry T. Wilks Conference Center on the Miami University–Hamilton campus. In keeping with his interest in art, Wilks has funded the art director's position at the Cincinnati Opera for several years. He has contributed greatly to life in Hamilton.

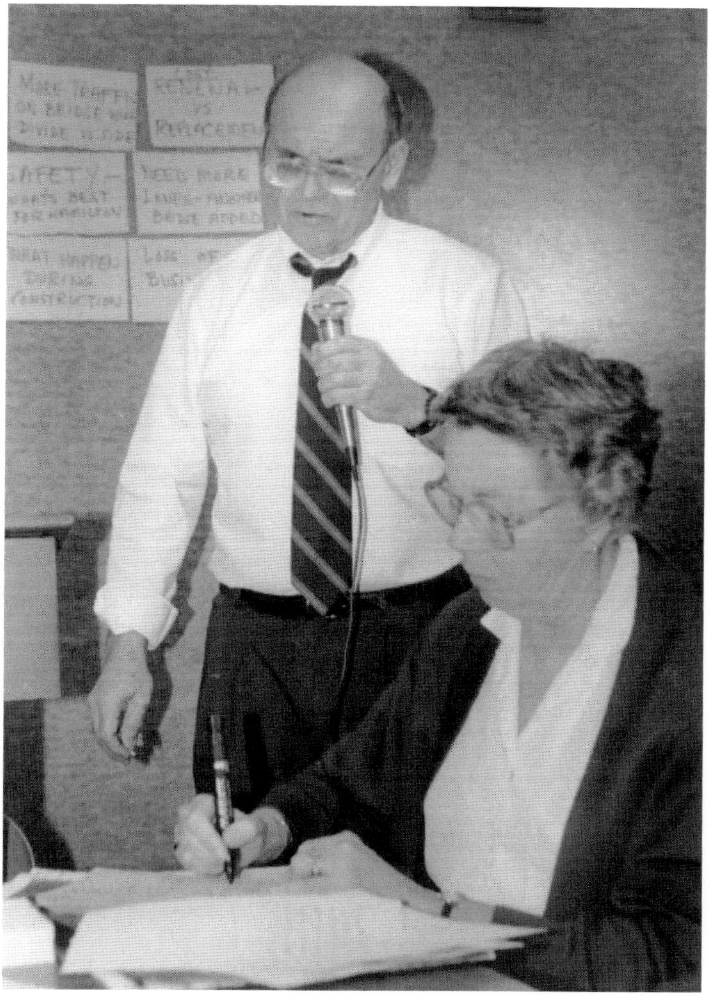

Ann Antenen and Jay Antenen
When Mayor Frank Witt died during a city council meeting in 1978, councilwoman Ann Antenen (1925–) became Hamilton's first and only (to date) woman mayor. She was elected to three terms on the city council, from 1976 to 1981. A talented artist and architect, she taught a popular art class at the Hamilton YWCA from 1959 to 1971 before turning her attention to restoring historic public and private buildings with a company she formed in 1971. Her husband, Jay Antenen (1923–2009), with his brother Dan Antenen, operated Antenen Construction Company, building commercial and industrial structures for more than 31 years. Ann and Jay were actively involved in the German Village Association and in the efforts to save the Anthony Wayne Hotel, Elisha Morgan Mansion in Fairfield, and several other historic buildings in Butler County. In 1983, the Antenens worked to organize Citizens for Historic and Preservation Services, the area's leading group dedicated to educating the public on the value of saving significant buildings and restoring neglected structures. They helped found the Heritage Hall Museum and served on the Butler County Courthouse restoration committee. Ann and Jay have served other groups and organizations, including the Ohio Arts Council, Ohio Municipal League, Fairfield Arts Center, United Way, Alcoholism Council, National League of Cities, and the Rotary Club. In 1996, the Antenen family made a lasting contribution to the residents of Butler County when they donated more than 130 acres to Butler County MetroParks for a nature preserve. Ann and Jay are seen here during a 1991 meeting of the "Save the Main Street–High Street Bridge" committee.

Sherry Corbett

One of Hamilton's most popular historic neighborhoods was championed by Sherry Lee Corbett (1947–2002). Corbett joined Miami University's Department of Sociology and Gerontology in 1974 and received two Outstanding Teacher awards from the university's student government, in 1989 and 1995. She had a passion for historic preservation and was a nationally known housing rehabilitation expert who represented Ohio as a delegate to the National Trust for Historic Preservation. In 1985, Corbett and city planning department associate Jim Boerke worked to create the Dayton-Campbell Historic District and to get it listed in the National Register of Historic Places. She purchased and personally supervised the complete restoration of 20 properties in the district, made up of homes built between 1875 and 1925. In doing so, she transformed the area into a vibrant neighborhood. Her contributions to the city were acknowledged when she was named Hamilton's Citizen of the Year in 1995. Dr. Corbett was shot to death in 2002 by Tonda Lynn Ansley, a former employee and tenant. Ansley was found not guilty by reason of insanity for the murder.

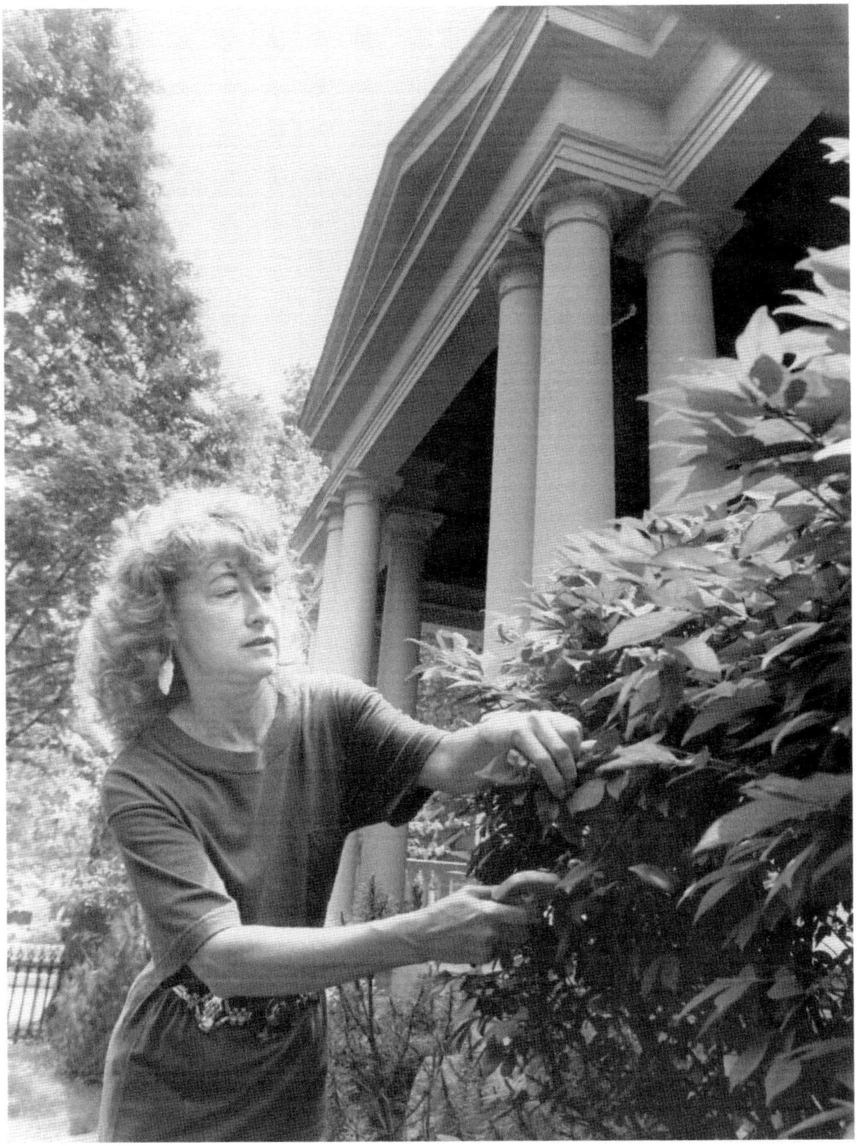

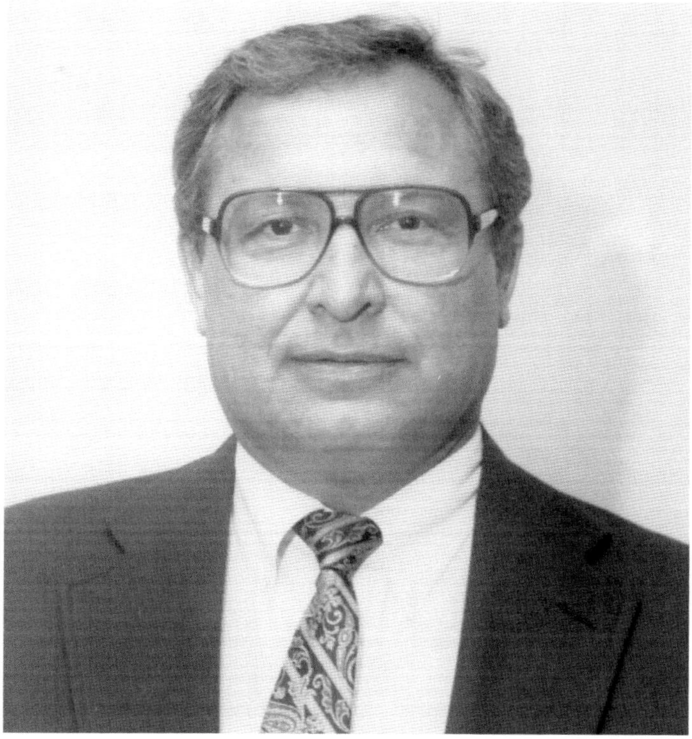

Jim Boerke
Boerke served in Hamilton's planning department from 1969 to 2001, including 12 years as department head. In 1985, he worked with Sherry Corbett to create the Dayton Lane Historic District. Boerke (1947–) directed the city's Vision 2020 comprehensive plan before becoming the head of planning and construction management for the Hamilton City School District in 2001. In that position, he supervised all school renovations and the construction of the district's state-of-the-art schools, at a cost of more than $235 million. Boerke retired from the district in 2012.

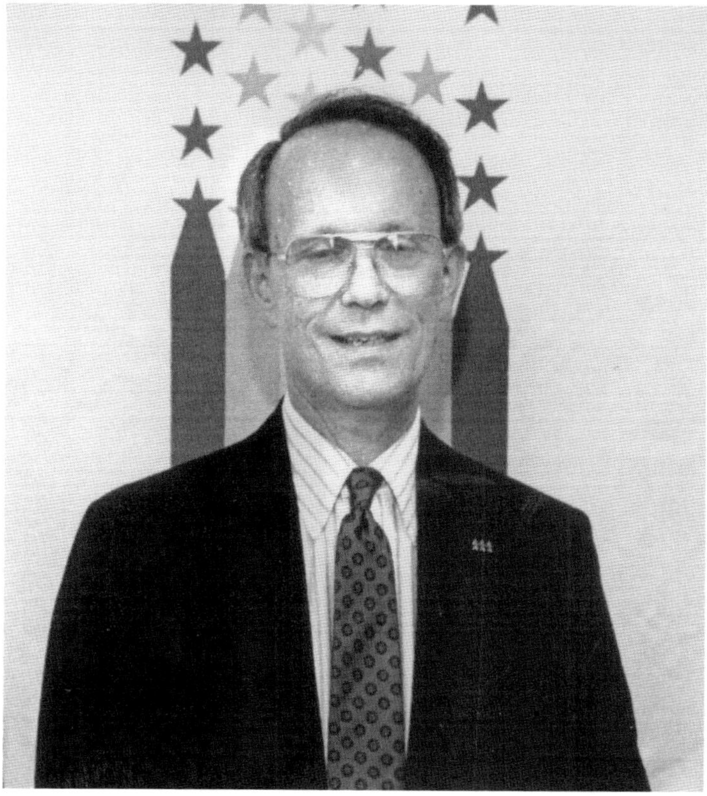

Jim Paulus
Paulus served as president and executive officer of the Butler County United Way from 1984 to 2000. He also served as director of planning and development for Fort Hamilton Hospital, executive director of the Butler County Alcoholism Council, and outreach coordinator for the Miami University–Hamilton campus. Paulus (1932–2012) was an active board member of the Hamilton Community Foundation, Emergency Money Fund, and Fitton Center for Creative Arts.

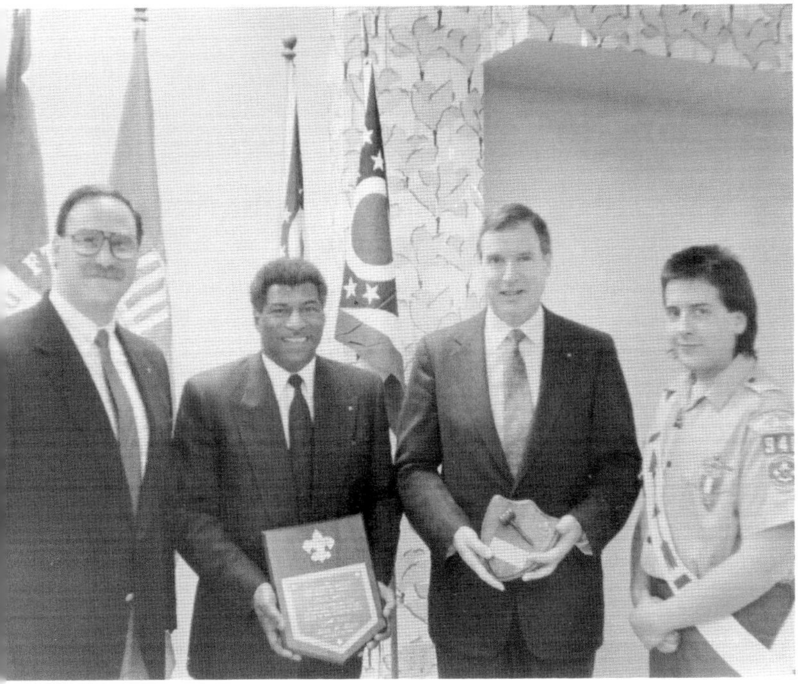

Neil Cohen
Cohen became co-owner of Hamilton Scrap Processors in 1975. He has served on the boards of the Hamilton Board of Education, Chamber of Commerce, Fort Hamilton Hospital, Junior Achievement of Butler County, and City of Sculpture. Cohen (1953–) provided the leadership for the successful 1986 school district levy campaign. He has donated space and materials for the City of Sculpture's Artist-In-Residence program and sponsored the Family Fridays program at the Fitton Center for Creative Arts. Attending a 1989 Eagle Scout luncheon are, from left to right, Cohen, James Brown, Dennis Sullivan, and Carl O'Neil.

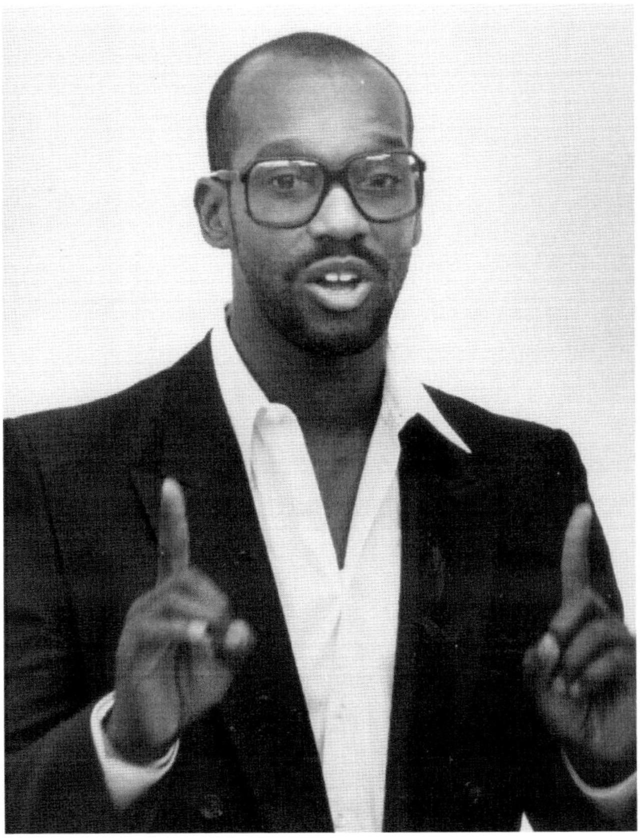

Bob Harris
Martial arts champion and photographer Bob Harris (1949–) began his efforts to improve Hamilton's Second and Fourth Wards in 1995, when he formed the Southeast Civic Association. He worked to improve the quality of life for the area's residents, to upgrade infrastructure, and helped to get a $1.9-million streetscape and walk of fame on Bailey Square. Harris, a frequent and outspoken critic of substance abuse, has operated the Moo Duk Kwan Karate Temple since 1969 and has won one national and two world karate titles.

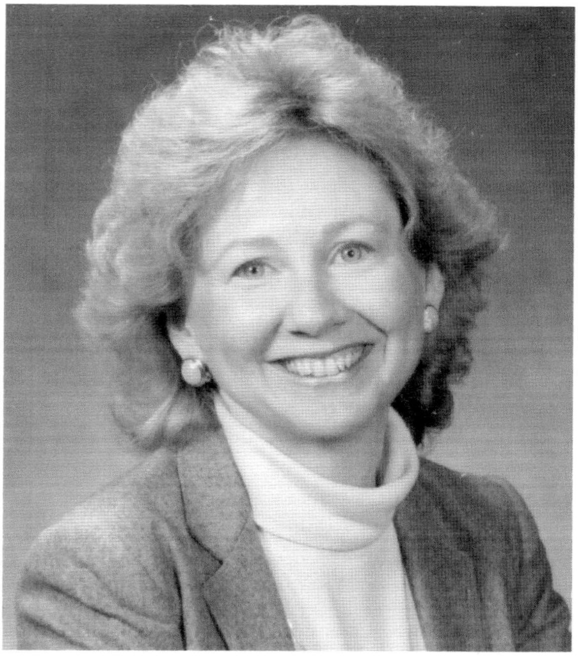

Nancy D. Wiley
Wiley (1950–), one of the most community-minded volunteers in Hamilton, has served on several boards and committees, including the United Way, Hamilton-Fairfield Symphony, Fitton Center for Creative Arts, Hamilton Community Foundation, and Historic Hamilton. She has been involved with the Rotary Club since 1988, serving as the group's president and as a producer or performer in several Rotary Revels. Wiley has worked to redevelop downtown Hamilton. Since 2001, she has been a key participant and president of the city's Vision 2020 Commission.

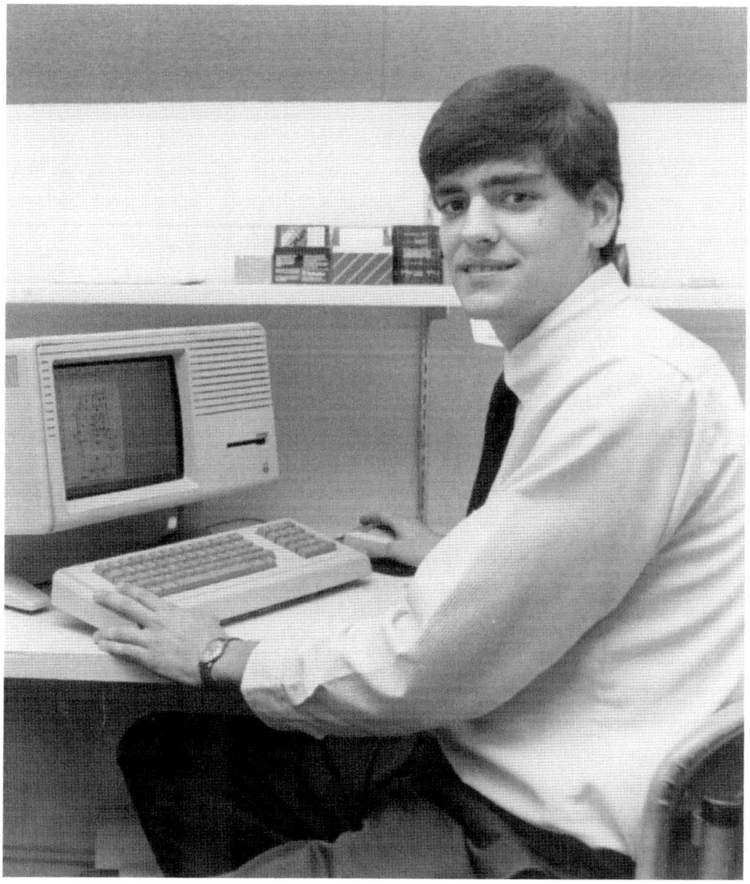

Michael P. Dingeldein
As lead architect for the Hamilton schools Master Facilities Plan, Dingeldein helped create the schools that students would be using for several decades. He was the lead architect for the Fitton Center for Creative Arts. Dingeldein has served on several boards, including the Hamilton Community Foundation, Vision 2020 Commission, Rossville Historic District, Hamilton-Fairfield Symphony Orchestra, and Citizens for Historic and Preservation Services. In 2012, he formed Community Design Alliance, a firm to help revitalize the city's urban core. Dingeldein (1961–) was named Hamilton's Citizen of the Year for 2012.

INDEX

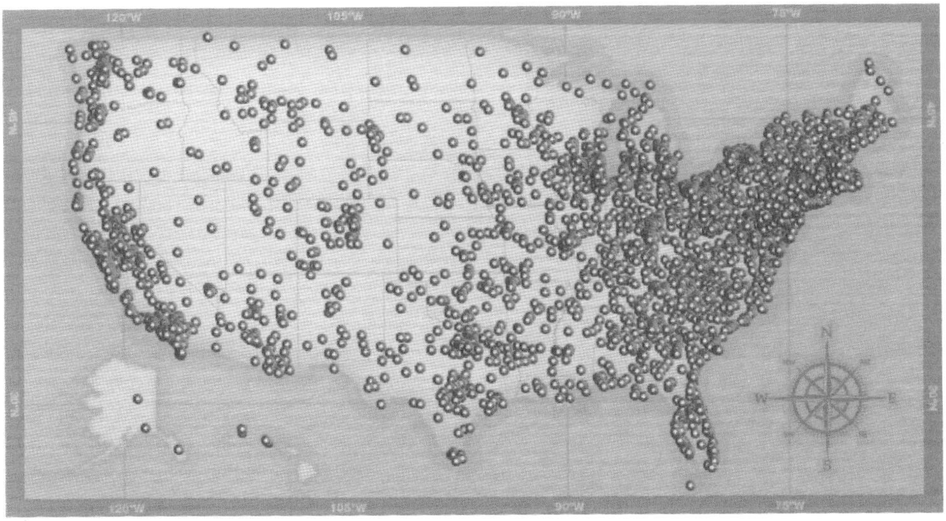

Consistent with our mission to preserve history on a local level, this book was printed in South Carolina on American-made paper and manufactured entirely in the United States. Products carrying the accredited Forest Stewardship Council (FSC) label are printed on 100 percent FSC-certified paper.

MADE IN THE USA